WORDSWORTH'S REVISITINGS

Wordsworth's Revisitings

BY

STEPHEN GILL

OXFORD
UNIVERSITY PRESS

PR
5881
. G55
2011

OXFORD
UNIVERSITY PRESS

Great Clarendon Street, Oxford OX2 6DP

Oxford University Press is a department of the University of Oxford.
It furthers the University's objective of excellence in research, scholarship,
and education by publishing worldwide in

Oxford New York

Auckland Cape Town Dar es Salaam Hong Kong Karachi
Kuala Lumpur Madrid Melbourne Mexico City Nairobi
New Delhi Shanghai Taipei Toronto

With offices in

Argentina Austria Brazil Chile Czech Republic France Greece
Guatemala Hungary Italy Japan Poland Portugal Singapore
South Korea Switzerland Thailand Turkey Ukraine Vietnam

Oxford is a registered trade mark of Oxford University Press
in the UK and in certain other countries

Published in the United States
by Oxford University Press Inc., New York

British Library Cataloguing in Publication Data
Data available

Library of Congress Cataloging in Publication Data
Data available

Typeset by RefineCatch Limited, Bungay, Suffolk
Printed in Great Britain
on acid-free paper by
Clays Ltd, St Ives plc

ISBN 978-0-19-926877-1

1 3 5 7 9 10 8 6 4 2

'It is delightful to remember these moments of far-distant days, which probably would have been forgotten if the impression had not been transferred to verse.'

'I would enshrine the spirit of the past
For future restoration.'

Acknowledgements

It is a pleasure to acknowledge help and kindnesses received during the writing of this book. I am very grateful to the Rector and Fellows of Lincoln College, Oxford, to the Trustees of the Zilkha Fund, Lincoln College, and to the Board of the Oxford University English Faculty for financial and other assistance. Thanks are due to the Trustees of the Wordsworth Trust for permission to reproduce illustrations of manuscripts in their collection and to the staff of the Jerwood Centre in Grasmere for help invariably offered with warm goodwill. Anyone who has ever called on the Curator, Jeff Cowton, for advice and practical help will know how heartfelt are my thanks to him.

I am grateful to many friends and academic colleagues for support of various kinds, but especial thanks are due to Richard and Fiona Gravil, Peter Manning, Peter McCullough, and Fiona Stafford. Clare Tilbury has given me support in all possible ways, not least by being such a patient listener. *Wordsworth's Revisitings* could not have come into being without the labours of all the editors of the Cornell Wordsworth Series, but I want particularly to pay tribute to James Butler, Jared Curtis, Stephen Parrish, and Mark L. Reed. Their scholarship has been an inspiration; their willingness to go well beyond the requirements of academic courtesy in helping me has been beyond praise. At Oxford University Press Jacqueline Baker could not have been more forbearingly helpful. My former tutor Jonathan Wordsworth would have been puzzled, I suspect, by my taking pleasure in Wordsworth's poetry after 1805, but I like to think that he would have appreciated the drift of this book. All of my work on Wordsworth began with him.

In writing this book I have revisited some of my own earlier work published as ' "Adventures on Salisbury Plain" and Wordsworth's Poetry of Protest 1795–97', *Studies in Romanticism*, 11 (1972), 48–65; ' "The Braes of Yarrow": Poetic Context and Personal Memory in

Wordsworth's "Extempore Effusion Upon the Death of James Hogg"', *Wordsworth Circle*, 16 (1985), 120–5; '"Affinities Preserved": Poetic Self-Reference in Wordsworth', *Studies in Romanticism*, 24 (1985), 531–49; 'Wordsworth, Scott, and "Musings Near Aquapendente"', *Centennial Review*, 36 (1992), 221–30.

Contents

Abbreviations

EQ	Edward Quillinan
HCR	Henry Crabb Robinson
MW	Mary Wordsworth
SH	Sara Hutchinson
STC	Samuel Taylor Coleridge
DW	Dorothy Wordsworth
WW	William Wordsworth
Curtis, *Fenwick Notes*	*The Fenwick Notes of William Wordsworth*, ed. Jared Curtis (London: Bristol Classical Press, 1993).
DWJ	Dorothy Wordsworth, *The Grasmere Journals*, ed. Pamela Woof (Oxford: Clarendon Press, 1991).
Norton Prelude	*The Prelude 1799, 1805, 1850*, ed. Jonathan Wordsworth, M. H. Abrams, and Stephen Gill (New York and London: W. W. Norton, 1979).
Prose	*The Prose Works of William Wordsworth*, ed. W. J. B. Owen and Jane Worthington Smyser, 3 vols. (Oxford: Clarendon Press, 1974).
STCL	*Collected Letters of Samuel Taylor Coleridge*, ed. Earl Leslie Griggs, 6 vols. (Oxford: Clarendon Press, 1956–71).
WL	*The Letters of William and Dorothy Wordsworth*, 8 vols. (Oxford: Clarendon Press, 1967–93). Individual volumes: *The Early Years 1787–1805*, ed. Chester L. Shaver (1967); *The Middle Years, pt. 1: 1806–1811*, ed. Mary Moorman (1969); *The Middle Years, pt. 2: 1812–1820*, ed. Mary Moorman and Alan G. Hill

(1970); *The Later Years, pt. 1: 1821–1828*,
ed. Alan G. Hill (1978); *The Later Years,
pt. 2: 1829–1834*, ed. Alan G. Hill (1979);
The Later Years, pt. 3: 1835–1839, ed.
Alan G. Hill (1982); *The Later Years, pt.
4: 1840–1853*, ed. Alan G. Hill (1988); *A
Supplement of New Letters*, ed. Alan G.
Hill (1993). The edition is referred to
serially as *WL*, I–VIII.

1799	*The Two-Part Prelude* of 1799.
1805	*The Prelude* in 13 books, version of 1805.
1850	*The Prelude*, in 14 books, published in London by Edward Moxon in 1850.

When quotations from poems are cited without reference to editorial
matter, the line number entry will be simply, for example, *Home at
Grasmere*, 66. Unless otherwise specified, the texts will be taken from the
relevant volume in the Cornell Wordsworth Series, General Editor Stephen
Parrish, 21 vols. (Ithaca and London: Cornell University Press, 1975–2007).
Volumes most frequently cited, listed by date of publication, are:

Gill, *SPP*	*The Salisbury Plain Poems of William Wordsworth*, ed. Stephen Gill (1975).
Darlington, *Home at Grasmere*	*Home at Grasmere*, ed. Beth Darlington (1977).
Parrish, *1799*	*The Prelude, 1798–1799*, ed. Stephen Parrish (1977).
Butler, *The Ruined Cottage*	*The Ruined Cottage and The Pedlar*, ed. James Butler (1979).
Osborn, *The Borderers*	*The Borderers*, ed. Robert Osborn (1982).
Curtis, *P2V*	*Poems in Two Volumes, and Other Poems, 1800–1807*, ed. Jared Curtis (1983).
Owen, *1850*	*The Fourteen-Book Prelude*, ed. W. J. B. Owen (1985).
Ketcham, *Shorter Poems*	*Shorter Poems, 1807–1820*, ed. Carl H. Ketcham (1989).
Reed, *1805*	*The Thirteen-Book Prelude*, ed. Mark L. Reed, 2 vols. (1991).
Butler and Green, *Lyrical Ballads*	*Lyrical Ballads and Other Poems, 1797–1800*, ed. James Butler and Karen Green (1992).

Landon and Curtis, *Early Poems*	*Early Poems and Fragments, 1785–1797*, ed. Carol Landon and Jared Curtis (1997).
Curtis, *Last Poems*	*Last Poems, 1821–1850*, ed. Jared Curtis (1999).
Jackson, *Sonnet Series*	*Sonnet Series and Itinerary Poems, 1820–1845*, ed. Geoffrey Jackson (2004).

Illustrations

Illustrations 1 courtesy of The Royal Collection © 2011 Her Majesty Queen Elizabeth II.

Illustrations 2 and 3 are reproduced courtesy of the Wordsworth Trust, Grasmere.

Introduction

Is there not
An art, a music, and a stream of words
That shall be life, the acknowledged voice of life?[1]

One passage of Wordsworth, that leads to the centre of his being as man and as poet, is the best entry point for this book. Written in 1800 for the pastoral poem 'Michael', but not used in the published version, the lines are about living and growing old among the mountains:

> thus it is
> That in such regions, by the sovereignty
> Of forms still paramount to every change
> Which years can bring into the human heart
> Our feelings are indissolubly bound
> Together, and affinities preserv'd
> Between all stages of the life of man.
> Hence with more pleasure far than others feel,
> Led by his son this Shepherd now went back
> Into the years which he himself had lived . . .[2]

Nothing was more important to Wordsworth than tracing the evidence that affinities had been preserved between all the stages of the life of man. Poetic creation was vital. Poems, whether published or not, remained as evidence of what survived time's depredation. The ploughshare turns over the ground on which Michael's cottage stood, but the poem survives, as a memorial both to the Shepherd and his family, and to the Poet, who fondly imagines his continuity with the 'youthful Poets, who among these Hills | Will be my second self when I am gone'. The creative imagination is the agent for ensuring continuity 'in spite of things silently gone out of mind and

things violently destroyed'.³ This is the subject of the following
chapters: Wordsworth's habitual return *as a poet* 'Into the years
which he himself had lived'.

★★★★★

On 20 June 1845 two of Wordsworth's friends, Isabella Fenwick and
Kate Southey, returned to his home, Rydal Mount, after a two-day
excursion into the south-western Lake District. The following
morning they described their visit to Furness Abbey and the mixture
of sensations it had unexpectedly prompted. Mostly there was
shock. The sacred ruin was being ravaged by the construction of
a railway line 'so near to the East window that from it Persons
might shake hands with the Passengers!!'⁴ But their distress at the
sight of great trees felled and churned-up turf had been tempered
by the 'picturesque appearance' of the navvies resting amidst the
ruins, as they took their mid-day meal. Wordsworth was 75 years
old and almost at the end of writing, but what he heard over the
breakfast table moved him to compose this sonnet before the day
was out:

> Well have yon Railway Labourers to THIS ground
> Withdrawn for noontide rest. They sit, they walk
> Among the Ruins, but no idle talk
> Is heard; to grave demeanour all are bound;
> And from one voice a Hymn with tuneful sound
> Hallows once more the long deserted Quire
> And thrills the old sepulchral earth, around.
> Others look up, and with fixed eyes admire
> That wide-spanned arch, wondering how it was raised,
> To keep, so high in air, its strength and grace:
> All seem to feel the spirit of the place,
> And by the general reverence God is praised:
> Profane Despoilers, stand ye not reproved,
> While thus these simple-hearted men are moved?⁵

When it appeared in his single-volume Collected Works of 1845,
'At Furness Abbey' cannot have been a surprise. In October the
previous year Wordsworth had published a sonnet in the *Morning
Post* inveighing against the proposal to push the railway from Kendal
to Low Wood, near the head of Windermere, and two months later
in two letters to the same paper had described as an 'outrage' the plan
to drive 'one of these pests' through 'part of the ruins of Furness
Abbey'. The letters were speedily reprinted as a pamphlet, *Kendal and*

Windermere Railway, and sonnets written as part of this campaign conclude the 'Miscellaneous Sonnets' division of the 1845 collection. With one voice they demand, 'Is then no nook of English ground secure | From rash assault?'[6]

No one could have mistaken the Poet Laureate's attitude to further railway penetration into the Lake District. It must have been clear, however, even to those unaware of the full extent of the Furness Railway Company's vandalism, that the threat of a railway through Furness Abbey touched Wordsworth especially deeply, for on the same page as 'At Furness Abbey' in the 1845 volume appeared another sonnet with the same title, from which the source of the poet's anger could have been readily inferred. On what turned out to be his last visit to Furness Abbey in July 1840, Wordsworth had been moved to compose a poem about the ruin and its setting.

> Here, where of havoc tired and rash undoing,
> Man left this Structure to become Time's prey
> A soothing spirit follows in the way
> That Nature takes, her counter-work pursuing.
> See how her Ivy clasps the sacred Ruin,
> Fall to prevent or beautify decay;
> And, on the mouldered walls, how bright, how gay,
> The flowers in pearly dews their bloom renewing!
> Thanks to the place, blessings upon the hour;
> Even as I speak the rising Sun's first smile
> Gleams on the grass-crowned top of yon tall Tower
> Whose cawing occupants with joy proclaim
> Prescriptive title to the shattered pile,
> Where, Cavendish, *thine* seems nothing but a name![7]

The poem celebrates the healing power of Time and Nature. At the dissolution of the monasteries 'rash undoing' caused 'havoc' at Furness Abbey, but how blessed once more is the spirit of the place now that Nature's 'counter-work' is in command. Having 'left this Structure to become Time's prey', what right can Man have to lordship here? But though the contrast between Nature's 'Prescriptive title' and Cavendish's nominal one makes for a fine conceit with which to end, a fine conceit is all it is and by June 1845, when Wordsworth wrote the second 'At Furness Abbey' sonnet, the emptiness of it was only too apparent. It was William Cavendish, Earl of Burlington and future 7th Duke of Devonshire, who owned the abbey grounds, not the birds, and as a prime mover in the newly formed Furness Railway Company he had authorized a line through his possession. He was even ready, if engineering needs demanded, to countenance demolition of some of the surviving buildings. The havoc of the past was being perpetrated once more, driven this time, the poet declares, not by religious zeal but by Mammon.[8]

Denunciation of his country's contemporary 'shame', its subservience to 'a Power, the Thirst of Gold | That rules o'er Britain like a baneful star',[9] places Wordsworth squarely in the 'Condition of England' discourse of the hungry-forties. 'To whom, then, is this wealth of England wealth? Who is it that it blesses?', Carlyle had asked in *Past and Present* (1843), a pertinent question as the wagons loaded with ore and slate began to rumble along the Furness Railway track. But though the context for Wordsworth's sentiment was new—contemporary industrial expansion—the sentiment itself from him was not. 'The world is too much with us; late and soon, | Getting and spending we lay waste our powers', he had declared forty years earlier and it was to be expected that the despoliation of such a beautiful place, on the threshold of the region he had made his own, would move the chief and sole surviving Lake Poet to 'the passion of a just disdain'.[10] But even with the evidence of two sonnets on Furness Abbey before them, Wordsworth's first readers could not have known quite how much the place meant to him, nor why. Clearly the dated 'At Furness Abbey' sonnet, 'Well have yon Railway Labourers', gestures to the undated one, 'Here, where of havoc tired', printed immediately before it. What remained concealed in 1845 was that both stood in relation to other poetry about Furness Abbey written much earlier and to richly sedimented memories from earlier still.

As he fashioned childhood memories in 1799 into the beginning of his autobiographical life's work, the posthumously published *Prelude*, Wordsworth drew on his first visit to the abbey ruins, a 'scheme of holiday delight', that must have taken place in the early 1780s. In the passage on Furness Abbey in what is now generally known as *The Two-Part Prelude*, II, 98–139, life and death are in counterpoint. The *memento mori* repose of the cross-legged knight and the stone abbot contrasts with the schoolboys' wanton energy. Living trees and ruined towers stand 'Both silent and both motion-less alike', sheltered by their valley setting from the sea-wind passing

overhead. And, most vivid memory of all, an invisible bird in the
nave banishes the gloom cast by the dripping ivy, singing so sweetly,

> that there I could have made
> My dwelling-place, and lived for ever there
> To hear such music.[11]

When he wrote these lines Wordsworth was primarily concerned
to chart with a show of chronological exactitude the stages of the
process by which Nature's ministry of joy and fear fashions the
human mind. The schoolboy's visit to Furness Abbey is placed on a
continuum which, within the opening books of the autobiographical poem, begins with a naked infant standing alone in a thunder-
shower and ends with a 17-year-old joining in the song of the
one life.

The significance of Furness for Wordsworth, however, was not
limited to this single childhood 'spot of time'. As the poem explored
further the stages by which the young adult became assured of his
poetic vocation it took in more, and more diverse, autobiographical
and historical materials and Furness was, so to speak, revisited. In
late summer 1794 Wordsworth had stayed at Rampside, a village
on the south coast of Furness faced by Piel Island with its castle, built
by the monks of Furness Abbey.[12] On a particularly beautiful day
Wordsworth walked east along the coast to Cartmel Priory and
there visited the grave of William Taylor, the Headmaster of
Hawkshead Grammar School who had encouraged his first attempts
at writing verse. Pausing at Chapel Island, on which the monks had
erected a chapel 'where in ancient times | Masses were said at the
hour which suited those | Who crossed the sands', Wordsworth
asked a passing traveller for news and heard the thrilling tidings that
'*Robespierre was dead*'. Uttering a 'hymn of triumph', Wordsworth
returned home and in the verse that records this event (*1805*, X,
539–66) he repeated, with verbal echoes and one line verbatim,
the conclusion to the earlier account of visiting Furness Abbey (*1805*,
II, 140 ff.):

> I pursued my way
> Along that very shore which I had skimmed
> In former times, when spurring from the Vale
> Of Nightshade, and St Mary's mouldering fane,
> And the stone abbot, after circuit made

> In wantonness of heart, a joyous crew
> Of schoolboys, hastening to their distant home,
> Along the margin of the moonlight sea,
> We beat with thundering hoofs the level sand.

The repetition of the line, 'We beat with thundering hoofs the level sand', is, Howard Erskine-Hill observes, 'Perhaps the most breathtaking poetic *coup* of *The Prelude*'.[13] In a section dealing with the conflicted and confusing experience and emotions of the adult Wordsworth in the 1790s, the recollection of the schoolboys as 'a joyous crew' invites the contrast of their innocent 'wantonness of heart' with the much more complex 'glee of spirit' in which the poet poured out his hymn of triumph. For it was sadly premature. With the fall of Robespierre it was possible for those who had welcomed the French Revolution to believe that its course would once again be guided by the ideals of liberty and equality and not the politics of terror. The rise of Napoleon ended such hopes—at least in most English breasts—and by the time he was recalling that hymn of triumph on Leven Sands Wordsworth could see how wrong he had been. 'Come ye golden times', he had exclaimed, but they had not come and in 1805 Wordsworth was drilling in uniform once a week, a member of the volunteer militia raised to repel a likely French invasion.

When Wordsworth revisited Furness Abbey in poetry over forty years later yet more painful contrasts were in play. To make their visit to the ruins and the sea the schoolboys had had to dissemble with the innkeeper who let them have their horses, 'for the intended bound | Of the day's journey was too distant far | For any cautious man'—the abbey is about twenty miles south of Hawkshead, where Wordsworth was at school. Now the railway system that was on the point of bringing tourists into the heart of the Lake District at Windermere was about to open up once remote Furness. Though primarily intended to transport industrial freight, the Furness Railway line was bound to join up with others to carry tourist passengers. And so it proved.[14]

Wordsworth's grief at the idea may seem unwarranted—even hypocritical, given that many of the tourists had with them the latest edition of his *Guide to the Lakes*—but it is understandable. Wordsworth had only to look at his sonnet written some five years before, 'Here, where of havoc tired', to be reminded of his much earlier attempt to capture in verse his recollection of visiting the 'sequestered ruin' of Furness Abbey when he was still a schoolboy. But though the poetry remained to 'enshrine the spirit of the past', as *The Prelude* put it, the 'holy scene' itself, as Wordsworth has learnt from Isabella Fenwick and Kate Southey, has changed forever.

'At Furness Abbey' ('Well have yon Railway labourers') is, however, more than the utterance of a private grief. The sonnet links up with all the other poems of his, from *Lyrical Ballads* onwards, in which Wordsworth has insisted on the 'world of ready wealth' open to the 'heart that watches and receives' ('The Tables Turned', 1798). The navvies are responding to something that cannot be measured or valued in cash terms—a sense, as Wordsworth had struggled to define it forty-five years earlier,

> Of majesty, and beauty, and repose,
> A blended holiness of earth and sky.[15]

All his writing life he had insisted on the 'profit' of listening to the 'sounds that are | The ghostly language of the ancient earth' (*1805*, II, 327–8). But now? The whistle of the train is not just a threat to the beauty of a particular spot, nor even harbinger of the world that Hopkins was to lament in 'God's Grandeur' as being 'seared with trade; bleared, smeared with toil'. It is the signal of the triumph of a particular cast of mind, one that thinks 'profit' means cash and does not care to see 'Proteus coming from the sea; | Or hear old Triton blow his wreathed horn'.[16]

'At Furness Abbey' was almost Wordsworth's last act of witness against this cast of mind, but not quite the last. The 1849–50 collected edition of his work included 'I know an aged Man', a short poem, written in 1846, about the isolation felt by an old man forced at last to enter a workhouse. While he could still manage to survive in his own cottage, the old man—wife, children, and kindred all dead—had formed a bond with a robin he fed daily,

> in love that failed not to fulfil,
> In spite of season's change, its own demand,
> By fluttering pinions here and busy bill;
> There by caresses from a tremulous hand.

Incarceration in the workhouse—he is termed a 'captive'—keeps the old man alive, but it severs him from relationship and love.

'I know an aged Man' is a Victorian poem—as he tremulously reaches out to the bird, the old man could be a figure in a painting by such a master of sentiment as Robert Martineau—and it appeared in a Victorian collection, Wordsworth's final edition of 1849–50. But Victorian though it is, this vignette on the pathos of old age also looks back half a century, to the first important collection that carried Wordsworth's name on its title-page, the 1800 *Lyrical Ballads*. In this collection 'The Old Cumberland Beggar' had contributed to the contemporary debate about vagrancy at a moment when, as Wordsworth later described it, 'The political economists were . . . beginning their war upon mendacity in all its forms & by implication, if not directly, on Alms-giving also.'[17] Acknowledging that the beggar will suffer if left to wander in the 'eye of Nature', the poem declares it better that he should live and die within a community that knows and succours him, rather than survive on loveless charity within a workhouse, and exhorts law-givers, 'ye | Who have a broom still ready in your hands | To rid the world of nuisances', to listen. But History, Economics, and Politics heard other voices. In 1834 the Poor Law Amendment Act regularized the provision of in-door relief through a revised workhouse system and all Wordsworth could do—in which he was joined by Carlyle and Dickens from the younger generation—was to condemn those elements of the new dispensation that violated the 'most sacred claims of civilised humanity'.[18] When 'I know an aged Man' was written the new-style workhouse system was a reality, which was not going to be altered by poetical protest. But though the tone of 'I know an aged Man' is muted compared with 'The Old Cumberland Beggar', the poem remains faithful to the kinds of affirmation that have characterized Wordsworth's poetry from *Lyrical Ballads* on, and which led to the declaration on his memorial in Grasmere church that [he] 'Tired not of Maintaining the Cause of the Poor and Simple: and so, in Perilous Times was raised up to be a Chief Minister, not only of Noblest Poesy, but of High and Sacred Truth'.[19]

'At Furness Abbey' and 'I know an aged Man' are paradigm acts of Wordsworthian revisiting, the subject of this book. Revisitings of various kinds are at the heart of Wordsworth's creativity. They might issue in published poems which directly or indirectly allude to earlier work in his evolving corpus. They might be acts of self-borrowing, or of self-reference, hidden from the world in manuscript, the kind of linkings which offer insights into the powerful and consistent vision the poet maintained that his imaginative creation was one evolving unity. Revisiting was also literal. Wordsworth could not bear to think that he had seen a place for the last time—the poignancy of his tour of Italy in 1837 comes largely from the knowledge that it was too late. Much longed-for, the tour had no antecedent he could revisit and the poet knew he would not be back. How different were the West Country, Scotland, the Alps, and France. Repeatedly Wordsworth went back to places that had mattered to him as man and as poet and tested his sense of the present and the intervening years in fresh acts of creation.

As I have tried to suggest in the discussion of 'At Furness Abbey' and 'I know an aged Man', Wordsworth's revisitings are of interest because of what they reveal about the obsessions and drives of a great artist. But that, though true, is a guardedly minimalist claim. The deeper reason why they are of interest is that they are fundamental to those elements in Wordsworth's poetry which maintain its continuing appeal. 'If my writings are to last', Wordsworth observed in 1835, 'it will I myself believe, be mainly owing to this characteristic. They will please for the single cause, "That we have all of us one human heart!" '[20] The one common bond of all human hearts is that we are mortal. What makes Wordsworth's poetry at its best so profoundly moving is the steadiness with which it confronts that fact and produces beauty from it. His poems about every kind of loss acknowledge 'the unimaginable touch of time' and yet uncover what sources of consolation and strength can be gleaned. Revisiting his own experience through the traces, both human and inanimate, of a life lived, Wordsworth continually checked his own sense of personal continuity against what Hardy called 'Time's mindless rote'— as human beings will. It is our good fortune that the resulting 'Thoughts that do often lie too deep for tears' were not too deep to be given shape in poetry.[21]

If the drive to revisit is so central to Wordsworth's imaginative life, however, how can the field of this book be anything less than his entire achievement? Aren't all Wordsworth's best poems revisitings?

In one sense the answer is, of course, yes. The full title of 'Lines written a few miles above Tintern Abbey | On revisiting the banks of the Wye during a tour, July 13, 1798' emphasizes that this is a poem of the present, the result of a visit *now*, only to reverse the emphasis in what follows, where retrospect is the keynote: 'Five years have passed . . . Once again', familiar locutions in quintessential Wordsworth territory—the present in relation to the past. 'Elegiac Stanzas . . . Peele Castle' begins with a similar kind of temporal gesture, 'I was thy Neighbour once, thou rugged Pile!', and again, as in 'Tintern Abbey', testimony about the present and prophecy about the future are extracted from analysis of what has changed between then, the earlier visit, and now, the writing of the poem. From its opening lines to its close *The Prelude* works in the same way. 'Oh there is blessing in this gentle breeze | . . . it beats against my cheek', the poet exclaims as he exults in his freedom, or so it seems. Fifty-four lines later it is revealed that this effusion is what the poet said and felt 'that day' (unspecified), and that these are words and feelings he needs to recall if he is to find the resources with which to fulfil the promise of his 'former years'. Thirteen books later, as the poem concludes, Wordsworth pledges himself and Coleridge anew to their great task and he does so by looking back, back to the Quantock Hills and the summer of *Lyrical Ballads*. Remember, Coleridge is exhorted, 'all which then we were', and there is scarcely a Wordsworth poem of any weight that does not tap into the limitless imaginative resource invoked here—retrospection.

Closely allied though they are, however, revisiting and retrospection are not the same and it is the difference between these two creative impulses that determines the focus as well as the boundaries of this book. *Wordsworth's Revisitings* is about the poet's continual return not to his past but to his past in his past writing. 'At Furness Abbey' draws Wordsworth's other writing about the ruin and the Furness coast into a poetic continuity. 'I know an aged Man' revisits and looks with a different eye at the old man with tremulous hands who was 'The Old Cumberland Beggar'. New creation is generated from earlier; our understanding and enjoyment of both are enhanced by perceiving the relationship.

For a revisit to be a revisit in terms of this book there must be an earlier Wordsworth text to which a later refers, or which it appropriates and revises. 'Tintern Abbey' and 'Peele Castle' are not in this sense revisitings, though both are, of course and unarguably, connected to each other and to every other poem of Wordsworth's that matters. Nor is his prose pamphlet *The Convention of Cintra*, published in 1809, a revisiting of the *Letter to the Bishop of Llandaff*, written in 1793 but never published by Wordsworth, even though both are polemics concerned with political justice, since there is no evidence that the *Letter* was worked over in preparation for *Cintra* or that its specific formulations of language contributed to the later text. Given that the *Letter* remained unknown in Wordsworth's lifetime, moreover, and, unlike *The Prelude*, was not prepared by him for posthumous publication, it is clear that the poet himself did not hope that after his death readers would benefit from studying both side by side.

Contiguity in itself does not indicate creative revisiting. From the collected poetical works of 1815 on, Wordsworth altered the presentation of his poems from edition to edition. In the cluster of 'Inscriptions', as finally ordered for the last authorized six-volume set of 1849–50, three poems appear in sequence (Inscriptions V–VII), 'Written with a Pencil upon a Stone in the Wall of the House (an Out-House), on the Island at Grasmere'; 'Written with a Slate Pencil on a Stone, on the Side of the Mountain of Black Comb'; 'Written with a Slate Pencil upon a Stone, the Largest of a Heap lying near a Deserted Quarry, upon one of the Islands at Rydal'. In the 1815 edition the order had been quite different—'Black Comb' was followed by four poems about Sir George Beaumont's grounds at Coleorton—but in 1820 the sequence was rearranged to the one that subsequently remained unchanged. 'Black Comb' was composed thirteen years later than the other pieces supposedly written with a slate pencil, but clearly Wordsworth thought it better on this occasion to ignore chronology and to present it flanked by, or as if in apposition to, the other inscriptions. It is clear why. All three poems can be read together productively; each is about ways of seeing, of making sense of natural phenomena and they observe a common generic convention. But textual revisiting is not involved. 'Black Comb' could have existed without the earlier poems; it does not depend on them for its meaning; they are not diminished when they are printed (as they usually are, if printed at all in a Wordsworth selection) without it.

Even with a rather strict definition of revisiting quite a lot more of Wordsworth's poetry could have been included—a proper study of the evolution of *The Prelude* alone, for example, would occupy a substantial monograph—but it is to be hoped that the discussion that follows of specimen areas of Wordsworth's *oeuvre* will demonstrate the interest of approaching it in this way and prompt further study of its more obscure byways. I would like to hope, too, that this book will contribute to the ongoing reassessment of the later Wordsworth, it being my conviction that imaginatively he remained impressively vigorous into old age and that the artistic stature of the poet in his later years, as opposed to his historical-cultural significance, tends to be underestimated. Chapter One, 'Second Thoughts', surveys a range of examples of creative revisiting and discusses both how revision worked in practice and what its significance was in Wordsworth's creative life. The second chapter revisits *The Ruined Cottage* and, contending that focus on its early incarnations is misplaced, seeks to bring out the importance of Wordsworth's struggles to decide on a satisfactory structure for the poem after 1799. Chapters Three and Four examine aspects of the development of *The Prelude* from 1804 to 1850. The attempt is made to show how the poet's sense of his own development and his response to contemporary events impel major revisions to the poem over his long working lifetime. In Chapter Five the focus is on the poetry of revisiting that springs from Wordsworth's connection with Sir Walter Scott. The final chapter, 'On Sarum's Plain', traces the history of the poet's engagement with an imaginative conception which first took shape when he was a 23-year-old republican, but which did not reach final form until he was, almost fifty years later, about to become Poet Laureate to Queen Victoria.

I

Second Thoughts

'My first expressions I often find detestable; and it is frequently
true of second words as of second thoughts, that they are the best.'[1]

(i)

On 1 September 1836 Edward Quillinan decided not to go out with his
gun. In his diary he recorded that 'Instead of partridge-shooting', he
was 'better employed in helping Mr. W "tinker", as he calls it . . .' .[2]
Quillinan's choice of pen over gun was shrewd. He was in the early
stages of courting Wordsworth's daughter, Dora, and could have found
no surer way of getting inside the defences her father was putting up
against this older, previously-married, Roman Catholic suitor than by
helping the poet as he worked at revision. For this is what 'family' had
always done—Dorothy Wordsworth, Mary and Sara Hutchinson,
Dora, and other relatives and friends had all at one time or another
been pressed into service as amanuenses.

In 1836 revision was a more than usually demanding affair for
everyone involved, from the family at Rydal Mount to the printers
in London, for Wordsworth had recently changed publishers from
Longman to Moxon and he was determined that Moxon's first
collected *Poetical Works* should be an event. In preparation for it he
looked over every line he had published with an eye to possible
improvement. He had done as much only four years earlier. Then a
set of the previous collected works, five volumes in 1827, had been
scrawled over in preparation for printing the four-volume set of 1832;
now a copy of that edition was inked and pencilled over for the new
collected poetical works of 1836–7.[3] Wordsworth didn't just revise,

he revised his revisions up the margins of the printed page he was using as base text and if indecipherability threatened, he sent the printers separate sheets with cross-references to the printed text, for them to make sense of, if they could. As requested, the printers sent revises, only to get them back—revised.

There was nothing unusual about this behaviour, nor did it arise from the increasing pernicketiness of age. Material circumstances accounted for a great deal of the harassment generated—paper was neither so cheap nor so easy to procure that it could be wasted; making multiple copies for safety's sake was time-consuming and laborious; getting manuscript and proof to and from London was complicated and hazardous. Even so, to these trials Wordsworth had always added self-generated ones. At the eleventh hour in the production of the second edition of *Lyrical Ballads* in 1800, for example, he wrote to the printer:

Mr Biggs,
Sir,
I sent off the three last sheets of the L.B. in a great hurry yesterday; and I have to request that you will take your pen and transcribe into the first sheet, which I sent yesterday, the three following verses, which I think I neglected to insert. They relate to the 4th Poem on the naming of places. If you look towards the end of that poem you will find these words

> 'was chang'd
> To serious musing and to self-reproach.'

Immediately after which ought to follow these 3 verses.

> 'Nor did we fail to see within ourselves
> What need there is to be reserv'd in speech,
> And temper all our thoughts with charity.
> Therefore, unwilling &c'

These three lines are absolutely necessary to render the poem intelligible. In the Poem of Michael about the middle of the first part you will find this line—

> '*The Clipping Tree*, a name which still it bears.'

Take a pen and alter the word '*still*' into the word 'yet' let the line be printed—

> '*The Clipping Tree*, a name which yet it bears.'

A few lines from the End of the first part of the same poem you will find this line—

'But when the Lad, now ten years old, could stand'

alter the manuscript with a pen and let it be printed thus

'But soon as Luke, now ten years old, could stand'[4]

And so on. This was only the last in a series of such letters and it can have been little comfort to Mr Biggs to realize that the anxiety such peremptory missives created in him was definitely less than that tormenting their sender.

Wordsworth's readiness to labour at revision, moreover, knew no limit. At one end of the scale revision might entail the termination of a poem's official existence—'Andrew Jones', for example, appeared from *Lyrical Ballads* 1800 to *Poems* 1815, but thereafter was culled; 'Among all lovely things my love had been' was dropped after a single appearance in 1807. Or it might mean radical textual reconfiguring, such as that which transformed the *Thanksgiving Ode*.

January 18th, 1816 was appointed a Day of General Thanksgiving for final victory against Napoleonic France. Such an outcome after more than twenty years of war was, Wordsworth believed, a 'great moral triumph' and he celebrated it with a 354-line ode.[5]

There are always problems of tone and content in any utterance in wartime, be it prayer, hymn, or poem, in which the Christian God is thanked for having furthered one's own efforts rather than the enemy's, and in his *Thanksgiving Ode* Wordsworth does not escape them. Most probably few people ever read the poem through, but Byron and Shelley did and they detested it. One passage in particular appalled them. It is one in which the poet confronts the mystery that God apparently employs evil, such as the slaughter at Waterloo, for ends man cannot discern and declares,

> We bow our heads before Thee, and we laud
> And magnify thy name, Almighty God!
>   But thy most dreaded instrument,
>   In working out a pure intent,
>   Is Man—arrayed for mutual slaughter,—
>   Yea, Carnage is thy daughter!   (277–82)

Shelley excoriated this passage in his parodic *Peter Bell the Third* of 1819; Byron singled it out in a scorching note to *Don Juan* in 1823.[6]

For Shelley and Byron the *Thanksgiving Ode* was confirmation of what they already felt about Wordsworth's direction, but there is no evidence that it slowed the rise of his reputation and after its appearance in 1816 in a slim volume consisting only of pieces 'chiefly referring to recent public events', the poem remained essentially unchanged through successive printings 1820 to 1843.

In preparation for the collected works of 1845, however, Wordsworth dismembered it. Savaging a copy of the 1836 edition (see Figure 1), he created two poems, one still bearing the original title, though now much different from the poem that had borne it for twenty-nine years, and the other called *Ode: 1815*, an alternative title, *Waterloo Ode*, having been scrapped. Wordsworth's final authorized collected poetical works of 1849–50 of course reprinted the *Thanksgiving Ode* and *Ode: 1815* in the identities they had recently assumed. Victorian readers new to Wordsworth's work might think that by consulting his *Thanksgiving Ode* in his latest edition they could find out how the Poet Laureate had responded many years earlier to a great moment in national history, but they could not. Something more than 'tinkering' had made sure of that.

At the other end of the scale revision consisted of playing with minutiae of phrasing within a line, in pursuit of nuances of diction and cadence. For example: since first publication in *Lyrical Ballads* 1800 one section of 'Michael' had begun,

> And in a later time, ere yet the Boy
> Had put on Boy's attire, did Michael love,

As he prepared copy for the edition of 1832, however, Wordsworth thought these lines might be improved and in the margins of the 1827 volume he was using for revision he tried out,

> In later day, yet ere the day was come
> That [?calld] the Boy to [?]

and

> In later day, yet ere [?that]
> Had put on Boy's apparel

and

> And ere the Boy did put on Boy's attire
> Michael, albeit

It is impossible to see what Wordsworth was troubled by in wording that had sufficed for thirty years, but clearly something displeased

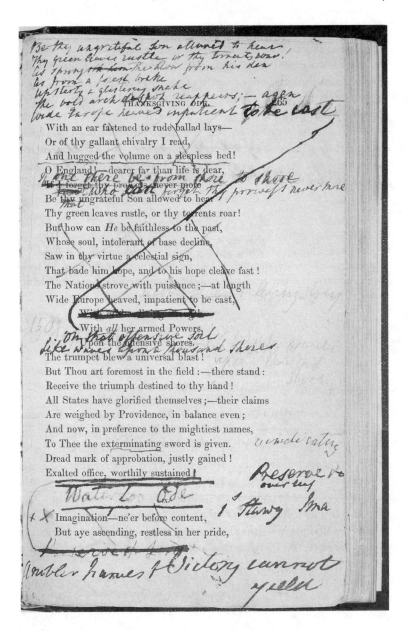

Figure 1. *Thanksgiving Ode*, MS 1836/45. Reproduced courtesy The Royal Collection © 2011 Her Majesty Queen Elizabeth II.

him. Whatever it was, these revisions made it no better—not one was carried through to the edition of 1832.

Such verbal fastidiousness was quite normal. On 24 January 1823 Wordsworth took the opportunity of a business letter to Lord Lonsdale to enclose 'a short Poem which I have just addressed to Lady le Fleming upon the occasion of erecting a Chapel at Rydal. I hope it will afford some pleasure to your Lordship and to Lady Lonsdale.' Perhaps it did. But one must wonder what were his Lordship's reactions when the very next day he opened another letter from Rydal Mount and read,

My Lord,
On reviewing the lines which I ventured to send yesterday, they seemed to me in some respect not sufficiently appropriate; I felt also that there was an abruptness in the mode of introducing the 4th stanza and that there was a disproportion between the middle and the other parts of the Poem. These several objections seem in a great measure obviated by the Introduction of a new stanza, as on the opposite page. It follows the third, ending,

> 'To interrupt the deep repose.'

> Ever most faithfully
> Your Lordship's
> W Wordsworth
A corrected copy is enclosed, of the whole.

In all his dealings with Lord Lonsdale Wordsworth was profoundly respectful, as befitted the greatest landowner and most prominent figure in the Lakes region, to whose friendship and patronage he owed much, but it is clear from this letter that Wordsworth expected Lord Lonsdale to be as respectful to him, as poet. The idea of Wordsworth worrying overnight about the abruptness with which he had introduced the fourth stanza is comical, but it is a mark of his seriousness about his art that he did and characteristic that he had no doubt that Lord and Lady Lonsdale would want to have what had just become the latest correct text.[7]

Though such textual scrupulosity was not just a symptom of old age, it was not until old age that Wordsworth divulged with complete candour just how driven he was. Throughout his writing life tetchy remarks in his letters—and sometimes in those of members of his family—reveal the toll in ill-health and bad humour that the concentrated effort of revision took on him and those around him.

His irritability stemmed in part from knowing that often there was little to show for his consumption of time and paper: 'The annoyance of this sort of work is, that progress bears no proportion to pains, and that hours of labour are often entirely thrown away', Wordsworth wrote to his publisher.[8] To a newly-made acquaintance in 1840, however, he put it more revealingly. Wordsworth had agreed to contribute to *The Poems of Geoffrey Chaucer, Modernized*, a venture promoted by one Thomas Powell, but when Powell insinuated that he would like him to take a watching brief for the whole volume, he was adamant in refusing to vet or in any way help with the other contributions.[9] His grounds were not age, or fatigue, or the pressure of other commitments, the usual white lies told by writers to editors, but this astonishing disclosure:

Little matters in Composition hang about and teaze me awkwardly, and at improper times when I ought to be taking my meals or asleep. On this account, however reluctantly, I must <u>decline</u> even <u>looking over</u> the Mss either of yourself or your Friends. I am sure I should find some thing which I should attempt to change, and probably after a good deal of pains make the passage no better, perhaps worse—This is my infirmity, I have employed scores of hours during the course of my life in retouching favorite passages of favorite Authors, of which labour not a trace remains nor ought to remain.[10]

'Scores of hours . . . course of my life.' As far as his own work is concerned, Wordsworth started revising it within a year of getting a first book published and he was stopped only by death. *An Evening Walk* appeared in 1793; by the following summer a copy of it had been mutilated in the process of reworking the whole poem. Such was the pattern until the final edition of Wordsworth's collected poetical works in 1849–50. Poems which had often gone through many versions in manuscript before appearing in print were scrutinized afresh each time a further collection was planned. Some editions were clearly more important than others. The two-volume *Poems* of 1815 gathered together Wordsworth's work so far in a classification system of his own devising. The six volumes of 1836 marked the beginning of a new era as Moxon's first complete *Poetical Works*. The edition of 1845 mattered a lot to Wordsworth because he hoped its single-volume format would enable him to reach readers unable to afford Moxon's multi-volume sets. But though he was more than usually painstaking about preparing text for these three editions, the effort he expended was special in degree only, not in kind.[11]

The unstinting effort put into revision of the poems matched that which went into their creation. Wordsworth often composed outdoors, noting lines on whatever bit of paper he had to hand, or holding them in his mind until he was able to write them down. Such an image of the poet lisping spontaneous numbers is almost too Romantic, but there is plentiful evidence to flesh it out in Wordsworth's case. The early lyric about his sister and the glow-worm, for example, 'Among all lovely things my love had been', was written as Wordsworth was crossing the northern Pennines, so wholly absorbed in concentration that he failed to notice when his fingers became numb with cold. Thirty years later what must have been a journey of extreme discomfort for a 60-year-old—two days on horseback from Lancaster to Cambridge, in tempestuous rain—engendered a sonnet, an elegy, and a few stanzas of an ode to May.[12]

Compared with what followed once a few lines had been written down, however, the pain and discomfort of cold and rain were as nothing. Gastric pains, eye trouble, insomnia, anxiety, and irritability flared up as Wordsworth coaxed a poem out of hiding. 'Wm wrote out part of his poem & endeavoured to alter it, & so made himself ill', Dorothy Wordsworth's journal entry for 26 January 1802, is one of many such; the manuscript photographs in any volume of the Cornell Wordsworth Series reveal the textual correlative of these bodily pains (see Figure 2). Crossings out, wholesale deletions, drafting in margins, asterisks, arrows, and brief memoranda are the messy track of the struggle to impose fresh ideas on to existing verse.

(ii)

Any study of Wordsworth's creative processes must touch on the topics just discussed and a great deal more exploration of them could be justified. How Wordsworth shaped poems in manuscript through successive versions until he was ready to publish them deserves further study, as does the systematic examination of how he repeatedly revised them once they were in print. What this chapter is

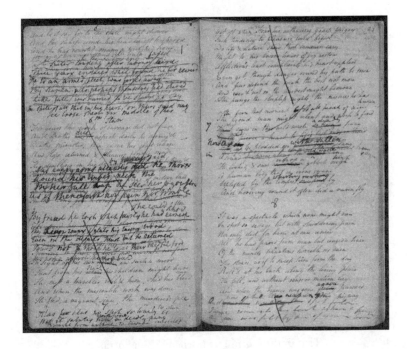

Figure 2. *Adventures on Salisbury Plain*, in Dove Cottage MS 16. Reproduced courtesy of the Wordsworth Trust, Grasmere.

concerned with, however, is in a sense neither and both of these topics. It is the compositional process in which Wordsworth continually made sorties across the boundaries that, separating manuscript from printed page, demarcate unpublished from published work.

Symptomatic moments on a small scale occur when the poet returns to work long done with and, one would have thought, forgotten. But Wordsworth did not forget. There is plentiful evidence that, at least in the realm of poetry, he never let go anything that had once interested or moved him.

At a London party in 1836, to take one instance, Wordsworth got into conversation with Elizabeth Barrett about the nature of the poetic life. They touched on Dante, and to support some remarks about his 'tenderness' Wordsworth 'softly & slowly & expressively' recited Dante's sonnet to Guido Cavalcanti ('Guido, vorrei, che tu, e Lappo, ed io'). Apologizing for not reciting it in Italian, Wordsworth drew on his memory of a translation by William Hayley, published as

far back as 1782. Given that in her record of this event Elizabeth Barrett commented on the Lake Poet's northern pronunciation of a word
in line 12, it may be assumed that Wordsworth summoned up the
whole sonnet.[13]

   Hayley is, at least in academic circles, a name. Who remembers
the work of Sneyd Davies (1709–69)? Wordsworth did. In 1830,
mulling over possibles for inclusion in an anthology of the British
Poets edited by Alexander Dyce, Wordsworth pleaded the case for
'an exceedingly pleasing poem' by Davies, which had taken his fancy
years earlier in a reader of elocution exercises.[14] Many other examples could be given of memory and confident critical judgement
working together in this way. And they did whenever Wordsworth
ranged over the whole body, not of what he had read, but of what he
had himself written.

   In 1821, for example, Wordsworth added a sonnet about transience
to the sequence soon to be published as *Ecclesiastical Sketches*. Mutability is the universal law for earthly things. 'Truth fails not', but her
outward forms

> melt like frosty rime
> That in the morning whitened hill and plain
> And is no more; drop like the tower sublime
> Of yesterday, which royally did wear
> Its crown of weeds, but could not even sustain
> Some casual shout that broke the silent air,
> Or the unimaginable touch of Time.[15]

In the imaginative hinterland of these lines loom the ruins of Peele
Castle ('And this huge Castle, standing here sublime') and Furness
Abbey with its grass-topped towers, but there is also another ruin,
one Wordsworth had conjured into being twenty-five years before.
In 1796 Wordsworth drafted what editors have since called 'A Gothic
Tale', a sequence of Spenserian stanzas connected in some ways to
his current enterprises, the narrative *Adventures on Salisbury Plain*
and the dramatic *The Borderers*: all three pieces of work remained
unpublished. One stanza describes a ruin:

> Whose walls had scattered many a stony heap.
> The unimaginable touch of time,
> Or shouldering winds, had split with ruin deep
> The towers that stately stood as in their prime,
> Though shattered . . .[16]

why after a decade's unsettled wandering he had returned to the Lake District to fulfil it. No longer in octosyllabic couplets but the blank verse of the *Two-Part Prelude*, the melancholy portentousness of the 17-year-old's deathbed farewell is critically placed by the adult who comments that the words themselves 'Were uttered in a casual access | Of sentiment, a momentary trance | That far outran the habit of my mind' (II, 164–78). Casual and momentary perhaps, but important enough to be included as early evidence of 'That sense of dim similitude which links | Our moral feelings with external forms', that is, nothing less than the ground of convictions whose origin and significance this autobiographical poem is devoted to exploring.

When the *Prelude* was expanded to its thirteen-book form by 1805, these lines were omitted altogether, and not like other passages from the two-book version of the poem moved elsewhere in the larger structure. In his first collected works, however, the *Poems* (1815), the farewell address was returned, so to speak, to its original context, by its publication as a fragment entitled, 'Extract: From the Conclusion of a Poem, Composed Upon Leaving School'. So it continued to appear in all subsequent editions to Wordsworth's death. But although the poem was now fixed, as it were, and given a titled identity for its existence in the public domain, Wordsworth continued to think of it in its blank verse embodiment as available for use and in his first major reworking of the thirteen-book *Prelude* in 1819 a place was found for the lines in Book Eight, 'Retrospect.—Love of Nature Leading to Love of Man.' Now there is no embarrassment or apology. The youth's effusion, described as 'a pure stream of words fresh from the heart', is produced as evidence that Nature might frame even an 'unconscious Boy' to 'pensive musings which might well beseem | Maturer years'. For thirty years Wordsworth's farewell address to his native mountains lived a double life, publicly as a youthful outpouring, classed among juvenile productions in the collected *Poetical Works*, and privately, in the manuscripts of the unpublished *Prelude*, as evidence that the poet was indeed a chosen son.

(iii)

Discussion of the movement of Wordsworth's apostrophe to his 'Dear native regions' between unpublished and published states over a period of years introduces another aspect of his creative process inseparable from the topic of revisiting. It is that throughout his working lifetime there were two Wordsworths. The one, who began publishing in 1793 as 'W. Wordsworth, B.A. of St. John's, Cambridge', and ended (in the most fulsome version of a variously worded title-page) as 'William Wordsworth, D.C.L., Poet Laureate, Honorary Member of the Royal Society of Edinburgh, and of the Royal Irish Academy, Etc. Etc.', was publicly embodied in sets of *Poetical Works*, which grew from two volumes in 1815 to six in 1849–50,[24] as successive discrete collections, such as *The River Duddon* (1820), or *Memorials of a Tour on the Continent, 1820* (1822), or *Yarrow Revisited* (1835), were allocated their place in the ever-expanding collected works. The emanation of the other Wordsworth existed in manuscript in the form of poems (and some prose) which Wordsworth retained, even after he had published a much revised version of them years after the moment of their original composition, or which he held back, never to publish at all.

Ostensibly Wordsworth would have disapproved of our interest in either of these categories of his work. 'I am far from laying it down', he declared in 1835, 'that writings which an Author may have excluded ought not to be in any shape reprinted, but I do think no Editor can incorporate them with his Works, without disrespect to his memory, and probably in the end, without injury to the interests of literature.' This statement notwithstanding, Wordsworth did preserve his manuscripts; they were part of the literary property bequeathed in his will; and from the 1880s on scholars have continued to engage in the activity he most condemned, 'raking together everything that may have dropped from a distinguished Author's pen'.[25]

What the surviving manuscripts reveal is how different might have been Wordsworth's career profile and perhaps the literary history of the Romantic period, had he made different decisions about publishing. What actually happened is a well-rehearsed tale. Wordsworth's career properly began with *Lyrical Ballads*. The 1798 volume attracted little attention, but the 1800 second edition did, not least because of its new polemical preface-cum-manifesto. By the third and fourth editions in 1802 and 1805 Wordsworth was clearly a rising star, what-ever the hostility already being voiced by Jeffrey and others. The 1807 collection of lyrics, however, *Poems, in Two Volumes*, was a disaster.

Many reviews, even when praising some poems, condemned others with such ridicule that Wordsworth withdrew into wounded silence. He did not publish another collection of lyric poetry for eight years.[26]

How very different is what might have been. By the summer of 1798 Wordsworth had completed versions of four substantial pieces: *Adventures on Salisbury Plain*, a narrative in Spenserian stanzas, embodying anti-war protest in a study of crime and guilt; *The Borderers*, a Shakespearian tragedy, set in the Middle Ages but clearly concerned with questions about power and personal responsibility brought into contemporary focus by the mutations of French revolutionary idealism; *The Ruined Cottage*, Wordsworth's most complex quasi-dramatic narrative yet, exploring suffering and ways of understanding it; *Peter Bell*, a fable like *The Ancient Mariner* about sin and redemption, but which offers the counterpoint of a local north of England setting to the supernatural one of Coleridge's tale.

Joseph Cottle was eager to publish some or all of these.[27] Had he done so, it would have been evident that the author known, if known at all, for two descriptive couplet poems published years before, had matured into a poet capable of dealing with big contemporary topics across a range of demanding verse forms. But Cottle published the anonymous slim volume, *Lyrical Ballads*, instead and all of these poems remained in manuscript, to be revisited some day, maybe.

Again, consider what is now generally regarded as Wordsworth's finest achievement, *The Prelude*. It would have been reasonable for readers of *Poems, in Two Volumes* in 1807 to believe that since the enlarged *Lyrical Ballads* collection of 1800 Wordsworth had done nothing but produce more of the same—more varied, more daring, but still shortish lyric poems. What such readers did not know, of course, was that between 1800 and 1807 Wordsworth had produced the era's signature poem, *The Prelude*, a personal epic of witness and testimony—witness of political events at home and abroad, testimony to convictions earned (so the poem insists) through suffering, breakdown, and recovery. *The Prelude* is the poem of the years leading up to Trafalgar, just as *Don Juan* is the poem of the era after Waterloo. But Byron published his masterpiece and Wordsworth didn't. He left it for a lifetime's revisiting.

There were of course good reasons why what actually happened did happen and I am not claiming that a different course of events would have been preferable. Speculation about what Wordsworth could have published but didn't is intended just to emphasize how odd the existence of the two Wordsworths is. On the one hand there is the poet of the published volumes, struggling against a great deal of adverse criticism to establish a readership and a reputation; on the other the poet keeping back a considerable amount of poetry good enough—to say the least of it—to publish. The reading public got to know the one but not the other.

In fact that last statement is only partially true. The reading public was allowed to discern the identity of the second Wordsworth, but only at a time of his choosing and in forms that concealed even as they apparently revealed. The story of Margaret and the Ruined Cottage was published in 1814, but as Book One of *The Excursion* its earlier identity is subsumed in the larger whole. A poem that originated in the anti-war discourse of the 1790s and which was contemporaneous with the *Lyrical Ballads* studies in suffering, stood in 1814 as the opening scene-setting of a philosophical work dominated by a poet-surrogate figure. Book One is entitled 'The Wanderer', not 'The Ruined Cottage'.

Adventures on Salisbury Plain and *The Borderers* were withheld until their author was sufficiently established that he could afford to make the backward glance to a turbulent period. In the 1842 *Poems, Chiefly of Early and Late Years* Wordsworth explains how *The Borderers* originated from a specific historical moment in the mid-1790s:

The study of human nature suggests this awful truth, that, as in the trials to which life subjects us, sin and crime are apt to start from their very opposite qualities, so are there no limits to the hardening of the heart, and the perversion of the understanding to which they may carry their slaves. During my long residence in France, while the Revolution was rapidly advancing to its extreme of wickedness, I had frequent opportunities of being an eyewitness of this process . . .

The tragedy written then, the poet discloses, has lain unregarded among his papers, 'without being mentioned even to my most intimate friends'. Unwilling to destroy the manuscript, Wordsworth has decided 'to undertake the responsibility of publishing it during my own life, rather than impose upon my successors the task of deciding its fate'. 'Accordingly', the poet adds, 'it has been revised with some care . . .'.[28] The candour here is less than total. By revising *The Borderers* and authorizing a version of it for publication, what

Wordsworth also did was interdict his 'successors' from putting out to the world the tragedy as actually written when the knowledge of what he witnessed in France was 'fresh upon [his] memory'.

In the same volume the Salisbury Plain poem was prefaced by an account of its genesis, which sets it in the context of the opening years of the war against France almost fifty years earlier. Again Wordsworth emphasizes that the poem embodies convictions forged in the heat of timely personal experience, namely, that he had lived in France and could judge the prevailing mood:

The struggle which was beginning, and which many thought would be brought to a speedy close by the irresistible arms of Great Britain being added to those of the allies, I was assured in my own mind would be of long continuance, and productive of distress and misery beyond all possible calculation. This conviction was pressed upon me by having been a witness during a long residence in revolutionary France, of the spirit which prevailed in that country.[29]

This historical context-setting, however, was disingenuous. As a later chapter will indicate in more detail, *Guilt and Sorrow; or, Incidents Upon Salisbury Plain*, as it was now titled, was not the poem the young Wordsworth had composed when, fresh from his time in France, he was proud to declare himself one 'of that odious class of men called democrats'.[30]

There was also a gulf between the composition and the publication of *The Prelude*, but in this case withholding did not mean concealment—at least, not entirely. Whereas Wordsworth told his readers nothing about the existence of his tragedy and the poems composed after his wanderings across Salisbury Plain, for forty years tit-bits of information about the autobiographical work were allowed into circulation. In an extraordinary fashion, the poem remained unknown and yet not a secret.

(iv)

What these specimens of Wordsworth's practice demonstrate most obviously is the control he was determined to exert over the shape of his published *oeuvre*. Wordsworth was as prone to anxiety as any writer has ever been about making the passage from manuscript to

printed page. When he had barely started out he claimed that publishing was something he 'dread[ed] as much as death itself',[31] and
forty-five years later, when his collected *Poetical Works* were appearing every few years in a new multi-volume format and he was about
to become Poet Laureate, the degree of anxiety displayed was, astonishingly, just as great. 'So sensible am I of the deficiencies in all that
I write, and so far does everything that I attempt fall short of what I
wish it to be', he declared in 1843, that 'I am inclined to believe I
should never have ventured to send forth verses of mine to the world
if it had not been done on the pressure of personal occasions. Had I
been a rich man, my productions . . . would most likely have been
confined to manuscript.'[32] The counter-balance to such anxieties was
to control all aspects of the existence of such productions as were
sent forth.

The most direct way of exercising continual control has already
been highlighted—revision of the text. Having taken great pains
over the creation of a poem, Wordsworth ushered it into the world,
but even as he did so he was wanting it back, for he clearly could
not conceive of the work as having now taken on an independent
existence. Every poem was always in a transitional state, open to
reconsideration. Not surprisingly careful readers felt the tug between
loyalty to the poet and loyalty to the poems as they knew them.
Henry Crabb Robinson, in one camp, did not seriously question the
poet's prerogative of revising his own work. The lawyer Barron
Field, in the other, did. Field justifiably thought he had earned the
right to make his challenge, for, as he told the poet, he had painstak-
ingly collated the five volumes of 1827 with all 'the previous editions,
correcting those editions with my pen, so as to shew the eye
hereafter the various readings at a glance'. An 'instructive lesson',
Field called it, and one of the things it taught him was that the poet
he so revered was betraying in his alterations 'a little disposition . . .
to mitigate that simplicity of speech, which you taught us was the
true language of the heart'.[33]

Field's long and detailed list of queries elicited considered replies,
which were for the most part, not surprisingly, justification of
changes the poet had made to his texts. In the face of one objection,
however, Wordsworth simply backed down. In the collected edition
of 1820 lines 13–16 of 'Elegiac Stanzas . . . Peele Castle' had been
changed from

Ah! THEN, if mine had been the Painter's hand,
To express what then I saw; and add the gleam,
The light that never was, on sea or land,
The consecration, and the Poet's dream;

to

Ah! THEN, if mine had been the Painter's hand,
To express what then I saw; and add a gleam,
Of lustre, known to neither sea nor land,
But borrowed from the youthful Poet's dream;

Field's objection was that the original lines had become creatures of the wild [*ferae naturae*], and he told the poet, 'I don't see what right you have to reclaim and clip the wings of the words and tame them thus.' This was courage verging on foolhardiness. Wordsworth was quite prepared to wrangle good-naturedly over verbal details, especially when the adversary was such a devotee as Field, but this, a question about his *right* to control his own work, was a fundamental challenge to his conception of his calling. But Field's courage paid off. The lines 'shall be restored', Wordsworth wrote tersely. 'I need not trouble you with the reasons that put me upon the alteration.'[34]

The poet's right of control, as creator, was exercised most imperiously through the power of determining what would emerge as the Wordsworth canon. As has already been suggested, this was partly a matter of including and excluding; and sometimes the reasons for the choice made are known or can be inferred, and sometimes not. 'Alice Fell', a wholly characteristic working-up of a real-life incident reported to Wordsworth, was dropped from editions 1820, 1827, and 1832, and the fact that it was reinstated after Coleridge's death in 1834 gives weight to the supposition that it was excluded not so much because of ridicule from those Wordsworth termed 'small critics', but because it had been censured in *Biographia Literaria* in 1817.[35] But why did 'The Convict' become, as its author rather brutally put it, 'a discarded poem', after appearing in *Lyrical Ballads* 1798?[36] Other pieces that were little more than make-weights in this hastily cobbled together volume survived, so why not this one? In the absence of any comment by Wordsworth or a member of the circle that would settle the question, conjecture has to focus on the poem's Gothic trappings, or its gallumphing metre, or the over-simplicity of its assertions about the social causes of crime. Whatever the reason, the fact is that 'The Convict' was not even given fresh life in the *Poems, Chiefly of Early and Late Years* collection, where it might have appeared with other pieces deemed to have historical and/or biographical interest. 'The Convict' was expunged because, though it once had been, it was no longer Wordsworthian.

Control was exercised, too, by a kind of dirigiste signposting, which few readers ever found helpful and which has recently been so completely obliterated (at least in British editions of Wordsworth) that a brief note about it might not be out of place.[37]

As so often turns out to be the case, the Preface to *The Excursion* in 1814 is a key document. It was here that Wordsworth unveiled the project of *The Recluse*, the great philosophical work that had been occupying him since its conception in 1798, and of course he did so not knowing that in fact *The Excursion* was to be the only part of it he would complete and publish. As he introduced the projected poem, *The Recluse*, and the one part of it actually realized, *The Excursion*, Wordsworth was already eager to ensure that the overall coherence of his productions not be missed. As long ago as 1805 he had told Sir George Beaumont that the autobiographical poem he had just completed might be 'considered as a sort of portico to *The Recluse*',[38] and now he developed the idea of building. His major life-work, the philosophical poem, might be considered, he suggested, as a Gothic church, to be entered through an ante-chapel, the as-yet-unpublished autobiographical poem. This image, he found, allowed still further suggestive elaboration:

Continuing this allusion, he may be permitted to add, that his minor Pieces, which have been long before the Public, when they shall be properly arranged, will be found by the attentive Reader to have such connection with the main Work as may give them claim to be likened to the little Cells, Oratories, and sepulchral Recesses, ordinarily included in those Edifices.

The work of properly arranging the minor pieces began in earnest the following year and occupied Wordsworth for the rest of his life.[39]

For his first collected *Poems* in 1815 Wordsworth organized the two volumes into categories designed, he asserted, echoing the previous year's declaration, to 'assist the attentive Reader in perceiving their connection with each other'. The classifications, which

corralled 'apparently miscellaneous' poems into arrangements made
'with reference to the powers of mind *predominant* in the production
of them; or to the mould in which they are cast; or, lastly, to the
subjects to which they relate',[40] were flexible and capacious enough
to absorb Wordsworth's prolific output over the next three decades.
New categories were added and poems might move between categories, but cumbersome and shaky though the structure was by the
1840s, it had served a vital purpose, namely that of effacing chronology. The temporal relation of poem to poem was unimportant.
What mattered was how each spoke to each and contributed to an
evolving whole, a whole which was reconsidered and freshly vali-
dated, so to speak, with the publication of each new collected *Poetical
Works*.

For those readers who perhaps might not be 'attentive' enough
Wordsworth provided one further guide—prompts in his own voice.
Lines 205–9 of Book Four of *The Excursion* read,

> Alas! the endowment of immortal Power
> Is matched unequally with custom, time,
> And domineering faculties of sense
> In all; in most with superadded foes,
> Idle temptations . . .

In 1814 and subsequently the passage was embellished with a note:

This subject is treated at length in the Ode at the conclusion of the second
volume of Poems by the Author.

The reference is to *Poems, in Two Volumes* of 1807, and it looks simple
enough, but in fact a manoeuvre of some significance is taking
place.[41] The Ode to which the note refers had no title in *Poems, in
Two Volumes*: it was just 'Ode'. When it next appeared in 1815 it was
very different. Now it had a title, 'Ode. Intimations of Immortality
From Recollections of Early Childhood', and an epigraph, extracted
from the first poem in the whole collection:

> The Child is Father of the Man;
> And I could wish my days to be
> Bound each to each by natural piety.

And in between the 1807 and 1815 versions of the Ode has come
Book Four of *The Excursion*, in which the Wanderer discourses on
the fading of our visionary powers wholly within the context of the

conviction that Man's progress is Heavenward. In short, the note to *The Excursion* brings into conjunction the 1807 Ode, 'There was a time', and the Wanderer's disquisition of 1814. The *Excursion* passage imposes a transcendental interpretation on the earlier ode. By 1815 the appropriateness of that interpretative field has been confirmed by a title which delimits the possibilities allowed. Readers in 1807 moved into a poem just called 'Ode' with 'There was a time when', an opening that beckoned to who knows what exercise of nostalgia, or lament; by 1815 the phrase 'Intimations of Immortality' had intervened to blazon at the outset what the poem was about.

Many other instances could be cited. In *Poems, Chiefly of Early and Late Years* (1842), for example, the reader is twice directed back in time, with specific page references to earlier editions, for poems that complement 'Address to the Scholars . . .' and 'Elegiac Verses'. Perhaps the most striking instance, however, came in 1820, when a new ode, 'Composed Upon an Evening of Extraordinary Splendor and Beauty', had a note appended to it: 'The reader, who is acquainted with the Author's Ode, intitled, "Intimations of Immortality, &c." will recognize the allusion to it that pervades the last stanza of the foregoing Poem.' The sub-text here, of course, is, 'and any reader unacquainted with the earlier poem had better look it up'. Rightly so, for the two odes do speak to each other. 'There was a time' rests on kinds of consolation for loss that fail in the later poem. In the earlier the creative imagination produces a visionary landscape—the children sporting by the shore—which is the climax of the poem, from which the poet returns to the actual landscape with renewed certainty. In the 1817 poem the actual landscape is not enriched by any landscape of the mind, so when night falls the vision fades and there is no proclamation of abundant recompense or of life and food for future years. The poignancy of 'Composed . . . Splendor and Beauty' arises very largely from the recognition of its own limitations embodied in verbal allusion to the earlier ode, even as it affirms its own kind of hope.

Signposting of this sort confirms all the other evidence that Wordsworth had a sense of his whole *oeuvre*—published and unpublished—as interrelated and interdependent. His constant revision indicates a sense also that the evolving whole had both a historic existence, but, much more importantly, a being in the continuous present. Revisiting is never an act of homage to past achievement

(Swift: 'Good God! what a genius I had when I wrote that book!'),[42] nor the memorializing of a long-gone experience, but a live engagement with the past that reactivates it into conjunction with the present.

(v)

Wordsworth publicly identified some poems as having issued rather more evidently than most from this desire to engage with a past poetic self by signalling through their titles that they were sequels.

For a sequel to be a sequel there must have been a lapse of time between the publication of the originating poem and its successor, a lapse to which the second poem draws attention. Such a definition will exclude 'Expostulation and Reply' and 'The Tables Turned', as well as 'Composed after a Journey across The Hamilton Hills, Yorkshire' ('Ere we had reach'd the wish'd for place, night fell:') and its pendant, 'These words were utter'd in a pensive mood'. Both of these pairings were printed as companion pieces when first published—the first two in *Lyrical Ballads* (1798); the second in *Poems, in Two Volumes* (1807)—and of course they ask to be read in the correct order. But any difference of attitude or viewpoint in the second poem in each case is not the product of reflection by a later upon an earlier self. The second poems are rather expressions of shifting thought and mood which readily cohere with those of the earlier. In the Hamilton Hills sonnets, for example, the 'pensive mood' of the second generates reflections about the transience of the glorious cloud vision just described, but these are no more than a natural continuation of the closing thoughts of the first poem and in manner the transition of thought is quite comparable to that which takes place in 'Tintern Abbey' (an Ode in all but name, as Wordsworth observed[43]) and the 'Ode: Intimations of Immortality'.

Another sequel that draws attention to itself as a sequel is, in fact, a variation of the type of non-sequel just discussed. In 1811 Wordsworth combated fatigue and melancholy while holidaying on the west coast of Cumbria by writing an 'Epistle to Sir George Howland Beaumont, Bart.' It was not published, as might have been expected, in 1815, nor thereafter, but for the *Poetical Works* of 1827 thirty-two lines were excised and presented, mendaciously, as a poem of the Scottish tour, 'Departure from the Vale of Grasmere. August, 1803.' Gathering together much unpublished material in 1841, however, Wordsworth revised the 'Epistle' and published it in *Poems, Chiefly of Early and Late Years* the following year. Revisiting the 1811 poem prompted further lines, 'Upon Perusing the Foregoing Epistle Thirty Years After Its Composition', and these were printed directly following the 'Epistle', before a prose note which marks off the 'Epistle' and its pendant 'Upon Perusing . . .' as a single unit.[44]

In the 'Epistle', in a relaxed, almost whimsically meandering fashion, Wordsworth had lovingly addressed Sir George and brought his own children into the scene. Now, exactly thirty years on, he informs the reader of the deaths of 'the dear young Ones' and of 'the Friend | For whom this simple Register was penned', but since this is the first occasion on which the reader has been told about the 1811 holiday or has been made privy to Sir George's house-building plans which are referred to in the note, a sense of the melancholy lapse of years, which clearly means so much to the poet as he reviews his earlier work, cannot be anything that the reader will bring to the poem.

In what I am terming true sequels, however, it is always the acknowledged lapse of time between the poems that is the vital generative agent, both for the poet and for the reader. Nowhere is this more true than in the sequence of Yarrow poems, in which one sequel even gives rise to another, but they and their associated poems are so rich that they claim a chapter to themselves in this study of Wordsworth's revisitings. There are other, lesser-known poems, however, that will serve to make the point and which are worthy of attention in themselves as specimens of this curious aspect of Wordsworth's *oeuvre*.

The sonnet 'Methought I saw the footsteps of a throne', composed in 1802 and published in 1807, clearly invokes Milton's 'Methought I saw my late espoused saint'. Both poems are dream visions about death. Milton sees his wife in a dream, 'as yet once more I trust to have | Full sight of her in heaven without restraint', but as he attempts to embrace her, he wakes, she flees, and the truth of his loss is reaffirmed. Wordsworth's dream poem seems to deny the pain of loss by presenting an image which can be taken either as an image of Death itself as beautiful—unlike the dread Death feared by the crowd at the beginning of the poem who terrifies all, 'Sick, hale, old, young'—or as an image of a dead woman, sleeping, as it were, calmly in the grave. In either reading, the sonnet seems to endorse the vision of death entertained in the 'Ode' ('There was a time'), where the grave can be presented as 'A place of thought where we in waiting lie', and the passage from Dorothy Wordsworth's journal, also of 1802, which Mary Moorman perceptively associated with it:

We then went to John's Grove, sate a while at first. Afterwards William lay, & I lay in a trench under the fence—he with his eyes shut & listening to the waterfalls & the Birds. . . . William heard me breathing & rustling now & then but we both lay still, & unseen by one another—he thought it would be as sweet thus to lie so in the grave, to hear the *peaceful* sounds of the earth & just to know that ones dear friends were near.[45]

The image of the 'lovely Beauty', 'one | Sleeping alone', returned to Wordsworth in June 1835, when he contemplated his dead sister-in-law, Sara Hutchinson, as he told Southey, 'within an hour after her decease, in the silence and peace of death, with as heavenly an expression on her countenance as ever human creature had'.[46] The poem that was conceived then begins as if it were issuing from an as-yet-unvoiced conversation with the earlier utterance: 'Even so . . .'. Since 1802 many deaths had touched Wordsworth very closely: the 'faith that looks through death' of the 'Ode: Intimations of Immortality' had been tested. The sonnet sequel, 'Even so . . .', however, does not rebuke or displace the earlier poem, but add to it. In Wordsworth's apprehension of his 'dear Sister' in death, it is as if the vision of the earlier sonnet is actually realized. Sara Hutchinson has become the beautiful woman imagined there. In death she has been granted a loveliness that both confirms the positive vision of the earlier sonnet while deepening it through the declaration that the true source of hope is the illumination of the 'lamp of faith'. This is the power that will continue both to underpin and fulfil the vision imagined into being in the earlier poem.

From 1836 onwards the two sonnets were printed as companion pieces, and they make a very strong pairing, for the second so roundedly completes the first—that is, there are no implications arising from or questions raised by the first that are not taken up and answered in the second that revisits it. With another striking example, however, the relationship between poem and sequel works rather differently.

'Beggars' was written in March 1802 and published in *Poems, in Two Volumes* in 1807. Out on a walk the poet encounters a vagrant woman, who possesses both the beauty of an Amazonian Queen and the stature and mien of a 'ruling Bandit's wife, among the Grecian Isles'. The story of woe she tells is clearly far-fetched, but the poet gives her some money, touched by her demeanour. The rest of the poem needs to be quoted, for its essential quality, its gaiety and fleetness of movement, cannot be conveyed in paraphrase.

> I left her, and pursued my way;
> And soon before me did espy
> A pair of little Boys at play,
> Chasing a crimson butterfly;
> The Taller follow'd with his hat in hand
> Wreath'd round with yellow flow'rs, the gayest of the land.
>
> The Other wore a rimless crown
> With leaves of laurel stuck about:
> And they both follow'd up and down,
> Each whooping with a merry shout;
> Two Brothers seem'd they, eight and ten years old;
> And like that Woman's face as gold is like to gold.
>
> They bolted on me thus, and lo!
> Each ready with a plaintive whine;
> Said I, 'Not half an hour ago
> Your Mother has had alms of mine.'
> 'That cannot be,' one answer'd, 'She is dead.'
> 'Nay but I gave her pence, and she will buy you bread.'
>
> 'She has been dead, Sir, many a day.'
> 'Sweet Boys, you're telling me a lie;
> It was your Mother, as I say—'
> And in the twinkling of an eye,
> 'Come, come!' cried one; and, without more ado,
> Off to some other play they both together flew.

This is one of the most appealing of Wordsworth's encounter poems. Unlike the little girl of 'We Are Seven' or the Leech Gatherer of 'Resolution and Independence', these 'joyous vagrants', as they are termed in one revision, do not admonish the poet, explicitly or implicitly—they just delight him. This, we are reminded, is the poet whose 'grand study' in educating little Basil

Montagu was 'to make him happy', who delighted in Hartley Coleridge, Six Years Old, 'exquisitely wild', and who in lyrics such as the extempore 'Written in March, While resting on the Bridge at the Foot of Brother's Water' exulted in the life of man, beast, and plant.[47]

Fifteen years later Wordsworth revisited 'Beggars' and so powerful is the recollection of 'Their daring wiles, their sportive cheer' that it was inevitable the sequel poem should open with the question, 'Where are they now, those wanton Boys?' The poet has no answer, but chooses to dwell on the 'genial hour' in which he met them and its significance for him now. It was March, 'When universal nature breathed | As with the breath of one sweet flower ... | Soft clouds, the whitest of the year, | Sailed through the sky—the brooks ran clear'. But 'genial' leads back to the 'genial faith, still rich in genial good' of 'Resolution and Independence' and with it the suggestion that the poet is recalling the spring-time of his creative life. 1802 was a turbulent year in which Coleridge's 'Dejection: An Ode' ('my genial spirits fail | And what can these avail | To lift the smoth'ring weight from off my breast?') was intertwined with Wordsworth's 'Where is it now, the glory and the dream?'. But it was also Wordsworth's second *annus mirabilis* as a lyric poet, and it is that which he celebrates in the sequel to 'Beggars'. Whatever was the underpinning of that creative year: 'to my heart is still endeared | The faith with which it then was cheered; | The faith which saw that gladsome pair | Walk through the fire with unsinged hair.'

Unbeknownst to his readers, this revisiting of 'Beggars' also involved reaching back to another earlier poem, for Wordsworth had made this biblical allusion before in a similar context. In Book Seven of *The Prelude* the memory returns to him of an infant he saw in a London theatre, placed upon a table amidst 'dissolute men | And shameless women' (387–8):

> but I behold
> The lovely Boy as I beheld him then,
> Among the wretched and the falsely gay,
> Like one of those who walk'd with hair unsinged
> Amid the fiery furnace. He hath since
> Appear'd to me ofttimes as if embalm'd
> By Nature; through some special privilege,

> Stopp'd at the growth he had; destined to live,
> To be, to have been, come and go, a Child
> And nothing more, no partner in the years
> That bear us forward to distress and guilt,
> Pain and abasement, beauty in such excess
> Adorn'd him in that miserable place.   (VII, 395–407)

In both of these allusions to Daniel 3: 23–6 similar ideas are in play—the baby and the little boys remain in Wordsworth's memory with their beauty and innocence untouched by the flames—but the tone and emphasis of the two are different. In the *Prelude* it is as if the poet is so burdened by a sense of the inevitability of life's course as 'distress and guilt | Pain and abasement' that he wishes for the child escape, even at the cost of premature death, 'embalmed', or, worse still, a stunted life, 'Stopped at the growth he had ... a child | And nothing more'. The 'Sequel' to 'Beggars' is less intense. As in its contemporary, the 'Ode, Composed Upon An Evening of Extraordinary Splendor and Beauty', the tone is melancholy, as if the product of a chastened realism, but also irradiated by a sort of reverent gratitude. The poet delights in the still fresh memory of the 'gladsome pair', and finds strength to affirm the continuing efficacy of the faith that had supported him then. In that poetic faith, he is able to acknowledge that the little boys cannot have walked unsinged through the fiery furnace, while building his prayer for their 'immortal bloom' on the hope that 'pitying Heaven' will protect them, they were 'so happy and so fair'.

Why did Wordsworth revisit 'Beggars' fifteen years after its composition? No evidence survives for a firm answer to this question, though the composition in the same year, 1817, of poems such as 'Ode.—1817', 'Ode: The Pass of Kirkstone', and 'Ode. Composed Upon an Evening of Extraordinary Splendor and Beauty', suggests one. These are all poems that in a sense involve retrospection: they definitely mark the emergence of the post-*Excursion* lyric Wordsworth. But these poems were all published soon after composition, in the 1820 volume, *The River Duddon*. The sequel to 'Beggars' wasn't. It lay in manuscript for another seven years before being issued in the five-volume *Collected Poetical Works* of 1827. It was printed in sequence with 'Beggars' as 'Sequel to the Foregoing. Composed Many Years After.' But the title was untrue. As any punctilious reader checking in their *Poems, in Two Volumes* would have discovered, 'Beggars' had been greatly revised for its appearance in 1827. Revisiting his 'Sequel' ten years after writing it had prompted Wordsworth to revisit its original after twenty-five.

One final example of further, rather than second thoughts in a sequel that cannot quite confess itself as such will serve to illustrate how inveterate, but also how various in its operations, was Wordsworth's compulsion to revisit.

In his 1822 gathering of *Memorials of a Tour on the Continent, 1820*, Wordsworth published 'The Three Cottage Girls', a celebration of the beauty and vigour of an 'Italian Maid' and 'The Helvetian Girl'.[48] The third Maid of the poem's title, however, had not been encountered on the 1820 tour, but in 1803 in Scotland. Having lived in Wordsworth's memory ever since, she was now summoned again for further poetic life in 'The Three Cottage Girls':

> 'Sweet Highland Girl! a very shower
> Of beauty was thy earthly dower,'
> When Thou dids't pass before my eyes,
> Gay Vision under sullen skies,
> While Hope and Love around thee played
> Near the rough Falls of Inversneyd!

A footnote directs the reader in 1822 to 'the Author's Miscellanous Poems, Vol. II'—that is, to the *Poems* of 1815.

While ostensibly recording fresh experience from the recent Continental tour, 'The Three Cottage Girls' in fact only becomes really eloquent with the declaration that the much earlier encounter remains so vivid to the inward eye, that

> Time cannot thin thy flowing hair,
> Nor take one ray of light from Thee;
> For in my Fancy thou dost share
> The gift of Immortality;
> And there shall bloom, with Thee allied,
> The Votaress by Lugano's side;
> And that intrepid Nymph, on Uri's steep, descried!

And when Wordsworth revised the poem fourteen years later for his 1836 collected *Poetical Works*, it was this declaration, and the figure of the Highland Girl that preoccupied him. The fifth stanza, consisting of the thirteen lines just quoted, was expanded to

> . . . rough Falls of Inversneyd!
> Have they, who nursed the blossom, seen

No breach of promise in the fruit?
Was joy, in following joy, as keen
As grief can be in grief's pursuit?
When youth had flown did hope still bless
Thy goings—or the cheerfulness
Of innocence survive to mitigate distress?

(vi)

But from our course why turn—to tread
A way with shadows overspread;
Where what we gladliest would believe
Is feared as what may most deceive?
Bright Spirit, not with amaranth crowned
But heath-bells from thy native ground,
Time cannot thin . . .

Revisiting the poem of 1822 in the comprehensive revision undertaken
for the 1836 collected edition Wordsworth registers the challenge to
him now—1836—of the prophecy about the Highland Girl made
then—1822—which was itself a return to the prophetic declaration
with which the original poem, 'To a Highland Girl', concluded in
1807. At each stage the affirmation of the closing lines of the first
poem is enlarged, strengthened, and reaffirmed. For readers in
Wordsworth's lifetime evidence of this particular process of revisiting
ended with 'The Three Cottage Girls'. In fact it did not end until 1843,
when the poet returned yet again to the Highland Girl and declared in
the privately recorded Fenwick Note: 'The sort of prophecy with
which the verses conclude has through God's goodness been realized,
and now, approaching the close of my 73rd year I have a most vivid
remembrance of her and the beautiful objects with which she was
surrounded.'[49]

This affirmation is in keeping with many others that Wordsworth
made to the special friend of his old age, Isabella Fenwick. Proud of
his well-trained memory, Wordsworth was understandably pleased
that in his last decade he could make such statements, as when he
declared, for example, of *An Evening Walk*:

There is not an image in it which I have not observed; and now, in my
seventy third year I recollect the time & place where most of them were
noticed. I will confine myself to one instance—.

> Waving his hat, the Shepherd from the vale
> Directs his winding dog the cliffs to scale.
> The dog bounds barking mid the glittering rocks
> Hunts where his master points the intercepted flocks.

I was an eye-witness of this for the first time while crossing the pass of Dunmail Raise.—Upon second thought, I will mention another image:

> And fronting the bright west yon oak entwines
> Its darkening boughs and leaves in stronger lines.

This is feebly & imperfectly exprest; but I recollect distinctly the very spot where this first struck me. It was in the way between Hawkshead and Ambleside, and gave me extreme pleasure.[50]

Nearly forty years earlier, a very important act of revisiting had engendered anxious thoughts about the Memory's staying-power. In their first incarnation in *The Two-Part Prelude*, the memories embodied in the two 'Spots of Time'—Penrith Beacon and Waiting for the Horses—had strongly supported the declaration that there are memories, reaching right back to earliest childhood, which retain their power to fructify 'our minds | Especially the imaginative power' (*1799*, I, 292–3). When Wordsworth returned to the lines in 1804, however, placing them in a new setting, one that gave even greater significance to the 'renovating' virtue of such memories, he added a transitional passage between the two 'Spots'. Whereas in *The Two-Part Prelude*, after the close of the episode on Penrith Beacon, the poet announces in three bald lines that he recollects 'Another scene which left a kindred power | Implanted in my mind' (*1799*, 329–30) and immediately begins to relate it, 'One Christmas time . . .', in *1805* the two descriptions of incidents in childhood are separated by a thirty-line passage of musings from the mature poet about growing-up. It includes this haunting moment of troubled candour:

> The days gone by
> Come back upon me from the dawn almost
> Of life: the hiding places of my power
> Seem open; I approach, and then they close;
> I see by glimpses now; when age comes on
> May scarcely see at all, and I would give,
> While yet we may, as far as words can give,
> A substance and a life to what I feel:
> I would enshrine the spirit of the past
> For future restoration.   (XI, 334–43)

In *1799* Memory was the redeeming agent; in *1805* it is Poetry that will preserve for future restoration.

Did the elderly poet recall this passage when he was reminiscing with Isabella Fenwick? Perhaps he might have done, when he remarked, for example, on the natural phenomenon celebrated in the sonnet 'November 1, 1815': 'Suggested on the banks of the Brathay, by the sight of Langdale Pikes. It is delightful to remember these moments of far-distant days, which probably would have been forgotten if the impression had not been transferred to verse.'[51] Such a comment, however, and the note on 'The Highland Girl', suggest that by this time Wordsworth's sense of the relation between primary experience and recollection of the experience through the medium of poetry was straightforward, or at least, that it did not demand theorizing at this stage in his writing life. But neither comment is without poignancy. Many impressions have been enshrined, 'transferred to verse', but how many must have been lost forever? And the Highland Girl? What Wordsworth remembers is the girl celebrated in the poem and in his sister's journal. Time cannot thin her flowing hair. Realized in poetry, she remains, like the baby in the theatre recalled in Book Seven of *The Prelude*, 'Stopp'd at the growth [s]he had' (VII, 402), but by 1843 the real Highland Girl, if still alive, must have been into her sixties. It seems unlikely that she had ever seen a copy of *Poems, in Two Volumes* or heard of its author. What she was in August 1803 Wordsworth, 'through God's goodness', could remember whenever he thought of his poem, but did she, one wonders, have any memory at all of the two English travellers, who took refuge in the ferry-house on Loch Lomond?

2

The Ruined Cottage Revisited

'You know what importance I attach to following strictly the last copy of the text of an author.'

(i)

In 1859 George Routledge brought out a new Wordsworth volume, *The Deserted Cottage*. Illustrated by Birket Foster, Joseph Wolf, and John Gilbert, and cased in splendidly decorated boards, it was a pretty book, one to be coveted, but amongst readers who bought books for their contents as well as their appearance it must have prompted a question—what was this poem?[1] In 1858, as soon as copyright law allowed publishers other than Wordsworth's designated one to enter the market, Routledge had issued a *Poetical Works*, but it had not included *The Deserted Cottage*. Nor had it appeared in Moxon's six-volume edition the year before. Routledge was making a name for himself in the book trade as a buccaneer. Had he perhaps just acquired a Wordsworth title that had eluded his official publisher? No. Routledge was book-making, repackaging long-familiar materials, as he admitted in his Preface.

'I have often wished,' was the observation of Mr. Coleridge, 'that the first two books of the Excursion has been published separately, under the name of "The Deserted Cottage." They would have formed, what indeed they are, one of the most beautiful poems in the language.' The wish of Coleridge is now fulfilled, and the Poem is before the Reader, who will find in it some of the most thoughtful and musical strains of the Author.

This self-serving declaration is worth a closer look. Routledge presents two books of a nine-book work, long in print, as a discrete poem. Coleridge is paraded to authorize this decision.[2] Wordsworth could not have been cited, for at no point in the long compositional and publication history of *The Excursion* did he ever think of the first two books as a separate poem. Nor did he ever use the title, *The Deserted Cottage*. In *The Excursion*, Books One and Two are called 'The Wanderer' and 'The Solitary'. Readers who were attentive, moreover, to the text of Routledge's production might have wondered what exactly they were getting. Apparently a reprint of the first two books of *The Excursion*, it is actually a reprint of a poem the author had discarded. In 1845 Wordsworth had substantially revised the first book of *The Excursion*, but copyright law prevented Routledge from reproducing that latest text, the text as it appears of course in the authorized Moxon 1857 edition. *The Deserted Cottage* had to consist of the first two books of *The Excursion* as they appeared on first publication in 1814. What Routledge packaged so attractively was neither a discrete poem, nor a Wordsworth title, nor a text that would have been approved by the poet who declared: 'You know what importance I attach to following strictly the last copy of the text of an author.'[3]

Had Routledge been challenged he might have mounted the defence that Wordsworth needed saving from himself. *The Deserted Cottage* is just too good a poem to remain unknown to all but those undaunted by the monumental *Excursion*. Such was Coleridge's view and who better to make a judgement on where this poet's strengths lie? On the question of choice of text, Routledge would have had to acknowledge that it was the Law that made the choice for him, but he might well have maintained that in fact his text was preferable to Moxon's authorized one, arguing that Wordsworth's late revisions to Book One of *The Excursion* were not in keeping with the original conception of the story of Margaret as it had appeared in 1814.

Routledge's little venture brings into focus issues that had accompanied the poem known in the Wordsworth circle first as *The Ruined Cottage* and later as *The Pedlar* right from its inception in 1797. The key question always was, What is the true identity of this poem? Wordsworth struggled with it for years in what was, after the labour of *The Prelude*, his most complex and demanding act of revisiting. And the question continues to engage anyone at all interested in

Wordsworth, because the period of revision that is most difficult to fathom spans almost the whole of his most creative period, and because this is not a matter of minor verse, but, as Coleridge said, of 'one of the most beautiful poems in the language'.

(ii)

Building on the work of Ernest de Selincourt and Helen Darbishire, Jonathan Wordsworth, Mark Reed, and James Butler have uncovered the history of *The Ruined Cottage* and *The Pedlar.* That there are some areas of disagreement between them is not in the least surprising. In his Cornell edition Butler lays out and analyses the surviving manuscript evidence as lucidly as possible, but the complexity of it all is quite bewildering. Evidence in one manuscript, or a comment in a letter or a journal, may hint at manuscripts now lost that are crucial to an understanding of the chronology of composition. Line numbers entered into manuscripts give a glimpse of the poet and his amanuenses actually at work totting up what has been prepared in fair copy, but, alas, the figures do not tell a wholly intelligible story. The dating of some passages of verse cannot be established with absolute certainty. And at one point in the history of composition it is not even clear whether members of the Wordsworth circle are being consistent in how they refer to the evolving body of work. Nonetheless, thanks to all five scholars, but primarily to Butler, a narrative of the poem's development has emerged. What follows is an outline.

The Ruined Cottage first took shape in 1797 as a tale that drew on Wordsworth's recent observation while living in the West Country of the hardships suffered by agricultural labourers and their families. From the outset the narrative structure was sophisticated. The earliest surviving manuscript contains sufficient to show three frames interacting: the poet relates to us his experience of meeting a Pedlar who tells him the core story of Margaret, an account that includes the voice of the now dead Margaret herself as she recounts her experiences to him. Musing on the ruins of a cottage, the Pedlar expounds its significance. It is all that remains of a family known to him that was destroyed by the inherent precariousness of peasant life—'Two blighting seasons when the fields were left | With half a

harvest'—compounded by 'A worse affliction in the plague of war'.[4]
Fragmentary evidence survives to indicate that the driver of further
development of the narrative was interplay between the Pedlar's recounting of a sequence of events in the past and his address to the
listener in the present. The structure became more complex still
when the history of the Pedlar himself, given by the poet-listener,
began to emerge as a strand in the poem's make-up.

By March the following year the poem had become a coherent
whole of 528 lines.[5] The plotting of the story is now clear: how
Margaret's husband is driven to desert his family; how she struggles
to maintain the cottage and her children, hoping for his return; and
how eventually she succumbs, dying in the cottage the Poet and
Pedlar are now contemplating, 'last human tenant of these ruined
walls'. As Butler observes, however, 'This version of the poem seems
to have pleased Wordsworth for only a short time' (p. 17), for it was
soon nearly doubled in length by three additions all to do with the
Pedlar. One is a passage in which he reveals that he continues to feel
poor Margaret's presence so familiarly that 'not seldom' a 'momen-
tary trance' comes over him as he broods upon her fate. Another is a
lengthy account of the Pedlar's childhood and youth among the
Cumbrian hills, that dwells upon his rapturous response to the
beauty of the natural world: 'In such high hour | Of visitation from
the living God | He did not feel the God: he felt his works' (p. 157).
The third consists of the Pedlar's exposition of his conviction that
converse with 'things that hold | An inarticulate language' is neces-
sarily productive of moral good, in which faith he is able to counsel
the Poet to 'no longer read | The forms of things with an unworthy
eye' but to be 'wise & chearful' (p. 277).

At the close of the Somerset *annus mirabilis* Wordsworth became
preoccupied with other work and activity—the preparation of *Lyrical
Ballads* and negotiations over publication of the volume, the sojourn in
Germany following eviction from Alfoxden, the earliest drafting for
what was to become *The Prelude*. Once back in England in 1799, however, Wordsworth, and Dorothy his amanuensis, again took up *The
Ruined Cottage*. For the fair-copy manuscript made now, the poem was
trimmed by cutting out the account of the Pedlar's psychological
growth and all but the conclusion to his homily on natural wisdom.[6]
The excised lines on the Pedlar's personal development were neatly
transcribed elsewhere in the notebook for consideration in the future.

It was to this material that Wordsworth turned late in 1801 with his attention now fixed solely on the Pedlar. Over the turn of the year he grafted on to the material excised in 1799 new lines to flesh out more fully the figure's identity. The account of the Pedlar's spiritual growth, essential to establishing his stature as a philosophic guide for the Poet, remains the core of the evolving work (pp. 327–63), but it is introduced with more mundane detail about his upbringing. The Pedlar—now named as Patrick Drummond—becomes a Scot, born 'Among the hills of Perthshire'. It had been his parents' wish that he should become a village schoolmaster, like his stepfather, but trial soon revealed the task to be 'A misery to him' and he had taken to the road. The Poet had known him from school-days, when the Pedlar had lodged in Hawkshead.

There the two discrete bodies of work, *The Ruined Cottage* and the material about the Pedlar, rested as Wordsworth's life entered a busy phase—he went to France, got married, toured Scotland, and wrote many lyrics. Late in 1803, however, work started again on the earlier composition towards a version that reunited its two threads into a whole in three Parts, referred to in the Wordsworth household as *The Pedlar*.[7] The whole of the First Part is given over to an account of the Pedlar, comprising both a chronicle of his life and a character sketch of his personality. The story of Margaret takes up the Second and Third Parts, the Pedlar's narrative being interrupted at a transition between the two by his disquisition on the purpose and morality of such story-telling. The poem concludes with the abbreviated passage of reconciling wisdom that had concluded the version copied out in 1799.

It is a long and entirely coherent version that melds the various elements Wordsworth had been struggling with ever since 1797, and as she fairly copied out the 883 lines in early 1804 Dorothy Wordsworth could have been forgiven for hoping that her brother would tinker with it no more. But he did, and almost at once. In the manuscript being prepared for Coleridge to take with him on his imminent departure for the Mediterranean, Wordsworth altered the presentation of the Pedlar yet again, the most important revision being a passage that gathers him into the company of those who are Poets by nature.[8]

At this point in its history the identity of this evolving body of poetry is both changed and yet simultaneously fixed. The change is that it ceases to be a discrete poetic mass: *The Ruined Cottage* and *The Pedlar* are subsumed into the greater whole of *The Excursion*. This poetry had long been associated with the *Recluse* project—Wordsworth had confirmed as much to Sir George Beaumont on Christmas Day 1804—but exactly what form the association might take had not been clear.[9] Now it began to emerge. The meeting of the Poet and the Pedlar—now called the Wanderer—and the latter's recital of the harrowing fortunes of Margaret were to be the lead-in to a quasi-dramatic poem in which narratives of exemplary life-histories would counterpoint the competing moral, philosophical, and ideological utterances of the protagonists, the Wanderer, the Solitary, and the Pastor. In the next complete manuscript copy of the poem *The Pedlar* has become 'The Wanderer' and is the first book of *The Excursion*, the only portion of *The Recluse* to be published in Wordsworth's lifetime.

What becomes fixed at the moment the poem loses its discrete identity is its shape. *The Excursion* appeared in numerous editions between 1814 and 1850, but in all of them the structure of Book One remained the same.[10] After a brief scene-setting introduction about meeting his old friend, the Wanderer, the Poet gives a long account of his upbringing and character before handing the narrative over to him. The story of Margaret follows, told partly in the Wanderer's and partly in Margaret's words, but the voice at the tranquil close of the book is once again the Poet's.

(iii)

The first question that arises from this complicated history is: When, if ever, was *The Ruined Cottage* completed? Given that Wordsworth did not publish it as an independent poem, might it not be deemed at some stage in its pre-*Excursion* evolution to have arrived at a state of wholeness that would justify scholars and critics treating it as a finished product, one he could have published had he chosen to do so?[11]

Helen Darbishire declared in 1949 that the opening book of *The Excursion* 'was completed in its first form as an independent poem entitled *The Ruined Cottage* in the spring of 1798', but ironically it was fidelity to Wordsworth's own view of the matter which prevented her from acting editorially on her assessment of when the poem first achieved independent life. To be consistent with the principles that had determined Ernest de Selincourt's Oxford edition which she was bringing to completion, Darbishire had to observe the poet's injunction about following an author's latest text and so could not present *The Ruined Cottage* as an independent poem. It appears as a textual variant—albeit a huge one—within the notes to *The Excursion*, Book One. That the Darbishire text of MS B of *The Ruined Cottage* is followed, moreover, by five pages of draft passages, all attempts at a conclusion to the poem, suggests very strongly that it is not quite warranted to describe *The Ruined Cottage* as 'completed' in the spring of 1798.[12]

Twenty years after Helen Darbishire, Jonathan Wordsworth took up again the issue of the poem's identity. Convinced that the 'tragic story of Margaret' is what he termed 'The *Ruined Cottage* proper' and that the study of the Pedlar's philosophical development has 'almost no bearing' on it, Jonathan Wordsworth divided the two. In *The Music of Humanity* he presented *The Ruined Cottage* as in the 1799 MS D, declaring it 'the first entirely coherent text', and created from the other material in the notebook a discrete poem he called, 'perhaps arbitrarily', *The Pedlar*.[13]

The choice of MS D for *The Ruined Cottage* was determined—or perhaps entailed—by the claim that the 'later history of the poem is one of odd local improvements and general deterioration' (p. 23).[14] Likewise for *The Pedlar*, there is, Jonathan Wordsworth insists, 'really no alternative to a text based on MS. D. MS. B is a working-manuscript in which the poetry has not yet taken its final shape, and in MS. E the shape has already been destroyed' (p. 168). The first of these statements writes off all of Wordsworth's intensive work on reshaping the poem during some of his most creative years and depends for its force upon there being agreement as to what constitutes 'deterioration'. The second strictly makes no sense at all. MS E is later than MS D; its version of the text cannot but be nearer to 'final' than an earlier one. Unpicked, what the statement means is that the version of *The Pedlar* judged superior on aesthetic grounds is the one to be considered 'final'.

The 1799 *Ruined Cottage* contains much fine poetry and Jonathan Wordsworth's discussion of it in *The Music of Humanity* remains the starting point for critical assessment. The position he takes, however, needs to be recognized for what it is. The textual scholar claims from the surviving manuscript evidence that two bodies of verse, *The Ruined Cottage* and *The Pedlar*, arrived at their first fully completed state in 1799; the literary critic claims in addition that this was their best state, almost all later revision being evidence of how far Wordsworth had travelled 'from his original impulse' (p. 25). Jonathan Wordsworth's was an aesthetic advocacy, but so imposing was the body of textual scholarship that supported the aesthetic argument of *The Music of Humanity* that its editorial implications were accepted too. It is fair to say that with its publication the Wordsworth canon changed. The 1799 version of *The Ruined Cottage* became *the* text of choice for subsequent editions of Wordsworth and anthologies. *The Pedlar*, too, was circulated by its editor in *The Borders of Vision* (1982) and in a frequently reprinted student text in 1985. At this point the reminder is needed: neither of these now canonical texts did Wordsworth regard as finished, publish, or prepare for publication.

In 1979 James Butler laid out all the surviving material pertaining to the history of *The Ruined Cottage* and *The Pedlar* from 1797 to 1804 and from it a quite different impression of their evolving identity can be gained from that given in *The Music of Humanity*. Butler presents clean 'reading texts' of *The Ruined Cottage* as it stood in 1798 and 1799, but the mass of drafts also presented, transcribed accurately and in full for the first time, and his analysis of their chronology of composition, demonstrate that both these versions of the poem are stages in a work-in-progress. The version of MS B (1798) had barely been copied out before it was being augmented by the additional work on the figure of the Pedlar already mentioned. Engrossing though the composition clearly was to Wordsworth, it was unclear how it was to be made to work alongside the story of Margaret, and MS D (1799) remains as a record of the moment when separation of them was entertained as an artistic possibility. That Wordsworth laboured so intensely over the Pedlar figure in 1802 and that Dorothy Wordsworth should refer to the 280 or so lines of verse that emerged as *The Pedlar*, suggests that a notion of this as a free-standing poem took shape. If so, as Butler observes (p. 30), it can only have been briefly. Very soon the Pedlar material was being thought of once again as an integral part of the poem about Margaret; a new version of the whole was created and transcribed in a text established firmly enough in manuscript for Butler to offer it as a further 'reading text' (MS E).

With the copying out of the 1804 manuscripts, Butler writes, 'the seven-year history of *The Ruined Cottage* and *The Pedlar* comes to a close' (p. 35). Insofar as this statement holds true, it is one that ought to give all readers of Wordsworth pause. The textual evidence marshalled in Butler's edition leads irresistibly to the conclusion that the poem conceived in 1797 arrived at its first fully worked out and stable state not in 1799 but in 1804. At this stage, as if in recognition of the importance of this moment when the mature identity of the poem was being acknowledged, Wordsworth renamed it. *The Ruined Cottage* became *The Pedlar*.[15]

In 1804 a seven-year history of composition did come to a close. This does not mean, however, that MS E is 'final', that Wordsworth's engagement with this poetic project at last came to rest in completion.[16] Far from it. As he began to work towards *The Excursion*, it could be argued, Wordsworth was keeping faith with *The Ruined Cottage* of the long past. By 1798 that poem was being conceived as contributing to the yet-to-be-focused *Recluse*. In 1804 it had reached a shape. Now it was being reshaped yet again for another identity within an increasingly clearly focused part of *The Recluse*. As *The Pedlar* becomes 'The Wanderer', Book One of *The Excursion*, the next stage of the work-in-progress begins. As the larger whole develops, the poem that constitutes its opening book does not remain unaltered in its 1804 identity, even though details of wording are little changed. The dramatic interplay of Solitary and Pastor, the eloquent formulations of the Wanderer in response to both, all have a bearing on the role and on the effect of Book One. The Pedlar's reconciling wisdom is the last word in *The Pedlar* of 1804, but it is not the last word in 'The Wanderer' of 1814. There it is provisional, subject to interpretation and perhaps modification in the light of the discourses to follow.

As he worked on *The Excursion* in arduous, though intermittent labour from 1806 to 1814, Wordsworth continued to develop his Pedlar figure, but, as has already been touched on, the publication of the poem in 1814 did not halt further work, substantial revision taking place for the 1845 edition. What can be said with certainty is that the development of the Pedlar-Wanderer figure and his poetic setting ended with the poet's death. Given the history of Wordsworth's involvement with it and the nature of its development, it would be presumptuous, though, to say that it had reached completion.

(iv)

The second question that arises from this complicated history is: What was it about *The Ruined Cottage* and *The Pedlar* materials that impelled Wordsworth to revisit them over so many years?

The unmerited suffering of Margaret intensifies as she sinks under the loss of her husband, material hardship, break-up of her family, mental collapse, and finally death from malnutrition, exposure, and sickness. But *The Ruined Cottage* is not trying to voice yet again the age-old human demand for an explanation to the problem of suffering. After the violent death of his brother John in 1805 an anguished Wordsworth did pose the fundamental question in the way countless others have done. Seeing that the 'great Cause and ruler of things' scatters pain so liberally about his creation, can it be, 'that we have *more of love* in our Nature than he has . . .?'[17] But this is not a question Wordsworth was given to dwelling on in this form and it is not the one raised by *The Ruined Cottage* in 1798. Margaret's sufferings are caused by the natural hazards of bad weather and blighted harvests and by the calamities of war, which in an unjust state of society press hardest upon the poor. These are givens. When the Pedlar observes that Margaret's children were her 'best hope next to God in Heaven', before immediately going on to relate that 'it pleased heaven' to add to 'blighting seasons' a 'worse affliction in the plague of war', the juxtaposition is not in the least Hardyesque. The narrator of *Tess of the D'Urbervilles* may ask, 'Where was the Providence of her simple faith' while Tess was being raped, but *The Ruined Cottage* does not mount a challenge to the ultimate dispensations of Providence, impugning neither the Almighty nor Margaret's 'hope . . . that heaven | Will give me patience to endure'. What Wordsworth found difficult to work out in this poem is not, I think, to be traced to an attempt to answer the unanswerable question.[18]

The questions the poem does raise, however, are, though not unanswerable, very difficult to answer. What is the proper response to a fate such as Margaret's? Given that the dispensations of Providence are what they are, and given that it is the duty of survivors to live beyond the grief engendered by natural human sympathy, how should the tale be dealt with? Can it be made productive? Troubling thought, but can Margaret's death be made to work for our good?

Can understanding how best to respond to her story help us lead a better life?

As he closes the first part of Margaret's story, in the first full version to survive, the Pedlar muses on the loveliness and peace of their surroundings and asks:

> 'Why should a tear be in an old Man's eye?
> Why should we thus with an untoward mind
> And in the weakness of humanity
> From natural wisdom turn our hearts away,
> To natural comfort shut our eyes and ears,
> And feeding on disquiet thus disturb
> The [calm] of Nature with our restless thoughts?'

But at the end of his narration he does not return to the question. Margaret's death is starkly announced and the poem stops. It is a stop, not a close.

That Wordsworth recognized the Pedlar's invocation of 'natural wisdom' as neither self-explanatory nor adequate as a sedative for 'restless thoughts' is evident from the effort he made in the spring and summer of 1798 to enlarge on it. In a dense and tightly argued passage the Pedlar sets out the convictions that underpin his concluding exhortation to the Poet to cease questioning the 'purposes of wisdom'. The passage, too long for quotation, yet difficult to excerpt from satisfactorily, is presented as an appendix below, pp. 213–15. What the Pedlar maintains is that the man who learns to love 'things that hold | An inarticulate language' will come of necessity to love mankind. Feeling the joy of such love he will be impelled to seek it everywhere. With sense 'A vital essence and a saving power', all objects will read 'Some sweet and tender lesson to our minds | Of human suffering or of human joy. | All things shall speak of man'. Nature will minister to the 'excursive power | Of Intellect and thought', sharpening Man's sense of the glory of 'this world of feeling and of life'. Once we are fully awakened from 'oblivious sleep', every day will 'Enlarge our sphere of pleasure and of pain' as the senses and the intellect supply mutual aid, invigorating and refining each other 'with a power that knows no bound'.

> 'Thus deeply drinking in the soul of things
> We shall be wise perforce, and we shall move
> From strict necessity along the path
> Of order and of good. Whate'er we see,

> Whate'er we feel, by agency direct
> Or indirect, shall tend to feed and nurse
> Our faculties and raise to loftier heights
> Our intellectual soul'.

The whole passage is finely wrought—as expository verse it is superior to even the best of Cowper and infinitely better than anything in Akenside or Young—and its propositions are central to all of Wordsworth's poetry in mid-1798. Its paean to awakened sense links it to 'Tintern Abbey'—'well pleased to recognize | In nature and the language of the sense | The anchor of my purest thoughts'. The demand, 'was it ever meant | That this majestic imagery, the clouds, | The ocean, and the firmament of heaven, | Should be a barren picture on the mind?' is also heard in 'The Tables Turned' ('Close up those barren leaves') and 'Lines Written in Early Spring'. As a declaration of faith it persuaded Coleridge, who transcribed the opening eighteen lines of it in a letter to his clergyman brother George, to add force to his assurance that he had 'snapped [his] squeaking baby-trumpet of Sedition', and was seeking only to 'set the affections in right tune by the beauty of the inanimate impregnated, as with a living soul, by the presence of Life'.[19]

Powerful though it is, however, the passage was set aside and in the next recension of *The Ruined Cottage* in 1799 the Pedlar was allowed only twenty-four lines in which to bring the Poet's thoughts and feelings to right tune at the conclusion of Margaret's story. Given that Wordsworth was never to repudiate the core message of the 'Not useless do I deem' lines, much of which was to appear in Book Four of *The Excursion*, why did he excise it in 1798–9?

The purely technical argument often advanced —the passage is so long it would unbalance the poem's structure—is not wholly persuasive. Eighteenth-century readers were accustomed to extended flights of meditative verse and both *The Prelude* and *The Excursion* demonstrate that Wordsworth relished this element of his Miltonic inheritance and was prepared to take poetic risks with it. There is, I suggest, a more persuasive explanation why Wordsworth cut the passage. It is that in composing the 'Not useless do I deem' lines Wordsworth was working against the grain of what he most wanted to achieve as a poet.

Indications of what that was are found in a prose fragment, dating from 1798, which is concerned with the nature of virtuous living and the role of 'that part of our conduct & actions which is the result of our habits'.[20] Treatises such as those by Godwin and Paley, which 'formally & systematically lay down rules for the actions of Men', are of no use, Wordsworth asserts, to which he adds that he knows of 'no book or system of moral philosophy written with sufficient power to melt into our affection[?s], to incorporate itself with the blood & vital juices of our minds, & thence to have any influence worth our notice in forming those habits of which I am speaking'. The essay peters out, but evidence of the significance to Wordsworth of this last declaration is abundant as he entered the most important years of his creative life, the period that defined him, to himself as much as to the world, as the kind of poet he aspired to be. In his lyrics Wordsworth repeatedly hymns the knowledge that comes from lived experience rather than from 'barren leaves':

> Let Nature be your teacher.
>
> She has a world of ready wealth,
> Our minds and hearts to bless—
> Spontaneous wisdom breathed by health,
> Truth breathed by chearfulness.
>
> One impulse from a vernal wood
> May teach you more of man;
> Of moral evil and of good,
> Than all the sages can.

'Chearfulness'—a keyword in the poetry of this period. It springs from openness:

> 'The eye it cannot chuse but see,
> We cannot bid the ear be still;
> Our bodies feel, where'er they be,
> Against, or with our will.'[21]

And 'Tintern Abbey' brings everything together in a personal testimony of truths 'Felt in the blood, and felt along the heart', as Wordsworth delivers his credo, his 'chearful faith that all which we behold | Is full of blessings'.

All these declarations of faith are opposed in form—importantly not in substance—to the lines beginning 'Not useless'. The latter are systematic, expository, syntactically insistent on the logical development of the argument: the lyrics and 'Tintern Abbey' are testamentary utterances, professions of faith. Wordsworth abandoned the idea of using the 'Not useless' lines as the run-in to the conclusion to *The Ruined Cottage*, I suggest, not because he stopped believing in them—he never did—but because he sensed something inimical in the mode of their expression. Wordsworth was shortly to declare that Poetry 'is the most philosophic of all writing' because while 'its object is truth', its particular power is to carry truth 'alive into the heart by passion'.[22] A better way had to be found poetically to convey the Pedlar's wisdom, if it were to incorporate itself with the blood and vital juices of our minds and so become active, practical knowledge.

While putting aside the 'Not useless' lines for the 1799 version of *The Ruined Cottage* eased one difficulty, however, it brought a bigger one into focus. It is the question of the authority of the Pedlar.[23] In the 1799 text almost all the biographical information about the figure has been excised: we learn his name, that he is a pedlar, and that he and the Poet are old friends, and that is all. During his narration he acts the part of an older and wiser man, but none of his remarks has indicated that his final counsel will be quite so astonishingly assured and comprehensive. Seeing how troubled the Poet is by Margaret's story, the Pedlar says,

> 'My Friend, enough to sorrow have you given,
> The purposes of wisdom ask no more;
> Be wise and chearful, and no longer read
> The forms of things with an unworthy eye.
> She sleeps in the calm earth, and peace is here.
> I well remember that those very plumes,
> Those weeds, and the high spear-grass on that wall,
> By mist and silent rain-drops silver'd o'er,
> As once I passed, did to my mind convey
> So still an image of tranquillity,
> So calm and still, and looked so beautiful
> Amid the uneasy thoughts which filled my mind,
> That what we feel of sorrow and despair
> From ruin and from change, and all the grief
> The passing shews of being leave behind,
> Appeared an idle dream that could not live
> Where meditation was. I turned away
> And walked along my road in happiness.'

'My Friend, enough to sorrow have you given.' To which a natural response might be that of the Scribes who heard Jesus teach in the synagogue and said, 'Whence hath this man this wisdom . . . Is this not the carpenter's son?' Or as a scornful Francis Jeffrey was to put it in his attempted demolition of *The Excursion* in 1814, does Mr Wordsworth expect us to attend to the 'wisdom and virtue' that is 'put into the mouth of a person accustomed to higgle about tape, or brass sleeve-buttons?'[24]

This question, the matter of authority, is one that Wordsworth so clearly had to confront, long before Jeffrey brutally posed it, that much of his writing over the period 1798–1805 is determined by engagements with it. Recollecting the origins of *The Recluse*, Coleridge said that the plan had been that Wordsworth should deliver 'upon authority' a 'system of philosophy'.[25] Such was Coleridge's claim in late life, but there is every reason to doubt that Wordsworth would ever have used the word 'system' in connection with the *Recluse* project. The phrase 'upon authority', though, cannot be dismissed quite so categorically as Coleridge's rather than Wordsworth's. It is clear from the firmness with which the young Wordsworth embraced the idea of the philosophic poem that he shared Coleridge's belief that he possessed extraordinary gifts and was marked out for special achievement. Looking forward eagerly to getting on with the project, Wordsworth announced, 'I know not any thing which will not come within the scope of my plan', a remarkable statement from a 28-year-old who has not much to show for his life so far, but it is one wholly in keeping with other such ambitious declarations made about *The Recluse* at this period.[26] And conviction carries authority. But such authority will collapse at the first challenge, if it is based on nothing more than an internal conviction of justification. The Revolutionary era threw up lots of self-styled prophets, with ambitions quite as grand as those to be embodied in *The Recluse*, a point not lost on Byron, who ranked Wordsworth with the maddest of them: 'this man is the kind of poet who in the same manner that Joanna Southcote found many thousand people to take her dropsy for God Almighty re-impregnated, has found some hundreds of persons to misbelieve in his insanities, and holds his art as a kind of poetical Emanuel Swedenborg or Richard Brothers or Parson Tozer, half enthusiast and half impostor.'[27] So what was Wordsworth's authority for believing he had something special to offer the world? What was the source of his conviction that he was called to be a latter-day Orpheus, singing 'some philosophic Song | Of Truth that cherishes our daily life, | With meditations passionate from deep | Recesses in man's heart'? It was a perfectly reasonable question the Scribes put to Jesus: 'By what authority doest thou these things?' (Matthew 21: 23).

Wordsworth's turn to autobiography was an attempt to engage with the issue. He declares explicitly in *The Two-Part Prelude* that these explorations of his past have taken shape in an attempt to understand himself and to explain to Coleridge 'how the heart was framed | Of him thou lovest'.[28] More particularly, the poet needs not only to understand but also to explain how he comes to be able to make the fervent *confessio fidei* with which the poem ends. Identifying the close of the 1790s as a time of 'dereliction and dismay', when fear is everywhere and millennial visions have become nothing more than a 'melancholy waste of hopes o'erthrown', Wordsworth finds grounds for a more than Roman confidence in Man, 'a faith | That fails not, in all sorrow my support, | The blessing of my life' (II, 479–91). And its source?

> the gift is yours,
> Ye Mountains! thine, O Nature! thou hast fed
> My lofty speculations, and in thee
> For this uneasy heart of ours I find
> A never-failing principle of joy
> And purest passion.   (II, 491–6)

To the unpersuaded or uncomprehending, such as Jeffrey commenting on *The Excursion* in 1814 or Macaulay on *The Prelude* in 1850, such a testimony—the 'old flimsy philosophy about the effect of scenery on the mind; the old crazy, mystical metaphysics'—would always smack of the 'mystical verbiage of the methodist pulpit', in which the speaker's own eloquence persuades him that 'he is the elected organ of divine truth and persuasion'.[29] For Wordsworth, to the contrary, there was nothing mystical about his conviction and sense of vocation. It was founded on personally verified data—that is, his own life—and *it made sense*. The 'Not useless' lines are an attempt to show how the claim that it did could be supported through the language of associationist philosophy. The autobiographical poetry of 1798–9 in *The Two-Part Prelude* seeks to show it from evidence drawn from lived experience. Everything in the poem is selected and structured to underpin the remarkable testimony with which it concludes. In Part One a flood of memories provide evidence not only of how vital are physical exploits and sensations of joy and fear in shaping the growing child, but of their continuing power for nourishment of the adult through recollection—'There are in our existence spots of time | Which with distinct pre-eminence retain | A fructifying virtue' (I, 288–90). The Second Part opens with further recollections, but these open out into meditations on why such experiences can be said to matter. Starting at the dawn of life with the baby at the breast, Wordsworth traces a development from the infant's growingly tenacious apprehension of the world outside itself, through to the ecstatic recognition by the poet in his seventeenth year that he participated in one life,

> the sentiment of being spread
> O'er all that moves, and all that seemeth still,
> O'er all that, lost beyond the reach of thought
> And human knowledge, to the human eye
> Invisible, yet liveth to the heart,
> O'er all that leaps, and runs, and shouts and sings
> Or beats the gladsome air, o'er all that glides
> Beneath the wave, yea in the wave itself
> And mighty depth of waters: wonder not
> If such my transports were, for in all things
> I saw one life and felt that it was joy. (II, 450–60)

The Two-Part Prelude records the growth of a 'chosen son', 1770 to 1787. The evolution of the poem itself, 1798 to 1799, records the chosen one's attempts to understand how he was chosen and what the implications of understanding it are.

Not surprisingly, all of Wordsworth's work on the figure of the pedlar follows the same pattern as the autobiographical exploration. In the 1798 version of The Ruined Cottage the Pedlar is described as a 'chosen son' (l. 76), whose lack of formal education is more than compensated for by his sense of one-ness with the active universe. Apparently poor, he is actually wealthy in all that makes for true aliveness—a creative mind, discrimination of feeling, a relationship with 'the God who looked into his mind' (89). That Wordsworth and the Pedlar are to be identified in essentials is demonstrated by the fact that most of the lines describing the latter were smoothly transferred to *The Prelude*, III, 121–67, where they serve to explain the poet's state of mind during his first year at Cambridge.

Work on *The Pedlar* of 1802 sought to sharpen the opposition set up in 1798 between 'dead lore' and vital knowledge, as if in recognition that for the pedlar figure to carry conviction as a prophet, more evidence had to be provided of how he has acquired a knowledge of the true. Altering his conception of him very strikingly, Wordsworth decided to enhance the account of the pedlar's development by exploring the relation between his experience of Nature's ministry and his formal education within the Christian faith. Formulations already tried out in the autobiographical verse were available for depiction of Nature's ministry, but for the account of the pedlar's Christian upbringing, Wordsworth moved into new territory— literally as well as figuratively.

As has been noted already, the Pedlar, previously said to come from the Lake District, now becomes a Scot.

In re-imagining his wisdom figure as coming from north of the border, Wordsworth was drawing on a mix of sources—as always, personal experience reinforced and interpreted through reading. In September 1801 Wordsworth visited Scotland for the first time, tracking the Clyde to Glasgow and moving on at least as far as Loch Lomond.[30] But Wordsworth had known something of Scotland from his schooldays acquaintance with Scottish pedlars. It was so common for pedlars to be Scottish, that in the parish registers he had examined, Hawkshead historian T. W. Thompson found 'they are almost always described as Scotchmen wherever they were born and bred'.[31] One of them, as Wordsworth recalled in the Fenwick Note to *The Excursion*, occasionally resided in Hawkshead 'while I was a school boy . . . with whom I had frequent conversations upon what had befallen him & what he had observed during his wandering life'.[32] Wordsworth also learned about such a pedlar from his future sister-in-law. On the death of her mother in 1783, Sara Hutchinson had been sent as a young girl to live with an aunt in Kendal, Mary Patrick. Her husband, James Patrick, had herded cattle in Perthshire before becoming a pedlar and subsequently a draper. 'My own imaginations', Wordsworth recalled, 'I was happy to find clothed in reality, and fresh ones suggested, by what she reported of this man's tenderness of heart, his strong and pure imagination, and his solid attainments in literature, chiefly religious, whether in prose or verse.'[33]

In the same note the aged poet also remarked with a certain wist-fulness that 'wandering' was always his passion and that 'had I been born in a class which would have deprived me of what is called a liberal education, it is not unlikely that being strong in body, I should have taken to a way of life such as that in which my Pedlar passed the greater part of his days.' It is a remark which reveals the continuing hold on Wordsworth's imagination of a passage from Robert Heron's *Observations Made in a Journey through the Western Counties of Scotland* (1793), which was acknowledged in a note to the 1814 *Excursion*:

In Heron's Tour in Scotland is given an intelligent account of the qualities by which this class of men used to be, and still are, in some degree, distin-guished, and of the benefits which Society derives from their labours. Among their characteristics, he does not omit to mention that, from being obliged to pass so much of their time in solitary wandering among rural objects, they frequently acquired meditative habits of mind, and are strongly disposed to enthusiasm poetical and religious.

Wordsworth will have been all the more likely to take this claim seriously because it came from the man who appreciated Burns's genius and was the first to write a biography of him.[34]

In his first working out of the pedlar Wordsworth had sought to contrast what the boy had gained by being free of the 'dead lore' of the schools. For the 1802 *Pedlar* he greatly enlarged the opposition, draw-ing on ideas about the figure's Scottish origins. When very young the boy has to earn his keep by herding cattle in the summer, but over the winter months he attends his stepfather's school, where he receives 'Needful instruction . . . [in] the ways | Of honesty & holiness severe'.[35] (Line references to the 1802 *Pedlar* are very difficult to follow in Butler's edition—due not to editorial failure but the great complex-ity of the manuscript materials being transcribed—so the following citations are of page numbers only.) His home is described (333) as,

Virtuous, & wanting little to the growth
Of a strong mind, although exceeding poor[.]
Pure livers were they all—austere & grave
And fearing God[,] the very children taught
Stern self-respect, a reverence for God's word
And piety scarce known on English land[.][36]

Tempering the severity of these shaping influences, however, is Nature's ministry, to which he is also exposed from his earliest years.

Alone among the hills, 'Intensely brood[ing]' on the shapes and forms of earth and sky, the boy becomes a living embodiment of the 'Not useless' exposition:

> he had felt the power
> Of nature and already was prepared
> By his intense conceptions to receive
> Deeply, the lesson deep of love, which he
> Whom Nature, by whatever means, has taught
> To feel intensely cannot but receive.   (345)

Nature's teaching is not in opposition to the Bible's. On the contrary, as 'Sensation, soul & form' melt into the boy,

> Oh *then* how beautiful how bright appeared
> The written promise; he had early learned
> To reverence the volume which displays
> The mystery[,] the life which cannot die[,]
> But in the mountains did he *feel* his faith[,]
> There did he see the writing.   (347)

The account of the boy's growth concludes with the rhapsodic passage about the joy of participating in the one life, already quoted. Such a man could never become a dominie; the confinement of the school-room is exchanged for the freedom of the pedlar's life.

The opposition of vital knowledge to dead lore in the figure of the Pedlar is clearly very important to Wordsworth's sense of the religious dimension to life, but equally so is the way in which the figure reflects Wordsworth's emerging conception of the Poet. The 1799 version of *The Ruined Cottage* was copied out just as Wordsworth was at work on his first treatise on poetry, the Preface to *Lyrical Ballads* 1800, and composition of *The Pedlar* overlapped the much revised version of the Preface for the third edition of *Lyrical Ballads* in 1802. The theoretical prose and the slowly evolving poetry about the Pedlar intertwine.

Two passages in particular link the figure to Wordsworth's concerns around the time of the 1800 Preface. In the 1798 composition the Pedlar is described as one who has wandered far from his native hills:

> much had he seen of men,
> Their manners, their enjoyments and pursuits,
> Their passions and their feelings, chiefly those

> Essential and eternal in the heart,
> Which 'mid the simpler forms of rural life
> Exist more simple in their elements
> And speak a plainer language.[37]

The lines are clearly the germ of the manifesto in the 1800 Preface for a particular kind of poetry concerned with fundamentals, the 'primary laws of our nature':

Low and rustic life was generally chosen because in that situation the essential passions of the heart find a better soil in which they can attain their maturity, are less under restraint, and speak a plainer and more emphatic language; because in that situation our elementary feelings exist in a state of greater simplicity and consequently may be more accurately contemplated and more forcibly communicated; because the manners of rural life germinate from those elementary feelings; and from the necessary character of rural occupations are more easily comprehended; and are more durable; and lastly, because in that situation the passions of men are incorporated with the beautiful and permanent forms of nature.[38]

This declaration—a theoretical gauntlet thrown down to be picked up later by Jeffrey, Hazlitt, and Coleridge amongst others—has many functions. It justifies the poet's retirement to a rural life among the mountains; it validates such a poem as the pastoral 'Michael'; and it emphasizes the significance of such a figure as the Pedlar, whose fictional life is imagined in conformity with all its propositions.

The Pedlar co-exists with the Wordsworth of *Lyrical Ballads* also when he pronounces sternly on what he believes to be the justification of his narrative. In itself Margaret's story is no more than

> a common tale,
> By moving accidents uncharactered,
> A tale of silent suffering, hardly clothed
> In bodily form, and to the grosser sense
> But ill adapted, scarcely palpable
> To him who does not think.   (290–5)

Reflection on the story, though, the Pedlar declares, may give rise to 'A power to virtue friendly' (288). The allusion to Othello's 'Of moving accidents by flood and field' anticipates the later use of the phrase in *Hart-Leap Well* (1800), where the poet disclaims sensation: 'The moving accident is not my trade', but the passage as a whole is linked to the many of Wordsworth's utterances about poetry around the moment of *Lyrical Ballads* 1800 which insist that in his poems 'the

feeling therein developed gives importance to the action and situation and not the action and situation to the feeling'; that the contemporary 'thirst after outrageous stimulation' is 'degrading'; that all his
poems have 'a worthy *purpose*'; and that there is a value in a poem
such as 'Michael', even 'though it be ungarnished with events'.[39]

In the Preface to *Lyrical Ballads* 1800 Wordsworth was concerned
primarily in defining the subject matter and the language of poetry
that might have the power 'to interest mankind permanently'.[40] Two
years later, however, what engaged him most was characterizing 'the
Poet' and again work on the Pedlar was integral to Wordsworth's
working out of his ideas.

The most remarkable of the many additions to the Preface for the
1802 *Lyrical Ballads* is the lengthy passage beginning, 'Taking up the
subject, then, upon general grounds, I ask what is meant by the word
Poet? What is a Poet?' One of the defining characteristics of the
Poet, according to Wordsworth's answer, is that he is 'a man pleased
with his own passions and volitions, and who rejoices more
than other men in the spirit of life that is in him; delighting to
contemplate similar volitions and passions as manifested in the
goings-on of the Universe, and habitually impelled to create them
where he does not find them' (138). This vision of a sense of life
so vivid that it impels the compulsion both to seek and to create it,
was first formulated in 1798 in the account of the Pedlar's religious
awakening and later served as autobiography in Book Three of
The Prelude:

> To every natural form, rock, fruit, and flower,
> Even the loose stones that cover the highway,
> He gave a moral life; he saw them feel
> Or linked them to some feeling. In all shapes
> He found a secret and mysterious soul,
> A fragrance and a spirit of strange meaning.[41]

Others, it is acknowledged, 'called it madness', but as Wordsworth
developed his idea of the Poet in the 1802 Preface and the contemporaneous work on *The Pedlar*, what he stressed most forcefully was
that this identification with the 'goings-on of the Universe' serves as
the foundation for a sympathetic openness to the goings-on of
human life, not as a mark of separation from it. In his itinerant
labour the Pedlar observes 'the progress and decay | Of many

minds[,] of minds and bodies too[,]' and 'Hence it was | That in our best experience he was rich | And in the wisdom of our daily life' (p. 361). Able to 'afford to suffer | With those whom he saw suffer', the Pedlar, like the ideal Poet, shares the 'general passions and thoughts and feelings of men'. And, Wordsworth asks in the 1802 Preface, what are they connected with?

Undoubtedly with our moral sentiments and animal sensation, and with the causes which excite these; with the operations of the elements and the appearances of the visible universe; with storm and sun-shine, with the revolutions of the seasons, with cold and heat, with loss of friends and kindred, with injuries and resentments, gratitude and hope, with fear and sorrow.

Or, as it is expressed in *The Pedlar*, 'he was alive | To all that was enjoyed where'er he went | And all that was endured.'

Working out this developing conception of the Pedlar proved very taxing. Day after day from January through March 1802 Dorothy Wordsworth recorded sleepless nights, illness, fatigue, and some bafflement as the poem resisted completion. 'William had had a bad night & was working at his poem. We sate by the fire & did not walk, but read the pedlar thinking it done but lo, though Wm could find fault with no one part of it—it was uninteresting & must be altered. Poor William!' (7 February). The entry a few days later offers a glimpse of what her brother's struggles cost her: 'William working again. I recopied the Pedlar, but poor William all the time at work . . . I almost finished writing The Pedlar, but poor William wore himself & me out with Labour' (12 February).[42] Eventually, however, the work halted. The Pedlar had become a type of the ideal Poet, one who through the nature of his early education and later experience is conversant both with God and higher truth and with ordinary men and women and their sufferings. He was invested with the authority he had earlier lacked.

By the spring of 1804 *The Ruined Cottage* and *The Pedlar* were united in the form that would survive through to the poem's incorporation into *The Excursion*. Even at this stage, though, when he was pulling together poetry that had already been heavily worked over, Wordsworth continued to revise, making two striking additions. The first reinforces the notion just mentioned—that the Pedlar becomes a type of the Poet.[43] In one manuscript, as the Poet is just beginning to explain his boyhood pleasure in the 'plain presence of [the Pedlar's] dignity', he exclaims,

> Oh! many are the Poets that are sown
> By nature, men endued with highest gifts,
> The vision and the faculty divine,
> Yet wanting the accomplishment of verse.

Many such men, born in low estate, the Poet claims to have known, who were 'as the prime and choice of sterling minds'. It is a claim Wordsworth repeated at greater length around the same time in *The Prelude*, XII, 220–77, where he pays tribute to Lake District shepherds, men 'rude in shew' but who are silent poets, performing 'high service' within themselves. The passage, a dense reworking of fundamental concerns about humble life, was of such importance to Wordsworth that he reprinted all fifty-four lines of it as conclusion to the Postscript to *Yarrow Revisited* in 1835, declaring the passage's timeless message relevant to contemporary social issues: 'it turns upon the individual dignity which humbleness of social condition does not preclude, but frequently promotes.'[44]

The Pedlar passage is also linked to the striking declaration in the 1802 Preface to *Lyrical Ballads* that a Poet 'is a man speaking to men: a man, it is true, endued with more lively sensibility, more enthusiasm and tenderness, who has a greater knowledge of human nature, and a more comprehensive soul, than are supposed to be common among mankind . . .'. The passage is generally taken to be an endorsement of the Poet's exceptionality, but in fact the last clause signals rather the opposite—that the qualities of mind and heart that make up the Poet are more common among mankind than is generally supposed. It was certainly what Wordsworth had in mind when he referred to his mariner brother, John, as a 'silent poet'.[45]

The second notable body of revision concerns once again the question of the Pedlar's identity. Perhaps in an attempt to universalize the figure, Wordsworth at this point strips the Pedlar of his name—Patrick Drummond—ironically so, because in the version of *The Pedlar* settled on now other defining aspects of his Scottishness are greatly emphasized. Many factors combined now in the realization of this development. Wordsworth had read John Stoddart's *Remarks on Local Scenery and Manners in Scotland* (1801), which weds an impassioned appreciation of landscape in general to a sensitive attempt to respond to the specific meanings of different manners, customs, and language. He had also read *Minstrelsy of the Scottish Border* (1802), in which Walter Scott's lament for the bards who had memorialized the deeds and heroes of the past spoke directly to the author of 'Michael'.[46] But much more important, he had learned a great deal more about Scotland at first hand. Wordsworth's first visit in 1801 had been as part of a wedding-party, travelling comfortably—sight-seeing from a coach, in fact—but his second, over the late summer of 1803, was much less comfortable and correspondingly much more valuable. Observing, reflecting, conversing or, as they crossed into the predominantly Gaelic-speaking Highlands, barely conversing, the tourists were bombarded with sensations and information of all kinds about environment, people, livelihoods, and customs.[47] Within weeks of his return, Wordsworth was at work on the Pedlar again.

From first conceivings, the Pedlar has been presented as one who loves Scottish poems and songs:

> His eye
> Flashing poetic fire, he would repeat
> The songs of Burns, and as we trudged along
> Together did we make the hollow grove
> Ring with our transports.[48]

At this stage he is a Cumbrian. When the Pedlar figure becomes Scottish, the growth of his imagination is attributed in part to his feeding on 'many a tale | Traditionary' and 'many a legend' of his native hills (343). Playing with the little girl at Hawkshead, he would be pleased

> to sing to her
> Scotch songs, sometimes, but oftener to repeat
> Scotch poetry, old ballads, & old tales[,]
> Love-Gregory, William Wallace & Rob Roy.   (329)

The 1804 version, however, alters the emphasis. While Love Gregory, Wallace, and Rob Roy remain, Burns is not mentioned, and the Pedlar and the Poet no longer make the groves ring with their transports.[49] Rather to the contrary:

> We walk'd, he talk'd about himself, or held
> Abstruse discourses, reasonings of the mind

> Turn'd inwards, or in other moods, he sang
> Old songs, and sometimes, too, at my request,
> Psalms and religious anthems, sounds sedate
> And soft, and most refreshing to the heart.   (386)

The more sombre note struck here is also sounded in material that expands the account of the Pedlar's specifically Scottish religious upbringing. As a boy he had 'read, and read again | Whate'er the Minister's old Shelf supplied | The life and death of Martyrs who sustain'd | Intolerable pangs' (396). In one of the two manuscripts made now the identity of the martyrs is made quite specific: 'The life and death of Martyrs who sustain'd | Intolerable pangs, the Records left | Of Persecution and the Covenant, | That, like an echo, ring through Scotland still' (397).[50] Absorbing himself in the history of the Covenanters, the young boy grows up in the Scottish Church, under the sway of 'The strong hand of her purity'. In 'his riper years' he remains grateful for the 'unrelenting eye' with which he was watched over in his youth. In the 1802 *Pedlar* Patrick is said to have gathered 'When a Boy | Some gloomy notions which in later life | Would come to him at times' (333), but in the 1804 composition what is stressed is that experience has tempered severity. Through experience—his wanderings, his loneliness, his goodness and kind works—'Whatever in his childhood, or in youth, | He had imbib'd of fear or darker thought | Was melted all away' (412). The Pedlar emerges as a deeply pious product of Scottish Presbyterianism, but one who has managed to combine its admirable seriousness with lightness of heart and love of all created things:

> surely, never did there live on earth
> A man of sweeter temper. Birds and beasts,
> He lov'd them all, chickens and household dogs,
> And to the kitten of a neighbour's house
> Would carry crumbs and feed it.   (412)

One small but highly significant revision confirms the growing importance to the poem of the Pedlar's Christian faith.[51] On one of his visits to Margaret, who is now alone and struggling, but not yet in irreversible decline, the Pedlar kisses her baby as he takes his leave. Both 1798 and 1799 texts read:

> I left her then
> With the best hope and comfort I could give;

> She thanked me for my will, but for my hope
> It seemed she did not thank me. (66–7)

In 1804, however, the lines are more explicit as to the source of the Pedlar's 'best hope':

> I counsell'd her to have her trust
> In God's good love, and seek his help by prayer.
> I took my Staff, and, when I kiss'd her Babe;
> The tears stood in her eyes. I left her then
> With the best hope and comfort I could give;
> She thank'd me for my will; but for my hope
> It seem'd she did not thank me. (438)

Within a year of the copying of MS M the need for Christian hope was brought home personally to Wordsworth on the violent death at sea of his brother John. It was the 'hope' St Paul offered to the Thessalonians when he assured them that Christians were not 'as others which have no hope'; it was embedded in the Book of Common Prayer's 'Order for the Burial of the Dead': 'O merciful God . . . who also hath taught us, by his holy Apostle Saint Paul, not to be sorry, as men without hope, for them that sleep in him.' And it was the hope with which 'Elegiac Stanzas, Suggested by a Picture of Peele Castle', Wordsworth's lament for his brother's passing, concludes:

> But welcome fortitude, and patient chear,
> And frequent sights of what is to be borne!
> Such sights, or worse, as are before me here.—
> Not without hope we suffer and we mourn.[52]

(v)

Once *The Pedlar* became Book One of *The Excursion* the text remained relatively stable. Revision was confined to verbal detail and, as Mary Wordsworth put it somewhat impatiently, 'too long-continued labour in the attempt to correct that he deems to be the faults (chiefly in the versification) of the Excursion'.[53] For the 1845 edition of his collected *Poetical Works*, however, Wordsworth made a substantial change that notably differentiates it from all previous texts of the poem that had begun life nearly fifty years ago.

In every version since 1798, both of the poem as independent creation and as Book One of *The Excursion*, it had been the Pedlar's task
to guide the Poet's sympathetic responses to the story of Margaret's
decline and to lead him at its close with her death to an acceptance
of realities deeper than the 'passing shews of Being'. At the mid-
point of his narration the sage old man invokes 'natural wisdom' and
'natural comfort' as powers to counter the tendency of Man's 'unto-
ward mind' towards 'feeding on disquiet'. At its close, he exhorts his
listener to 'read | The forms of things with an unworthy eye' no
longer, in the passage already quoted, beginning (in the 1814 text),
'My Friend! enough to sorrow you have given | The purposes of
wisdom ask no more'.[54]

Such was the text of *The Excursion* that made Keats rejoice and
Mary and Percy Shelley mourn. It was what Tennyson and Darwin
read. This was the text invoked by Matthew Arnold when trying to
console his sister on the death of their mother.[55] But it was a text that
by 1845 no longer satisfied its creator. In a final revision the terms of
the Wanderer's concluding words of wisdom were altered. Margaret,
he now declares, had been one

> 'Who in her worst distress, had ofttimes felt
> The unbounded might of prayer; and learned with soul
> Fixed on the Cross, that consolation springs,
> From sources deeper far than deepest pain,
> For the meek Sufferer. Why then should we read
> The forms of things with an unworthy eye?'

To read the forms of things with an unworthy eye would be to
disregard the boon of divine grace which Margaret had acknowledged in her lifetime and which supports the Wanderer as he relates
her story. As he assures the Poet in his new last words, 'all the
grief | That passing shows of Being leave behind' appears an idle
dream to him 'Whose meditative sympathies repose | Upon the
breast of Faith'. Such was the final authorized text of *The Excursion*,
Book One. But what is the significance of Wordsworth making this
change now?

In 1814 Francis Jeffrey's review of *The Excursion* had opened with
'This will never do', and very little of the poem survives his demonstration of why not. It is important to note, however, that Jeffrey has
no quarrel with its theology. The weakness of *The Excursion* in
Jeffrey's judgement is that truisms are buried in an exposition 'more

cloudy, wordy, and inconceivably prolix, than any thing we ever met with', which confirms that, like the worst sort of Methodist preacher, Mr Wordsworth has become so intoxicated with his own eloquence that he believes the truisms to be his own discovery. But the religious doctrine is sound. It is

the old familiar one, that a firm belief in the providence of a wise and beneficent Being must be our great stay and support under all afflictions and perplexities upon earth—and that there are indications of his power and goodness in all the aspects of the visible universe, whether living or inanimate—every part of which should therefore be regarded with love and reverence, as exponents of those great attributes.[56]

Prolixity; the pretension of the 'Prospectus'; the mystical verbiage; these and many other aspects of *The Excursion* were targeted by reviewers, but the fundamentals of its stance towards God and Nature were not. It is not surprising—they were congruent with the long-established parameters of mainstream thinking. In his first draftings for what would become *The Two-Part Prelude* of 1799 Wordsworth pointed to what might demand a loftier song:

> How oft the eternal spirit, he that has
> His life in unimaginable things
> And he who painting what he is in all
> The visible imagery of all the worlds
> Is yet apparent chiefly as the soul
> Of our first sympathies. . . .[57]

The topics touched on here are not at all startling *as topics*. Over the previous century they had been the stuff of innumerable treatises, sermons, hymns, and poems that explored how far Locke's declaration that 'The works of Nature everywhere sufficiently evidence a Deity' could be regarded as true and in what ways it could be brought home as a truth to the minds and hearts of ordinary human beings.[58] The discourse of Natural Theology was fully capable of encompassing most shades of dispute and it went on robustly generating contributions until well into the nineteenth century. The Wanderer's passage of reconciling wisdom in 1814 was one such. However distinctive it may have been as poetry, as an utterance about God, Nature, and Man it existed within the same conceptual framework as Paley's *Natural Theology; or, Evidences of the Existence and Attributes of the Deity* (1802).[59] Most readers were comfortable with the well-worked-over Natural Theology of *The Excursion*, but for some it was not in itself sufficient. Charles Lamb might appreciate the poem's lack of doctrinal specificity, believing it a virtue that it had 'the character of an expanded and generous Quakerism', but less accommodating Christians looked for more certainty. Reviewing the poem in 1815, for example, the evangelical poet James Montgomery found much to praise. He placed *The Excursion* amongst the finest of those works that throughout the ages have honoured the Deity through loving attentiveness to the visible creation, 'the veil of glory which he has cast round the thick darkness wherein he dwells withdrawn from mortal sight, yet makes his presence felt, wherever there is motion, breath, or being'. There is much more commendation in this vein and not for a moment is the poet's belief in God doubted, but Montgomery is perturbed by a crucial weakness. 'Every system of ethics which insists not on the extinction of sin in the human soul, by the only means through which it can be extinguished, and everlasting righteousness substituted, is radically defective ... We do not mean to infer, that Mr Wordsworth excludes from his system the salvation of man, as revealed in the Scriptures, but it is evident that he has not made "Jesus Christ the chief corner-stone" of it'.[60]

From the other end of the Anglican spectrum, John Taylor Coleridge welcomed *The Excursion* in the High Church organ, the *British Critic*, for intending to enforce the principles 'which seem to us to shine like a glory round every page of true poetry ... that whatsoever material or temporary exists before our senses, is capable of being associated, in our minds, with something spiritual and eternal; that such associations tend to ennoble and purify the heart'. By 'considering all things sensible with respect to some higher power', he avers, 'we are more likely to get an insight into final causes, and all the wonderful ways of Providence'.[61] However, while the future biographer of Keble remained a fervent admirer, not doubting that Mr Wordsworth was 'a great moral teacher', he could not but think that the poet failed to see the implications of some of his flights of fancy and he insisted that he ought to have seen them. In a later essay for the *British Critic*, Taylor Coleridge considers, for example, the assertion in the 'Ode: Intimations of Immortality' that the child enters the world 'trailing clouds of glory ... | From God, who is our home'. This may be finely imaginative poetry, he concedes, but if it is true, 'what becomes of original sin, and the fall of man, and if they are abandoned, where is the atonement—in one word, (and the consequence cannot stop shorter,) where is Christianity?'[62]

John Taylor Coleridge was not a Philistine. He knew that poetry differed from moral philosophy and he had the highest regard for Wordsworth as a poet, but poets were no more to be exempted from the test of truth than philosophers and so he pressed his questions home very firmly. They were posed again in 1828, with less sympathy and rather more doggedness, by someone who was moving from being one of Wordsworth's earliest and most fervent admirers to being a captious critic, John Wilson. Reviewing Montgomery's *The Christian Psalmist* and *The Christian Poet*, and John Keble's *The Christian Year*, for *Blackwood's Magazine*, Wilson, writing as 'Christopher North', took the opportunity to consider the nature of 'Sacred Poetry'. At one point in his argument about the possibilities of the genre, he turns to the 'great and lamentable defect' in Wordsworth's presentation of human life, namely, the absence of Revealed Religion. Wordsworth is a great poet and Wordsworth is a Christian, but, Wilson declares, if one examines his most important work, *The Excursion*, 'He certainly cannot be called a Christian poet.' Consider the story of Margaret. Was she a Christian?

Let the answer be yes—as good a Christian as ever kneeled in the small mountain chapel, in whose churchyard her body now waits for the resurrection. If she was—then the picture of her and her agonies, is a libel not only on her character, but on the character of all other poor Christian women in this Christian land. Placed as she was, for so many years, in the clutches of so many passions—she surely must have turned sometimes—ay, often, and often, and often, else had she sooner left the clay—towards her Lord and Saviour.[63]

Although the combative tone of the piece most probably disguised it, Wilson was trying to make a discrimination between an attack on Mr Wordsworth's personal beliefs and his publicly expressed ones as a poet. Was he a '*Christian poet*', both words equally stressed? Over a decade later Wilson reissued his challenge and he may have been determined to do so by the appearance of another article on Wordsworth's poetry and the Christian religion, which arrived at a markedly more positive assessment. *Dearden's Miscellany* proclaimed itself a literary magazine that exercised the privilege 'of appealing to and taking our stand upon, universally acknowledged Christian

truths, as the fountains of right judgment', so its assessment of Wordsworth in 1840 naturally concentrated on him as religious poet. High
praise for *The Excursion*, above all, is accompanied by an attack on
those who have accused its author of 'being without Christianity'.
All too often, the anonymous writer [Henry Alford] declares, critics
confound 'two very different things, namely *religious poetry*, and *versi-
fied religion*'.[64] Whether or not Wilson knew the article in *Dearden's
Miscellany*, exhumation of his own 1828 *Blackwood's* piece for his
Recollections of Christopher North in 1842 put back into circulation
the argument, powerfully made, that at least on the evidence of
The Excursion Wordsworth 'certainly cannot be considered a
Christian poet'.

In the course of his polemic, Wilson singles out the Wanderer's
most important words to the Poet in Book One for particular scorn.
' "Where meditation is!" What meditation? Turn thou, O child of a
day! to the New Testament, and therein thou mayest find comfort.'
That Wordsworth revised his lines to make it explicit that the
meditation was a Christian one was almost certainly prompted by
Wilson's needling.[65] It is doubtful, though, whether Wordsworth,
who had such an imperious view of his own poetic authority, would
have moved in the direction of greater explicitness had he not
himself come to believe that the key passage in *The Excursion*, Book
One was no longer satisfactory. By 1845 he knew that the Christian
elements which had been increasingly important in the development
of *The Ruined Cottage* and *The Pedlar* 1802–4, and which had seemed
clear enough then, needed to be made clearer still, for in the thirty
years since the first publication of *The Excursion*, the intellectual
context—and specifically the religious context—into which the
poem was received had changed very greatly.

On one topic Wordsworth had been little more than an informed
observer of developments in thought. The debate as to how far and
in what ways God could be known from his Creation—the Argument from Design—was further sophisticated in the first half of the
nineteenth century, notably by geologists who were also clergymen.
As John Wyatt has shown in *Wordsworth and the Geologists*, the poet
was an acknowledged influence on some of the leading figures in this
field of science, but Wordsworth played no real part in determining
the trajectory of research in this area.[66] For the 1842 edition of the
Guide to the Lakes, a long-time friend of the poet's honoured a

twenty-year-old promise by providing 'Three Letters upon the Geology of the Lake District'. This was quite a coup, for the friend, the Reverend Adam Sedgwick, was the Woodwardian Professor of Geology at Cambridge and the evidently highly-informed letters, which gave every appearance of being up-to-the-minute science, strengthened the *Guide* by aligning it with an increasingly important area of research. But no one was likely to buy this edition of Wordsworth's *Guide* thinking that it would make an innovative contribution to debate about God and Nature; nor did it. 'All nature bears the impress of one great Creative Mind': the words are Sedgwick's, in the opening to his first letter; they could have been Wordsworth's; and they would have received a nod of assent from Paley.

In another area of religious discourse, however, Wordsworth was much more than just an observer of developments. He was actively involved and was in a small way an agent of change. The 1845 revisions to *The Excursion* come as the culmination of decades of activity in which the poet had played a part in defining the religious spirit of the age.

Though a full study of Wordsworth and the Church is much needed, for the purposes of this chapter it will be enough to highlight two aspects of this very large topic. The first is Wordsworth's growing interest over the last thirty years of his life in the story of Christianity in the British Isles and in particular in the creation and evolution of the Church of England. His interest was never disinterested. The sequence of 102 sonnets he published in 1822, *Ecclesiastical Sketches*, was prompted by concern over the newly-surfacing agitation for Catholic Emancipation and it records the history of the Christian faith in Britain from its first arrival through to the present day from the standpoint of one convinced that the evolution of the Church of England testified to Providential design.[67] It is particularly notable for the honoured place given to Laud (Part II, XXXV), an early revelation of leanings that affiliated Wordsworth to the old High Church party, in which his brother Christopher and nephew, Christopher, were prominent, and endeared him to the younger generation of reformers in both the ancient universities.[68] The ecclesiological movement of the 1830s and 1840s fostered scholarly interest in the Church as a visible fabric—its historical buildings and parsonage houses—and the poet's evident concern for these was such a strong recommendation that the President of the Cambridge Camden

Society thought he 'might be considered one of the founders' of it.[69] To those in Oxford who eventually emerged from 1833 onwards as the Oxford Movement, Wordsworth's importance was many-faceted, but it was epitomized in a single note in *Ecclesiastical Sketches*. Appended to a sonnet about church building, it read: 'The Lutherans have retained the Cross within their Churches; it is to be regretted that we have not done the same.' A simple statement, but one that carried a powerful charge. One's attitude to a Cross within an Anglican church, which had long been a gauge of the degree of one's High Churchmanship, was about to become a furiously contested badge of sectarianism.[70] To Henry Crabb Robinson and Frederick William Faber, one a Unitarian who was dismayed and the other a Tractarian who was delighted, Wordsworth's note delivered the same message—that the poet was to be counted among those Anglicans who were sympathetic to a more Catholic approach to forms of worship and symbols of the faith.

A variety of further evidence of Wordsworth's attachment to the Church of England could be produced. Government decisions on 'the Catholic Question'—most notably Catholic Emancipation in 1829 and the Maynooth Endowment Grant of 1845—prompted a great deal of serious thought and discussion in correspondence with senior Churchmen.[71] What Wordsworth witnessed of the piety of Catholic worshippers during a visit to Ireland in 1829 prompted many expressions of his anxiety for the future of the Anglican Church.[72] In 1835 a large part of the prose 'Postscript' to *Yarrow Revisited* was devoted to a consideration of the importance of curates in the ministry of the Church of England and how they should best be rewarded. Though a rather dry topic, one might think, with which to end a new collection of poems, it was one of current concern on which Wordsworth had decided views he was deter-mined to air.[73] A year later the poet was throwing himself into a campaign to build a new church in his birthplace, Cockermouth.

By the 1840s Wordsworth's fame as a Poet was so firmly associated with his identity as Anglican that he was being honoured by those whose own agendas were in reality wideningly divergent. On the one hand he was acclaimed by John Keble and others within the Oxford Movement—it was Keble who delivered the Creweian Oration in 1839 when Wordsworth received an Honorary Degree from Oxford University.[74] On the other he was the brother of the ultra-orthodox Master of Trinity College, Cambridge and uncle to the author of *Theophilus Anglicanus* (1843), a defence of traditional High Churchmanship which Christopher Wordsworth, senior, deemed more likely than anything else he had read 'to arrest the progress of the evils threatened to us from Newman and Newmanism'.[75] The admiring uncle acknowledged the gift of his nephew's treatise appropriately—with a sonnet, that opens:

> Enlightened Teacher, gladly from thy hand
> Have I received this proof of pains bestowed
> By Thee to guide thy Pupils on the road
> That, in our native isle, and every land,
> The Church, when trusting in divine command
> And in her Catholic attributes, hath trod.[76]

The other aspect of Wordsworth and the Church can be dealt with more briefly, even though it is central to all the work of his last three decades. It is that Wordsworth became increasingly ready to invoke Christ and the doctrines of the faith. In his published writings and private letters up to his middle years Wordsworth is chary of doing so. He speaks of God the Father, to whose will he and his family must resign themselves after the death of his brother in 1805 and the deaths of two of his children in 1812, but not of the Son.[77] From *Ecclesiastical Sketches* on, however, Jesus Christ and the specific doctrines associated with his name are invoked more frequently, sometimes rather generally, as in 'holy faith and Christian hope', sometimes quite specifically, as in 'A Gravestone upon the Floor in the Cloisters of Worcester Cathedral', which ends, 'Stranger, pass | Softly!—To save the contrite, Jesus bled.'[78] In the 1843 Fenwick Note to *The Excursion*, the poet regretted that he had not carried out his plan of writing further about the Solitary so as to show him returning to 'the Christian Faith in which he had been educated'.[79] Just as he was revisiting his poems for the 1845 edition, the poet and the Reverend R. P. Graves, resident curate of Windermere, had conversations about the place of the Christian faith in his work, which Graves summed up as follows: 'In point of fact you believed that the truths developed by you would be found to be, like all other truths of natural religion, beneficially adapted to particular stages of human experience, and at the same time not only in harmony with but preparative for the higher truths of Revelation, to your own belief in which your later poems, especially, afforded abundant testimony.'[80]

Graves's language, as befits a clergyman, is exact and there is no evidence that Wordsworth demurred from it. 'Revelation'—the truth about Mankind's redemption through Christ, revealed by God in the life of his Son and in the Bible—requires 'belief'. In the revision to Book One of *The Excursion* in 1845, the Wanderer confers upon the suffering Margaret the faith that the poet was fully ready at this point in his life to proclaim. It was a source of rejoicing to Frederick Faber that he had persuaded the 75-year-old Wordsworth to fix a Cross in his bedroom so that he could look at it first thing in the morning and last thing at night. Margaret dies with her 'soul | Fixed on the Cross'.[81]

With this one revision alone Wordsworth turns *The Excursion* into a witness of the 1840s, a decade in which questions of religious allegiance became frenzied. The poem ought to be included in any discussion of the years in which John Henry Newman left the Church he had adorned, when Arthur Hugh Clough destroyed his academic career for conscience's sake, and when James Anthony Froude declared that he and the best and bravest of his contemporaries 'determined to have done with insincerity, to find ground under [our] feet, to let the uncertain remain uncertain, but to learn how much and what we could honestly regard as true'.[82] This stirring passage has long been recognized as an authentic voice of the 1840s, but the Wanderer's words in *The Excursion* of 1845 are another.

3

The Prelude: 1804–1820

                                              so wide appears
        The vacancy between me and those days,
        Which yet have such self-presence in my mind
        That, sometimes, when I think of them I seem
        Two consciousnesses, conscious of myself
        And of some other Being.[1]

(i)

Wordsworth died on 23 April 1850. Three months later *The Prelude, or Growth of a Poet's Mind; An Autobiographical Poem* was published in London. On 2 August the poet's widow selected a volume from the first consignment of copies to arrive at Rydal Mount and inscribed it: 'John Carter, an affectionate & grateful Memorial, from his friend, Mary Wordsworth'. There must have been pleasure—the first edition of *The Prelude* is an unadorned but handsome book—and pride—here was indeed a fitting 'Memorial' of the late Poet Laureate. But there must have been a feeling, too, of enormous relief. Mary Wordsworth was now 80 years old and she had lived with manuscripts of this poem for the forty-eight years of her married life. John Carter had joined the staff at Rydal Mount in 1813 and his thirty-seven years of service had included the labour of making one of them, a fair-copy of no fewer than 333 pages. At last it was published.[2]

At last, also, the poem had, so to speak, settled down: it had acquired a proper title. For many years it was identified by its addressee, referred to as 'the poem to Coleridge'. In elegant calligraphy the title-page of one of the fair-copies made of the poem as completed in 1805 reads: 'Poem/Title Not Yet Fixed Upon/by William Wordsworth/Addressed to S.T.Coleridge'. But it was also 'a Poem on my own earlier life', as Wordsworth termed it in letters in 1804, a descriptive title which became a little more specific in later years in versions of (this from one of his daughter Dora's letters) 'The Growth of his own Mind'.[3] But though he prepared the poem for publication after his death, Wordsworth did not pronounce on the question of title and so left his family and executors a problem. What were they to call it?

That there was a problem was not divulged in 1850. The 'Advertisement' (prefatory words) to the first edition drew attention only to the question of the poem's place in Wordsworth's work overall, not mentioning that the poem lacked an authorized title. The explanation Wordsworth had himself provided in 1814 of the relation of the autobiographical poem to *The Recluse* was repeated in full and the editorial comment, 'It will thence be seen, that the present Poem was intended to be introductory to the RECLUSE . . .', so clearly indicated that the title, *The Prelude*, meshed with Wordsworth's thinking about the poem that there was no reason for it to enter any reader's mind in 1850 that it had not been settled on by the author half a century earlier.

A year later, however, in his biography of his uncle, Christopher Wordsworth revealed the truth. Having recapitulated the early history of the poem's composition and its relation to that of *The Excursion*, he continued:

Its title, 'The Prelude', had not been fixed on by the author himself: the Poem remained anonymous till his death. The present title has been prefixed to it at the suggestion of the beloved partner of his life, and the best interpreter of his thoughts, from considerations of its tentative and preliminary character. Obviously it would have been desirable to mark its relation to 'The Recluse' by some analogous appellation; but this could not easily be done, at the same time that its other essential characteristics were indicated. Besides, the appearance of this poem, *after* the author's death, might tend to lead some readers into an opinion that it was his *final* production, instead of being, as it really is, one of his *earlier* works. They were to be guarded against this supposition. Hence a name has been adopted, which may serve to keep the true nature and position of the poem constantly before the eye of the reader; and 'THE PRELUDE' will now be perused and estimated with the feelings properly due to its preparatory character, and to the period at which it was composed.[4]

Christopher Wordsworth's uneasiness is plain. There is something odd about this publication and the reader needs to be alerted. Although the poem occupied Wordsworth for much of his life, it seems that it retained its 'tentative and preliminary character'. It never had a title. Although prepared for publication at the height of the poet's maturity and now published at his death, *The Prelude*, the reader is cautioned, is not a late production, but 'one of his *earlier* works'.

Christopher Wordsworth's desire to push *The Prelude* back in time, to play down the fact of its existence in the middle of the century by emphasizing its much earlier origins, has been shared by commentators and editors ever since. William Knight printed the 1850 text in his, the first-ever scholarly edition of Wordsworth's collected works, but the accompanying parade of evidence drew attention to how intriguing was the history of the poem's composition in the opening years of the century.[5] In 1926 Ernest de Selincourt revealed a new text of *The Prelude*, the version in thirteen books completed in 1805, and although parallel text printing of the fourteen-book 1850 text opposite the new thirteen-book one indicated that there were now two versions of the autobiographical poem for scholars and critics to consider, the compare-and-contrast exercise in his introduction made it clear that the earlier was to be preferred.[6] In the 1970s a still earlier version in two books was established from manuscripts which, as finished fair-copies, seemed complete enough to warrant separate publication.[7] More recently the claims of earlier or more elusive versions of the poem have been urged. Duncan Wu has reconstructed the text of the five-book version and issued it as an edition and Jonathan Wordsworth has printed the earliest draftings of 1798, claiming both that they are a 'self-contained poem', and that they contain 'in embryo the discussion of the education through nature central to all later versions of *The Prelude*'.[8]

If the 'Was it for this' lines of 1798 are the embryo, the thirteen books of 1805 are clearly the version with which *The Prelude* reached maturity. On 3 June 1805 Wordsworth reported to Sir George Beaumont that he had 'finished' work on it a fortnight earlier; over the coming months the poem with the title not yet fixed upon was transcribed in two beautiful fair-copy manuscripts.

Understandably this is the poem that has engaged most attention in recent years. How exactly, scholars have asked (and are still asking), did a few passages recalling childhood exploits evolve into a multi-genre poem almost nine thousand lines long; why did key passages change their place in the developing structure; why was so much serviceable blank verse jettisoned as the work of shaping the whole continued? But there are other questions to be asked and another narrative to be pieced together about the poem's life, for it did not stop in 1805 any more than Wordsworth's did.

The strangeness of the relationship between poet and poem in this case, and the source of its fascination, emerges if some dates are considered. *The Prelude* as autobiographical chronicle traces Wordsworth's life from 1770 to 1798, from the infant listening to the river Derwent flowing past his birthplace at Cockermouth, to the poet 'wanton[ing] in wild poesy' among the Quantock Hills. But in addition to being a chronicle of past time, the poem is also a variegated record of the present—of the years of the poem's making, 1798–1805.

The impress of the present is most obvious when it announces itself as such. Book Seven, for example, begins with the admission that five years have passed since Wordsworth uttered in dithyrambic fervour the words which open the poem. Readers of epic recognize this well-established literary device, the pause for renewal mid-way through a long poem, but the way in which Wordsworth domesticates it with personal detail is astonishing. He confesses he has done little or nothing over the summer, partly because he wanted a holiday and partly because things got in the way—here editors note 'birth of daughter in August'. But more recently, he says, well, actually it was yesterday evening, nature's sights and sounds have quickened him to feel that he could 'now resume with cheerful hope'.

Other gestures similarly locate the poem in present time. Lines towards the end of Book Ten pour scorn on Napoleon's coronation as Emperor by Pope Pius VII on 2 December 1804 (930–40). At the beginning of the same book Wordsworth struggles to convey how his feelings see-sawed in response to the increasing violence of the French Revolution. His conviction, he says, was that 'one paramount mind' might have 'quelled | Outrage and bloody power' and that this remains a 'Creed which ten shameful years have not annulled'. Given that 'Tintern Abbey' has the date July 13 1798 as part of its full title, the poem's opening words, 'Five years have passed', demand that readers immediately calculate that the poet's first visit to the Wye took place in 1793. So it is here in *The Prelude*. 'Ten shameful

years'—which are they? Since the most recent datable events mentioned have been the massacres in September and Louvet's denuncia-
tion of Robespierre in October 1792, it is clearly to be inferred that
the poet is making this heartfelt utterance after the failure of the
Treaty of Amiens and the resumption of hostilities in May 1803.

Historical markers such as these serve to point up the process of
the poem's composition. What the poet refers to as 'our long labour'
(XIII, 172), we are reminded, has taken some years to arrive at 'its
appointed close' (XIII, 270), that is, at the moment in 1798, now
some years ago, when he and Coleridge conceived of 'building up
a work that should endure' (XIII, 274). Then, the poem tells us,
Coleridge was writing 'The Ancient Mariner' and Wordsworth
'The Idiot Boy'. What *The Prelude* does not explicitly remind us at its
close is that since then—during the years it has taken to arrive at
completion—Wordsworth has also written (amongst much else)
'Resolution and Independence', the 'Ode to Duty', and the 'Ode:
Intimations of Immortality'.

If not explicit, this knowledge is embedded in the text of *The
Prelude* in passages which suddenly invoke other Wordsworth poems.
Take, for example, the presence of the 'Intimations' ode, in Book V,
531–47:

> Our childhood sits,
> Our simple childhood sits upon a throne
> That hath more power than all the elements.
> I guess not what this tells of Being past,
> Nor what it augurs of the life to come;
> But so it is: and in that dubious hour,
> That twilight when we first begin to see
> This dawning earth, to recognize, expect;
> And in the long probation that ensues,
> The time of trial, ere we learn to live
> In reconcilement with our stinted powers,
> To endure this state of meagre vassalage;
> Unwilling to forego, confess, submit,
> Uneasy and unsettled; yoke-fellows
> To custom, mettlesome, and yet not tam'd
> And humbled down, oh! then we feel, we feel,
> We know when we have Friends . . .

It's a wonderful passage, but not one Wordsworth could or would
have written in 1798. With its emphasis on learning to live in

'reconcilement with our stinted powers', the whole treatment of the child entering on life's probation associates the lines with the tone and sentiment of the 1804 ode and not with those of 'Tintern Abbey' in 1798.

The 'Intimations' ode is strikingly present also in Book Eleven. Lines 258–79 declare what the poet's imaginative growth has owed to 'spots of time, | Which with distinct preeminence retain | A renovating Virtue'. Such moments date from childhood, and lines 279–315 proceed to recount one, the incident on Penrith Beacon. A second 'spot of time' is recalled in lines 345–88, the episode of the waiting for the horses shortly before the poet's father's death. Both of these passages were written in 1799 and belong to Wordsworth's earliest conception of an autobiographical exercise framed to explain himself to Coleridge. But at that stage the first spot flowed into the second with only a brief, workmanlike transition, 'Nor less I recollect . . .' (*1799*, I, 327). By the time these incidents took their place in the developing structure of *The Prelude* in 1804–5 they were separated by poignant lines in which the poet acknowledges his fear that direct access to the sources of his power is weakening, as distinct preeminence becomes glimpses and flashes, and his hope that poetry might stem the loss by enshrining what was once so bright. Every word of the transition passage between the two spots of time in the thirteen-book *Prelude* chimes with the 'Intimations' ode, 'There was a time'. What the passage proclaims is that though *The Prelude* ends with an enthusiastic recapitulation of plans formed in the joyful summer of 1798, the poem has actually been brought to its conclusion by a different poet from the one who began it when they were fresh and when what they promised was a stimulus and not a burden.

Chronicle: 1770 (birth) to 1798 (*Lyrical Ballads* and plan for *Recluse*). Composition: 1798 ('Was it for this') to 1805 (*Prelude* in thirteen books finished). These are clearly *The Prelude*'s crucial dates. But the poem had a continuing existence after 1805. The chronicle element remained largely unchanged—that is, when the poem was first published in 1850 it ended as it had done in 1805 with the summer of *Lyrical Ballads*. Between 1805 and 1850, though, the making of the poem had continued, for Wordsworth could not in any sense let it go. He could not publish it, but nor could he let it lie forgotten in a bottom drawer.

His principal argument against publication was rehearsed on many occasions—an appeal to literary decorum. This, he maintained, forbade the poet from presenting himself as an object of interest until a work should have been created that would legitimate curiosity about its creator. As he wrote to Richard Sharp in 1804: '. . . it seems a frightful deal to say about one's self, and of course will never be published . . . till another work has been written of sufficient importance to justify me in giving my own history to the world' (29 April 1804). In the late 1830s, by which time Wordsworth had accepted that he never would write *The Recluse*, a further pragmatic argument supervened—hoped-for changes in the law of copyright might mean that posthumous publication of *The Prelude* would guarantee the longest possible period in which his surviving family could enjoy the royalty income from it.

Whatever the reason, Wordsworth did not publish his autobiographical poem. But exactly because it was an autobiographical poem it continued bone of his bone. For much of his life after 1805 Wordsworth brooded over his formative years and from time to time he revisited the poem in which they were chronicled. They could not alter, but perspectives on them could and with each revisiting of *The Prelude* changes were made which themselves reflect developments in Wordsworth's own life as poet and in the cultural milieu in which he was becoming a significant figure.[9]

Wordsworth's revisitings of *The Prelude* were thorough-going, characteristically, and any full account of the revisions inscribed in the surviving manuscripts would be voluminous and indigestible. What the rest of this chapter does is attempt to convey a sense of the poet's continuing engagement with his autobiography by focusing on one moment in each of the four decades in which Wordsworth and his poem grew older together.

The first is the moment in 1804 when Wordsworth reviewed a poem that was now nearing completion in an elegantly coherent form and so radically rethought it that in the process of more than doubling in size the autobiography took on a quite new character. It was at this moment that the structure of *The Prelude* as given to the world at last in 1850, first became discernible.

The second specimen revisiting dates from 1819. With *The Excursion* (1814) and *Poems* (1815) published, Wordsworth—admire his work or not—was clearly a poet who mattered. His *Excursion* was one of the 'three things to rejoice at in this Age', in Keats's famous judgement.[10] But unbeknownst to his (few) readers, Wordsworth was in straits. That Coleridge was profoundly disappointed in The Excursion was a stumbling block to any further progress on The Recluse and it could not be said that a few substantial odes written around 1817 were any sign that serious work towards the next stage of the project was about to begin. What he did was what Wordsworth always did when blocked by the obstacle of The Recluse—he revisited The Prelude, and revised.

In 1831–2, the third moment, Wordsworth reviewed his autobiographical poem from the darker perspective of his late middle age. Two aspects of it were troubling. It was still a work avowedly preparatory to another and a greater; it still concluded with hope for Man's redemption 'surely yet to come'. But after a decade of reminders from his family that 'After fifty years of age there is no time to spare',[11] Wordsworth was in fact on the verge of acknowledging that The Recluse never would be completed, and the gloom that this engendered was more than matched by that arising from his reading of current social and political affairs. Man's redemption might be yet to come, but in the meantime it seemed to him that his own beloved country was going to the dogs.

Finally there is the revisiting of 1839, when The Prelude was prepared for posthumous publication. As the 69-year-old poet looked back at the figure of himself as a young idealist, the 'ingenuous Youth' who had burnt with outrage at injustice in France, did he still recognize him and his ideals? Were there after all affinities preserved between what Wordsworth had felt then and what he felt now about the new age of Benthamism triumphant, workhouses and railways?

(ii)

The textual history of The Prelude in 1804 is complicated but, at least in essentials, no longer obscure.[12] In brief: by 1800 Wordsworth had written two books of what Coleridge termed 'the biographical, or philosophico-biographical Poem to be prefixed or annexed to the Recluse'.[13] By the beginning of 1804 he had returned to it and, describing its scope as being 'my own earlier life', now conceived of

it as demanding 'five parts or books' for completion.[14] Early in
March Wordsworth was confident that he was safe, nearly there: by
12 March he had set off on a fresh venture into new terrain, not safe
at all.

The momentousness of this, the most important artistic decision of
Wordsworth's life, needs to be registered. Wordsworth was doing
what he should not have been doing—and he knew it. What he
'should' have been doing was making progress with the philosophical
poem. That was what Coleridge wanted—'O let it be the tail-piece
of "The Recluse", for of nothing but "The Recluse" can I hear
patiently'[15]—and frequent references in letters to the subsidiary nature
of the autobiographical work confirms that the belief early in 1804
was that Wordsworth was exerting himself mightily to tidy away
something that, though important in its own way, was hindering him
from what he was really eager to get on with. By late March this
comfortable model of poetic life at Grasmere had been shattered. The
autobiographical poem was what he was getting on with and that
with amazing energy. Three thousand lines have been added to it
in ten weeks, he told Richard Sharp in late April, acknowledging,
moreover, that the whole was going to 'turn out far longer than I
ever dreamt of'.[16] Wordsworth is like an explorer who has an idea
of his goal but, astonished and enthralled by what is being discovered
on the way, has to revise all notions of how long it will take to
reach it. He may have confessed to Sharp that it seemed a frightful
deal to be saying about himself, but he went on saying it. A
beautifully copied manuscript of all Wordsworth's recent poetry
was prepared for Coleridge to take with him on his Mediterranean
travels, but it contained neither a completed philosophico-
biographical prefix to, nor any evidence of further work on *The
Recluse*.[17]

What caused so unpredictable a turn of events? Why didn't
Wordsworth finish the poem in five books, ready for Coleridge to
take with him? The autobiographical retrospect was addressed
to him and one of its declared functions was that it should help
Coleridge 'to know | With better knowledge how the heart was
framed | of him thou lovest' (*1799*, I, 456–8). Would not the five-
book poem have done that? Books One and Two trace the progress
of the child's development from the mother's breast to seventeen
years of age and conclude with the affirmation that whatever has

helped the adult Wordsworth retain hope for the future in these present times of dereliction is to be traced to his formation by Nature 'among the hills where I was born'. In Book Three the education offered by Cambridge is cast both as an opportunity and a snare which the poet, conscious though he was of his own inner resources, only partially escaped. Wordsworth will have savoured composition of this book the more for being conscious that he was addressing another Cambridge man whose academic career had been less than glorious. Book Four continued the theme of education, in part by direct assault on fashionable theories, but more subtly by the recollections of further formative moments in the poet's own life. Book Five was to confirm all the brightest promises of the previous books, recounting experiences which demonstrate the continuing power of Nature's agency and the profundity of the creative imagination. Accounts of the climbing of Snowdon and the 'spots of time' serve to explain and to underwrite the poet's conviction that he was a chosen son:

> I made no vows, but vows
> Were then made for me—bond unknown to me
> Was given, that I should be, else sinning greatly,
> A dedicated spirit.[18]

One sin would be not to write to *The Recluse*.

Why, then, did such a philosophico-biographical poem come to seem inadequate? One reason, perhaps of a number of reasons, must be that while the five-book poem accounted for Wordsworth's sense that he had a vocation to be a poet, it gave no clue as to why the chosen son should think he at only 28 years of age had important things to say on 'Nature, Man, and Society', nor what 'the knowledge of which I am possessed' might be that it should be an imperative duty to utter it 'in these times of fear, | This melancholy waste of hopes o'erthrown'.[19] What gave Wordsworth any special claim to be not a poet, but the poet of *The Recluse*?

If an answer were to yield itself it would have to come from Wordsworth's experiences in post-Revolutionary France and in England in the years following the outbreak of war between the two countries in 1793, but these were not only in themselves the most turbulent experiences of Wordsworth's life, they were also the ones least likely now to make for comfortable revisiting. At one

particularly dense moment of narrative-cum-explication in Book
Ten (878–82) Wordsworth declares to Coleridge that

> Time may come
> When some dramatic Story may afford
> Shapes livelier to convey to thee, my Friend,
> What then I learn'd, or think I learn'd of truth
> And the errors into which I was betray'd
>
> . . .

and the hesitation is doubly revealing. At a crisis in his intellectual
and moral life the poet learned about truth—or rather, he thinks he
learned about it; maybe this autobiographical blank verse, despite
there being thousands of lines of it, will not be adequate to convey
whatever it is that must be conveyed—which is what? 'Strange question', as Wordsworth observes elsewhere at a similar moment of
opacity, 'but it answers not itself'.[20]

The hesitancy of this transitional passage epitomizes the uncer-
tainty as to direction and aim, the equivocations and recapitulations
that characterize the books of *The Prelude* written after the five-book
structure was abandoned. No one can read them, especially Books
Nine to Twelve, without asking, why has the poem become so hard
to follow—so difficult, with a quite different kind of difficulty from
that presented by the earlier books?

The cause in part was, obviously, that the events Wordsworth was
attempting to recollect were tumultuous and difficult to chronicle at
all clearly, let alone interpret. In the struggle for clarity of focus and
exactitude of interpretative recall, Book Ten enacts the poet's own
difficulties—and compounds the reader's—by going over the same
period twice. Beginning as France becomes a republic in September
1792, the narrative proceeds with an optimistic Wordsworth returning to England only to be shattered by the declaration of war in 1793.
France now 'waxed mad', but on the death of Robespierre in July
1794 'Authority put on a milder face', and Wordsworth's hopefulness
rekindles. At this point in the book, however, instead of continuing
chronologically, Wordsworth returns to the period in 1792 when he
was most deeply engaged with thinking 'upon management | Of
nations' and recalls in a rhapsodic passage—'Bliss was it in that
dawn to be alive, | But to be young was very heaven!'—a sentiment
that pre-dates the events already chronicled earlier in the book.
Wordsworth sums up at line 757, with a date,

> In the main outline, such, it might be said
> Was my condition, till with open war
> Britain opposed the Liberties of France.

and thirty or so lines later he moves the narrative on with another datable reference,

> And now, become Oppressors in their turn,
> Frenchmen had changed a war of self-defense
> For one of conquest . . .

With this 'And now', however, all chronological signposting stops. 'This was a time when . . .', the next verse paragraph begins, but nothing in the dramatic account of crisis–collapse–recovery that follows indicates what time that was. The most significant testing of Wordsworth's adult life is presented as consequent upon and subsequent to certain historical events, but in itself untrammelled by material specificity. Something of great moment happened, something that resulted in the project of *The Recluse* and the actuality of *The Prelude* currently in process, but where and when it happened, and over how long a period, the retrospective account, though evidently struggling to 'trac[e] faithfully | The workings of a youthful mind, beneath | The breath of great events' (X, 942–4), does not, or cannot tell.

The root cause, however, is that the difficulty of treating these events, which were dauntingly complex in themselves, was compounded by the distance between their historical moment and that in which they were being recollected, and by the distance between the Wordsworth who experienced and the Wordsworth who recalled them.

On 18 May 1803 war resumed after the brief respite afforded by the Treaty of Amiens. At once preparations for a French invasion of England began: 'Let us be masters of the Straits of Dover for six hours', Napoleon declared, 'and we shall be masters of the world.'[21] As invasion fever mounted, Wordsworth enlisted with the Ambleside Volunteers on 3 October, joining nearly half a million men nationwide who pledged themselves to defend their country against the Corsican upstart. Cumbria did not matter strategically, but, as Wordsworth declared in a sonnet of October 1803 to the 'Men of Kent' who, of course, would bear the brunt of the aggression, what their northern countrymen could do was demonstrate solidarity of mood and purpose:

> In Britain is one breath;
> We all are with you now from Shore to Shore:-
> Ye Men of Kent, 'tis Victory or Death!

So Wordsworth buckled on a sword and alongside the other men of Grasmere mustered for drill. 'Surely', his sister declared, 'there never was a more determined hater of the French.'[22]

How very different had been his feelings and behaviour ten years before. 'My heart was all | Given to the people, and my love was theirs'—the people who stirred this generous emotion were French, the foremost 'caravan', as Wordsworth believed, of those currently travelling 'forward towards Liberty'.[23] The declaration of war on 1 February 1793, which revealed just how far askew he was from political reality and national sentiment, stunned Wordsworth into total disorientation. A stranger in his own country,

> I rejoiced,
> Yes, afterwards, truth painful to record!
> Exulted in the triumph of my soul
> When Englishmen by thousands were o'erthrown,
> Left without glory on the Field, or driven,
> Brave hearts, to shameful flight. It was a grief,
> Grief call it not, 'twas any thing but that,
> A conflict of sensations without name,
> Of which he only who may love the sight
> Of a Village Steeple as I do can judge
> When in the Congregation, bending all
> To their great Father, prayers were offer'd up,
> Or praises for our Country's Victories,
> And 'mid the simple worshippers, perchance,
> I only, like an uninvited Guest,
> Whom no one owned, sate silent, shall I add
> Fed on the day of vengeance, yet to come?

This (X, 258–74) is not the most difficult passage of verse in *The Prelude*, but it is surely the most astonishing. For two years Wordsworth had been composing sonnets that celebrate various aspects of Englishness. On the French coast itself (during the 1802 lull in the war), Wordsworth had looked across the Straits of Dover and, seeing the Evening Star, had yearned to be home:

> There! that dusky spot
> Beneath thee, it is England; there it lies.
> Blessings be on you both! one hope, one lot,

> One life, one glory! I, with many a fear
> For my dear Country, many heartfelt sighs,
> Among Men who do not love her linger here.[24]

When he did get back, everything he saw or heard said one thing, 'All, all are English'.[25] And a year later he imagined what would happen if Napoleon did cross the Channel—it would be a victory, a rout of the enemy, in which the whole nation would rejoice over the bodies of the invaders left 'lying in the silent sun, | Never to rise again!':

> Come forth, ye Old Men, now in peaceful show
> And greet your Sons! drums beat, and trumpets blow!
> Make merry, Wives! ye little Children stun
> Your Grandame's ears with pleasure of your noise!
> Clap, Infants, clap your hands! Divine must be
> That triumph, when the very worst, the pain,
> And even the prospect of our Brethren slain,
> Hath something in it which the heart enjoys:-
> In glory they will sleep and endless sanctity.[26]

The title of this sonnet is 'Anticipation'. As Wordsworth remembered in 1804, he had once feasted on anticipation of a different victory and 'the day of vengeance, yet to come'. Communal ritual, the parish church, young men in uniform dying for their country— the *Prelude* passage assembles the most potent emblems that could be conceived and turns the poet's relationship to them, as depicted in his recent sonnets, inside out.

It must have cost Wordsworth a great deal, not to recall how opposed he was to the war against the fledgling republic, but to dramatize it in this fashion. The passage admitting that he had once prayed for French victories was hardly one he could have passed around at a meeting of the Ambleside Volunteers or shown to his new friend Sir George Beaumont. But that he wrote it at all is a mark of the real strength of this part of the autobiographical poem. Wordsworth was determined to honour both selves—the self he had become and the self he had once been. Firm pointing throughout— 'Such was my then belief, that there was one, | And only one solicitude for all' (X, 227–8)—accompanies the sifting of what could still be regarded with pride from what had now to be seen as misguided.

In the political books 'juvenile errors are my theme' (X, 637), but it had not all been error and though Wordsworth wanted to be rigorous, he was not about to don the hair-shirt of total recantation. When he exclaims, 'Bliss was it in that dawn to be alive, | But to be young was very heaven!', there is no hint of ironic knowingness. The poetry that follows (X, 701–8) challenges everyone *not* to respond to a moment when

> Not favor'd spots alone, but the whole earth
> The beauty wore of promise, that which sets,
> To take an image which was felt, no doubt,
> Among the bowers of paradise itself,
> The budding rose above the rose full blown.
> What temper at the prospect did not wake
> To happiness unthought-of? The inert
> Were rouz'd, and lively natures rapt away.

Similarly, when Wordsworth and Beaupuis meet the hunger-bitten girl and Beaupuis exclaims, ' " 'Tis against that | Which we are fighting" ' (IX, 519–20), the emotion that fires Wordsworth's politics at that time is admirable, not foolish:

> I with him believed
> Devoutly that a spirit was abroad
> Which could not be withstood, that poverty,
> At least like this, would in a little time
> Be found no more . . .

It would have been shameful had Wordsworth not been able to recall, 'my heart was all | Given to the People, and my love was theirs' (IX, 125–6).

Buttressing the positive presentation of experience in which the seeds of juvenile error may have germinated is the claim that the Pitt government had 'from the very first' looked 'with ungracious eyes' upon 'regenerated France' and by declaring war had incurred a mighty guilt:

> Oh! much have they to account for, who could tear
> By violence at one decisive rent,
> From the best Youth in England their dear pride,
> Their joy in England.   (X, 275–8)

Worse was to follow. Things were done 'in those days' likely 'To turn all judgements out of their right course' (X, 638–9)—i.e. not just those of young idealists—the poet of 1804 declares, adding that even now the remembrance of them stirs up feelings of scorn and condemnation inappropriate to verse. But he cannot not remember and the passage (X, 645–56) that begins,

> Our Shepherds (this say merely) at that time
> Thirsted to make the guardian Crook of Law
> A tool of Murder . . .

flows into a denunciation of the government's determination in the 1790s 'to undermine | Justice, and make an end of Liberty', that betrays in its vehemence exactly the passion the poet has just said he hoped not to give way to.

What Wordsworth was remembering in this chronicle of the 1790s, and alluding to specifically in his attack on false shepherds, was the largely successful government attempt to suppress radicalism and popular dissent. The Treason Trials of 1794, in which men Wordsworth actually knew battled for their lives; the suspension of Habeas Corpus in 1794 and the 'gagging acts' (The Treasonable Practices Bill and the Seditious Meetings Bill) the following year; the hounding of figures such as Muir and Palmer in Scotland—both transported; the deployment of an army of spies, informers, and *agents provocateurs*—all these measures were signs of authority's determination to eradicate symptoms of the French disease.[27] That a spy was sent to check up on the suspicious comings and goings at Alfoxden and that Wordsworth lost the lease of the house, becoming homeless once again, because he was tainted with the odour of radicalism, explains what he meant when he observed that his recollections of the 1790s were touching on 'passion over near ourselves, | Reality too close and too intense' (X, 640–1).

In his survey of this period, however, Wordsworth was also revisiting his own writings. The stage by stage narrative of *The Prelude* Books IX–XII goes: enthusiastic commitment to the cause of liberty—alienation and turmoil—emotional and intellectual crisis—recovery and recognition of 'true self'. But during this period Wordsworth was also writing and though he published nothing, what he was able to show Coleridge at the beginning of their friendship convinced him that Wordsworth was 'the first poet of the age'.[28] Little more than a year later, after hearing his most recent work, Coleridge went further. 'Wordsworth', he declared, 'is a great man.'[29] From his viewpoint in 1804 Wordsworth was able to assess the part these writings had played in the drama of crisis and recovery that had made him the poet he now was. His artistic master-stroke was to include revisitings of the major compositions of that period in the expanding *Prelude* of 1804. The allusions are no more than a few lines, but they carry a powerful charge. They signal, first, the intrinsic importance of these works in Wordsworth's intellectual development; and, second, the inestimable importance of the fact that it had been the warmth of Coleridge's response to them that had quickened his sense of poetic vocation and given it direction.

The first allusion surfaces in one of the many opaque passages of Book Ten. After 1794, when 'Frenchmen had changed a war of self-defense | For one of conquest' (792–3), Wordsworth responded to the particular situation of France ('I read her doom') by dwelling still more intently on general principles. But, the poet of 1804 asserts, it was a dangerous time to engage 'in heat | Of contest' over political and social ideas, for the mess and turmoil of public affairs made doubly alluring 'the Philosophy | That promised to abstract the hopes of man | Out of his feelings, to be fix'd thenceforth | For ever in a purer element' (806–9). Wordsworth recalls very clearly the bait tempting the 'young ingenuous mind':

> what delight!
> How glorious! in self-knowledge and self-rule
> To look through all the frailties of the world
> And, with a resolute mastery shaking off
> The accidents of nature, time, and place
> That make up the weak being of the past,
> Build social freedom on its only basis,
> The freedom of the individual mind,
> Which, to the blind restraint of general laws
> Superior, magisterially adopts
> One guide, the light of circumstances, flash'd
> Upon an independent intellect. (818–29)

As has long been recognized, the last two lines are taken verbatim from the villain Rivers's speech in *The Borderers*, in which he assures the duped Mortimer that he has attained freedom by throwing off the 'tyranny | Of moralists and saints and lawgivers' to obey the 'only law that wisdom | Can ever recognize: the immediate law | Flashed from the light of circumstances | Upon an independent intellect'.[30] I don't want, though, to reconsider here the familiar questions these lines tend to prompt: how far Wordsworth was ever a disciple of Godwin; whether indeed this section of Book Ten does refer primarily to Godwin; or in what ways *The Borderers* of 1796–7 is to be read as Wordsworth's exploration of forces unleashed by the French Revolution and its immediate aftermath.[31] I want rather to make a point about the function of *The Borderers*, not as it was in the 1790s but as it is in *The Prelude*. Why does Wordsworth introduce a memory of it here in Book Ten in 1804?

The answer, I think, is twofold. The first strand is that the allusion to a key moment in the play acknowledges its equally key place in Wordsworth's development in the second half of the previous decade. As Wordsworth looked back from 1804 to the 1790s, and, more important, to *his* 1790s, he discerned in his experience a dynamic of crisis and recovery. What he also recognized was that his own writing had been a primary agent in his salvation. *The Borderers* surfaces in *The Prelude* where it does in recognition that Wordsworth's capacity to write it was the sign that whatever the crisis had been, he had come through. He had taken command of his experience in part through the process of turning its raw stuff into a play.

The first person to sense the significance of this was Coleridge, and that is the second reason for the allusion in Book Ten. When Wordsworth looked back at the end of *The Prelude* what he saw 'in clearer view | Than any sweetest sight of yesterday' (XIII, 391–2) was Coleridge 'on Quantock's grassy hills', towards the close of the *annus mirabilis* 1797–8. It had opened with the two poets reading their plays to each other in the first week in June 1797. '[Coleridge] repeated two acts and a half of his tragedy *Osorio*', Dorothy Wordsworth reported. 'The next morning William read his tragedy *The Borderers*.'[32] It was within days that Coleridge delivered the judgement already quoted, 'Wordsworth is a great man.'

The echo of a few lines from *The Borderers* might almost be a private gesture from Wordsworth to Coleridge, a graceful even if veiled confirmation that their first days together at Racedown had not been forgotten. The second allusion to earlier poetry to be dwelt on, however, Book Twelve, lines 312–53, though it too has a private significance for the two poets, is much more important: it both affirms Coleridge's crucial role in Wordsworth's development as a poet and, even more important, suggests the terms in which that role might be best appreciated.

Short though it is and devoid of poetic splendours such as the Spots of Time, Book Twelve is nonetheless the keystone of the autobiographical poem. Books Nine and Ten have traced the young idealist's *Sturm und Drang* period, roughly 1792 to 1796. Book Eleven has detailed the agencies by which an 'impaired' Imagination was 'restored', closing with the dramatic affirmation, 'Behold me then | Once more in Nature's presence, thus restored . . .'. The function of Book Twelve is to explain what happened next and thus how the poet of *Lyrical Ballads* and *The Recluse* came to recognize his proper field of action.

The sequence goes: having recovered from whatever the turbulence was chronicled in Books Nine and Ten, the poet seeks 'a temperate shew | Of objects that endure' (35–6). Nature re-establishes a 'wiser mood' more deeply in his soul (45–6) and thus 'moderated, thus composed' (53), the poet looks once more to man and the 'familiar face of life' (67). The 'utter hollowness of what we name | The wealth of nations' having been perceived (79–80), an anxious wish was bred,

> To ascertain how much of real worth
> And genuine knowledge, and true power of mind
> Did at this day exist in those who liv'd
> By bodily labour, labour far exceeding
> Their due proportion, under all the weight
> Of that injustice which upon ourselves
> By composition of society,
> Ourselves entail.   (98–105)

Experience of humble people encountered on lonely roads convinces the poet 'How little that to which alone we give | The name of education hath to do | With real feeling and just sense' (169–71), which leads to the declaration that such people, 'When all the external man is rude in shew' (227), must be the matter of his song. Very powerful lines, 237–77, echo and complement both the Preface to *Lyrical Ballads* (1800) and the 'Prospectus' to *The Recluse*, investing Wordsworth's choice of life with an aura of the sacred, 'It shall be my pride | That I have dared to tread this holy ground, | Speaking no dream but things oracular' (250–2). The climax to the passage is a linked series of assertions: that the 'genius of the Poet hence | May boldly take his way among mankind | Wherever Nature leads' (294–6); that Poets, though 'Connected in a mighty scheme of truth'

(302), enjoy each one 'for his peculiar dower a sense | By which he is enabled to perceive | Something unseen before' (303–5); that to this poet in particular was vouchsafed a hope that a work of his 'Proceeding from the depth of untaught things, | Enduring and creative, might become | A Power like one of Nature's' (310–12).

All of these declarations of faith in the dignity of common man are familiar to anyone who knows the poetry and prose of Wordsworth's early maturity. In *The Ruined Cottage* of 1797–8, for example, the wise Pedlar is introduced as one who had seen much of men,

> Their manners, their enjoyments and pursuits,
> Their passions and their feelings, chiefly those
> Essential and eternal in the heart,
> Which 'mid the simpler forms of rural life
> Exist more simple in their elements
> And speak a plainer language.[33]

It is an early statement of a conviction expounded in the most familiar passages of the Preface to *Lyrical Ballads*—'Low and rustic life was generally chosen ... speak a plainer and more emphatic language'; in the declaration to Charles James Fox that 'men who do not wear fine cloaths [*sic*] can feel deeply' (letter, 14 January 1801); in the reproof delivered to John Wilson about his criteria for literary judgement: 'People in our rank of life are perpetually falling into one sad mistake, namely, that of supposing that human nature and the persons they associate with are one and the same thing'; and throughout the *Lyrical Ballads* and *The Prelude* itself. Many more similar quotations could be adduced and all—the poetry and the complementary prose—would date from 1798 and after; none from 1793, when Wordsworth crossed Salisbury Plain, or 1794–5, when he wrote about it. So why does Book Twelve now introduce Druids, Britons in wolf-skin vests, and sacrificial wickers, a far remove, one might think, from humble life and Nature's power to consecrate?

It is, the poet insists, because assurances of conviction came to him 'Once above all' when he was a traveller 'Upon the Plain of Sarum' (313–14). As he roamed Salisbury Plain for three summer days, Wordsworth recalls, he had visions of the barbaric past, in which warriors armed with stone-axes strode across the wold while in the darkness flickered the flames of sacrificial altars fed with living men.

Very differently, at other moments he was intrigued by markings on the plain that gave evidence of the Druids as early astronomers and mathematicians and charmed by glimpses of the 'bearded Teachers, with white wands | Uplifted, pointing to the starry Sky | Alternately, and Plain below' (349–51).[34] Throughout the passage (XII, 312–53), reworkings of and direct quotations from the Spenserian *Salisbury Plain*, lines 172–98, and *Adventures on Salisbury Plain*, lines 36 and 157–9, are deftly folded into the blank verse. The whole seamlessly registers the engagement of the poet of 1804–5 with his experiences of 1793 and with the effort of composition that ensued.

The highly-wrought visions on Salisbury Plain constitute an engaging section of an otherwise rather dryly discursive book of *The Prelude*, but it is not at all clear in what way the poet's hallucinatory encounters in his solitude might have 'raised' him to the 'mood' evoked in the previous thirty-four lines (278–312), the mood in which he dares to hope that work of his 'might become | A power like one of Nature's' (311–12). What is very clear, however, is that in 1804–5 Wordsworth had come to think them crucial to his development as a poet. 'To such mood, | Once above all, a Traveller at that time | Upon the Plain of Sarum, was I raised' (312–14). In a poem that includes so much poetry more obviously concerned with dedication to 'the holy life of music and of verse', such as the glad preamble, the dedication walk, the Spots of Time and the meditation on the ascent of Snowdon, the emphatic 'Once above all' is astonishing.

In the lines which conclude the Salisbury Plain episode and bring Book XII to a close (354–79) Wordsworth tries to explain why he now places such value upon what he has just detailed. He begins by recalling Coleridge's delight in the 'imperfect verse' that stemmed from his friend's 'lonesome journey' across the Plain. It witnessed to original force, a 'higher power' to transform the 'actual world of our familiar days' in ways not hitherto reflected in books. Perhaps, the poet concedes, such high esteem was testimony to new friendship rather than true discrimination, but hardly has that concession been granted before Wordsworth, characteristically, withdraws it and reinforces the first proposition, insisting that in fact his memory concurs ('the mind is to herself | Witness and judge') that there was something special about that moment:

> I remember well
> That in life's every-day appearances
> I seem'd about this period to have sight
> Of a new world, a world, too, that was fit
> To be transmitted and made visible
> To other eyes, as having for its base
> That whence our dignity originates,
> That which both gives it being and maintains
> A balance, an ennobling interchange
> Of action from within and from without,
> The excellence, pure spirit, and best power
> Both of the object seen, and the eye that sees.

From the beginning of the Salisbury Plain sequence to its end chronological markers have conveyed a sense of historical exactitude—'About this time' (278), 'at that time' (313), 'I must then have exercised' (360), 'about this period' (370)—but they are treacherous guide-posts. Do they point back to 1793 when Wordsworth actually crossed Salisbury Plain? 1794 when the first imperfect verse was completed? 1795 when Coleridge, now first met, was able to read a revised version of it? or some later time at Racedown or Alfoxden, when he and Wordsworth certainly did muse on the relation of 'the object seen, and the eye that sees'. And the answer is that it doesn't matter, because what is taking place in the whole sequence is not so much a reshaping of history as a broad-brush re-colouration of it. First, all trace of the socio-political anger that fuelled Wordsworth's writing in the years following his return to England from France at the end of 1792 is expunged. In 1793–5 he did 'have sight | Of a new world', but it was one to which the execution of a king might have to be an excusable prelude (*Letter to the Bishop of Llandaff*), one which could come about when the Heroes of Truth have done their work of tearing down the Temples of Superstition (*Salisbury Plain*), one in which press-ganged sailors would not be driven to crime by an unjust society and gibbeted by the agents of violated Justice (*Adventures on Salisbury Plain*). Though echoes from the Salisbury Plain poems are permitted into the text of *The Prelude*, the nature of the poems they represent in the chronicle of those years is wholly concealed. Next, in lines 354 to 379, the concluding passage addressed to Coleridge, Wordsworth transfers to the years 1793–1796/7 the growing assurance of vocation and the sense of intellectual and artistic power, which possessed him over the *annus mirabilis* of greatest creative intimacy with Coleridge, 1797–8. Wordsworth then did have a vision of a new world fit to be transmitted, but it was one in which Paradise was to be looked for in the 'simple produce of the common day' and its prophet, singing the spousal verse of the wedding of the mind of man to the goodly universe, was to be the poet of *Lyrical Ballads*, not of *Salisbury Plain*.[35]

This depoliticized vision of the Salisbury Plain poems was endorsed by Coleridge in *Biographia Literaria*, when he came to look back on his first encounter with Wordsworth in 1795—that is, when a version of *Adventures on Salisbury Plain* was in circulation. Recollecting the 'sudden effect' produced by Wordsworth's recitation of 'a manuscript poem, which still remains unpublished, but of which the stanza, and tone of style, were the same as those of the "Female Vagrant" as originally printed in the first volume of the "Lyrical Ballads"', Coleridge tries at some length to identify what it was that struck him so profoundly, before eventually arriving at one of his most memorable tributes to the particular character of Wordsworth's poetic power:

It was the union of deep feeling with profound thought; the fine balance of truth in observing with the imaginative faculty in modifying the objects observed; and above all the original gift of spreading the tone, the *atmosphere*, and with it the depth and height of the ideal world around forms, incidents, and situations, of which, for the common view, custom had bedimmed all the lustre, had dried up the sparkle and the dew drops.[36]

This is beautiful, but it may be doubted whether a single reader has ever responded to the angry, sensationalist *Adventures on Salisbury Plain* in quite this way. What Coleridge's tribute does is present, as if it were his response to the poem in 1795, a version of the judgement made in *The Prelude*—a judgement which that poem attributes to Coleridge.

There is a Chinese box effect here. Coleridge in 1817 repeats what Wordsworth said in 1804–5; there can be no doubt, however, that the terms Wordsworth uses in *The Prelude* are very Coleridgean and reflect his absorption of Coleridgean modes of thought through the on-going discussion about poetry the two had been having ever since 1797. But who originated the terminology is not the point at issue here; nor is it what language of praise Coleridge actually used when the two poets first became friends.[37] What matters for this discussion is that in 1804 Wordsworth should have highlighted Coleridge's role as poetic mentor at this stage in *The Prelude* and that he should have formulated in this way the terms in which his encouragement was expressed.

It is important because the passage in *The Prelude* has a far-reaching effect. It transmutes the social and political dimension of the two Salisbury Plain poems entirely. Poems which arose from historically specific protest against tyranny, priestcraft, and injustice, and which demonstrated above all the 'calamities of war as they affect individuals',[38] are transformed into works whose real significance is that they demonstrate that their creator's sensibility is that of a 'higher power'. Coleridge's praise, Wordsworth declares, in the passage already quoted (XII, 368-79), also very importantly acted as timely confirmation of what he himself was experiencing—nothing less than an awakening to a renewed sense of life and with that a heightened sense of duty:

> I remember well
> That in life's every-day appearances
> I seem'd about this period to have sight
> Of a new world, a world, too, that was fit
> To be transmitted and made visible
> To other eyes . . .

What Wordsworth is 'remember[ing] well', in fact, is the period during which, as he and Coleridge began to conceive an enormously ambitious project that would transmit a vision of a new world and work for Man's redemption, he assumed the mantle of philosopher-prophet-poet. The stridency that characterizes the Salisbury Plain protest poems has no place in Wordsworth's new poetic dispensation, but the poems themselves have an important place in his 1804-5 recollection of his formative years. They figure in *The Prelude* Book Twelve not because the poet wants to recapture the anger that produced them, but because what he recalls is that Coleridge's whole-hearted responsiveness 'about this period' was what confirmed his sense of vocation and focused it on the specific project to which the autobiographical poem was but a prelude.

Placing the Salisbury Plain revisited passage where it is, and using it to formulate artistic and ideological concepts which in fact date from the period of *Lyrical Ballads* onwards, has, moreover, further important effects. It affirms that whatever crisis and disruption

Wordsworth may have suffered in the 1790s, there is a more than counter-balancing continuity between those turbulent years and the now in which *The Prelude* is being brought to completion; that since for this reason the 1790s have to be included in any account of the growth of the mind of the poet of *The Recluse*, the limited five-book structure planned for it will not do; and that Coleridge's contribution to his development cannot be over-valued. Human love, especially Dorothy Wordsworth's, and Nature 'saved' Wordsworth, *The Prelude* insists. What Book Twelve adds is that it was Coleridge's distinction to see at the very beginning of their friendship what he had been saved for.

(iii)

In January 1807 Wordsworth read *The Prelude* to Coleridge and it was this act that marked the completion of the first stage of the poem's life. It was 'finished', Wordsworth had announced to Beaumont; now the 'gift', 'this offering of my love' (XIII, 411, 426), had been delivered to its addressee, Coleridge. Preserved in two fair-copy manuscripts, the autobiographical poem with the title not yet decided upon was a task completed.

A little over a decade later, however, Wordsworth was stirred to look it all over once more. Early in 1819 his clerk, John Carter, began to make a further copy of the poem. As Mark Reed, *The Prelude*'s greatest modern editor, points out, what prompted Carter is not known, but what is clear is that 'Wordsworth's inflammable propensities for revision ignited'. The poem was revisited and after the familiar process of 'tinkering', much of which was eventually discarded, what Reed calls 'the "C-Stage *Prelude*"' emerged as a version of the poem in its own right.[39]

The revisions that embody an 'imaginative tendency', which, as Reed puts it (p. 89), is 'well defined and strongly impelled', are generally small in themselves. Two changes at this stage of the poem's evolution, however, were substantial, and both say a great deal about Wordsworth's state of mind as he approached his fiftieth birthday. The first was made in MS C itself, a lengthy addition to Book Six about the expulsion of the monks from the Grande Chartreuse. The second only took effect after work on MS C had lapsed, but there can be no doubt that it originated in the creative fervour of revision. The change was the consequence of the decision taken to release a part of the poem, the Vaudracour and Julia episode in Book Nine, and thereafter to excise it from the overall structure.

In *The Prelude* of 1805 Wordsworth's account of his visit in 1790 to the monastery of the Grande Chartreuse could hardly be brisker. He and his companion, Robert Jones, bid farewell to a group with whom they have been travelling and

> the Convent of Chartreuse
> Receiv'd us two days afterwards, and there
> We rested in an awful Solitude;
> Thence onward to the Country of the Swiss.   (VI, 422–5)

It being no part of the poet's 'present purpose to retrace | That variegated journey step by step', the verse hastens on to Mont Blanc and the Simplon Pass.

In 1819, however, the Chartreuse becomes a figurative as well as a literal resting place. An interpolation at *1805*, VI, 424/5 brings the travel narrative to a halt as the poet focuses on the moment in 1792 when government troops took over the monastery and eventually expelled the inhabitants. The silence and solitude of the sacred place were violated by 'Arms flashing, and a military glare | Of riotous men commissioned to expel | With senseless rapine'.[40] Nature implores the soldiers to 'Stay [their] impious hands'. Honouring the 'Patriot's zeal' and acknowledging that in this time of revolution 'galling chains' have to be broken, she nonetheless urges them to spare this 'embodied Dream'. Too dense for paraphrase, Nature's apostrophe can only be followed in full quotation:

> 'But spare, if past and future be the wings
> On whose support harmoniously conjoin'd
> Moves the great spirit of human knowledge, spare
> These courts of mystery where a step advanc'd
> Between the portals of the shadowy rocks
> Leaves far behind the vanities of life,
> Where if a Peasant enter or a King
> A penitential tear or holy thought
> Has power to initiate—let it be redeem'd
> With all its blameless priesthood for the sake
> Of faith and meditative reason resting
> Upon the word of heaven-imparted truth

> Triumphantly assured; for humbler claim
> Of that imaginative impulse sent
> From these majestic floods—those shining cliffs
> The untransmuted shapes of many worlds,
> (Cerulian Æther's pure inhabitants);
> The forests unapproachable by death,
> That shall endure as long as man endures
> To think, to hope, to worship and to feel,
> To struggle, to be lost within himself
> In trepidation; from the blank abyss
> To look with bodily eyes and be consoled.'⁴¹

In later development of the passage up to its first appearance in 1850 these words are uttered by the poet. He claims to have heard Nature's ejaculation, 'Stay, stay your sacrilegious hands', *then* (1790) and to hear it still *now* (the time of writing), and it wrings from a poet 'by conflicting passions pressed' the apostrophe just quoted, in reinforcement of Nature's plea. The 1850 version is rhetorically more dramatic, but no one reading the 1819 text is going to be in any doubt that Nature's and the poet's voice are one and the same.

Why did Wordsworth make this addition to Book Six now? Hard evidence is lacking; that is, nothing in his current reading, or any conversation, so far as is known, can be adduced as the specific prompt to a meditation and historical retrospect on the Grande Chartreuse. What is clear, though, is that the well-springs of this new composition are to be found in revisiting of his own earlier poetry on the Chartreuse and on monasticism that had been taking place sporadically for some years. The history of this revisiting, briefly, is as follows.

Wordsworth and Jones visited the monastery of the Grande Chartreuse over the 4th and 5th of August 1790. Though Dorothy Wordsworth was later to claim that no 'spot which he visited during his youthful Travels with Robert Jones made so great an impression on his mind',⁴² there is no record of what the 20-year-old Wordsworth actually saw and felt when he was there. Maddeningly, the letter one most wants, the one Wordsworth wrote to his sister from the monastery, has not survived; the remark in his next letter that the travellers had stayed two days at the Grande Chartreuse 'contemplating, with encreased pleasure its wonderful scenery' is no compensation for its loss.⁴³

Two years later, however, when he was once again in France, Wordsworth returned to the monastery in memory and imagination and on this occasion a little more is vouchsafed. Lines 53–79 of *Descriptive Sketches* present Nature's alarm as the 'death-like' peace of the Grande Chartreuse is shattered by the military incursion:

> The cloister startles at the gleam of arms,
> And Blasphemy the shuddering fane alarms;
> Nod the cloud-piercing pines their troubl'd heads,
> Spires, rocks, and lawns, a browner night o'erspreads.[44]

This is atmospheric, but the Gothic animation is not based on eye-witness and the account in the thirteen-book *Prelude* returns to factual accuracy, observing only, as has already been noted, that Wordsworth and Jones rested at the Grande Chartreuse before pressing on towards Switzerland.

The monastery though, and its setting amidst what Gray described as 'the most solemn, the most romantic, and the most astonishing scenes' he had ever beheld,[45] continued to figure powerfully in Wordsworth's imagination and in 1808 he returned there in his most sustained attempt to unlock its meaning for him nearly two decades after his actual visit. In *The Tuft of Primroses*, a poem intended for *The Recluse* but never completed, Wordsworth wrestles with the truth, made all too apparent locally in the recent felling of many of Grasmere's ancient trees, that

> the best
> And Dearest resting places of the heart
> Vanish beneath an unrelenting doom.[46]

A long meditation follows on the motives that lead men, St Basil for example, to choose a life of seclusion, which concludes in a lament at the destruction of sacred houses such as Fountains Abbey, the 'stately Towers | And branching windows gorgeously array'd, | And aisles and roofs magnificent that thrill'd | With halleluiahs'. This leads seamlessly to a dramatic episode (ll. 507–25) in which Wordsworth represents himself and his 'Fellow-pilgrim' as having been possibly the very last travellers to have been received in peace at the Grande Chartreuse before violence engulfed it; and this in turn concludes with an incomplete passage (ll. 526–92) recording Nature's plea that the monastery 'With all its blameless priesthood' be reprieved.

This was the passage, written eleven years earlier, that Wordsworth returned to in 1819 and commandeered for the 'C-Stage' of the autobiographical poem. But this was not the first time since writing *The Tuft of Primroses* that Wordsworth had revisited his poetry on the Grande Chartreuse. For his first ever collected poetical works, the two volumes of 1815, he extracted passages from *Descriptive Sketches*, published in 1793, one of which included (revised of course) the lines on the Chartreuse. In the prose discourse which closed the collection, however, the *Essay, Supplementary to the Preface*, a reflective observation quoted from manuscript,

> '—Past and future, are the wings
> On whose support, harmoniously conjoined,
> Moves the great Spirit of human knowledge—'

is taken from the *Tuft of Primroses* material already quoted. In short Wordsworth reviews his 1790 experience through the lens of both the poetry of 1808 (*The Tuft*) and of 1792–3 (*Descriptive Sketches*).

Only a year before the 1815 *Poems*, moreover, *The Tuft of Primroses* must have had renewed presence in Wordsworth's mind, for at last *The Excursion*, which made use of much of it, was published. In Book Three the Solitary speaks feelingly of the human longing for peace,

> The central feeling of all happiness,
> Not as a refuge from distress or pain,
> A breathing-time, vacation, or a truce,
> But for its absolute self; a life of peace,
> Stability without regret or fear;
> That has been, is, and shall be evermore!

His words ring with echoes of the earlier *Ode to Duty* and *Elegiac Stanzas . . . Peele Castle*, but they are drawn from the *Tuft of Primroses* material on monastic retirement already referred to. And it is notable that the whole passage (III, 367–461) on 'The universal instinct of repose, | The longing for confirmed tranquillity' (397–8), stands out as the finest poetry in the book.

The argument being pursued is that on a number of occasions in 1814 and 1815 Wordsworth returned to his Chartreuse material and it was these revisitings that prompted the big addition to *The Prelude* in 1819. But even if this sequence of occasions be admitted, the question remains, why did this earlier writing speak to Wordsworth now?

The passage added to the 'C-Stage' *Prelude* consists of an impassioned advocacy of the monastery and its environs as the human embodiment of a spiritual ideal. In 1793, when Wordsworth had returned to England from France an ardent radical, he had concluded his protest poem *Salisbury Plain* with a call for the 'Heroes of Truth' to engage in battle without quarter against Error and Superstition and had looked forward to the day when Reason's emblem should rear 'High o'er the towers of Pride'.[47] Now, in the 1819 interpolation, Nature is presented as having then (when Wordsworth and Jones were at the Grande Chartreuse) likewise bid the 'purging fires' of revolution ascend 'Up to the loftiest towers of pride', but the monastery, she insists, is exempt and must be saved. The life within it equalizes Peasant and King, an emblem of true radicalism; its 'blameless priesthood', far from being living proof of what in 1793 was termed 'Superstition's reign', ministers to 'heaven-imparted truth'. And of hardly less importance is the imaginative impulse given by the mountains and forests, which speak to the present and will speak to generations yet unborn, enduring,

> as long as man endures
> To think, to hope, to worship and to feel,
> To struggle, to be lost within himself
> In trepidation; from the blank abyss
> To look with bodily eyes and be consoled.
> ('C-Stage', 476–80)

Absolute peace; permanence; endurance—Wordsworth had wrought poetry from such words and concepts ever since *Home at Grasmere* in 1800. As a counter to an ever-present consciousness of mutability, Wordsworth responded profoundly to evidence of mute survival—the ruins of Michael's sheepfold, or Peele Castle. Survival, though, was never a value in itself. Although Wordsworth was certainly moved by the spectacle of whatever just resisted time—the rocks on the Kirkstone Pass, for example, or the flow of the River Duddon, 'Still glides the Stream, and shall for ever glide'—he was drawn imaginatively to emblems of survival by the deepening conviction that values could not be nurtured other than by continuity of transmission across the generations.

Such a conviction underpins the *Two Addresses to the Freeholders of Westmorland* which Wordsworth composed during the general election campaign in 1818. White-hot to support the existing Lowther interest against the pretender Henry Brougham, and clad in the rhetorical mantle he had last worn for *The Convention of Cintra* (1809), Wordsworth urged the electors to recognize that the Lowther family and the landed interest constituted the best elements in the 'ancient frame of society' (169), in which, by a process of slow, natural wisdom, 'Time is gently carrying what is useless or injurious into the background' (173).[48] The choice before the electors was not a local matter merely of 'comparative insignificance' (189), but one on whose outcome depended the continuance of Britain's 'tranquillity and freedom; the maintenance of justice and equity for which she is pre-eminent among nations; and the preservation of her social comforts, her charitable propensities, her morals and her religion' (189).

In the peroration concluding his second address Wordsworth sought to identify Brougham as one of those reformers whose practices had 'led to the destruction of all that was venerable in a neighbouring Country' (189). Allusions to the havoc caused by the revolution in France colour the whole of Wordsworth's impassioned appeal to his fellow countrymen, but it is in this one sentence that the connection is most clearly exposed between his reading of events in Kendal in 1818 and those at the Grande Chartreuse in 1792. 'Stay your impious hands . . .', Nature says to the French soldiers in the 1819 *Prelude* interpolation, but she could as well be speaking to Henry Brougham.

Wordsworth didn't just support the Lowther cause in print. In a surge of energy he campaigned, visited waverers, reported back to headquarters. He was rarely at home, as Keats found to his dismay when he called at Rydal Mount only to find that the poet was out canvassing. Those near to Wordsworth were alarmed. It was 'pitiable', his wife, Mary, thought that he 'should thus be diverted from his natural pursuits',[49] but it is quite clear that Wordsworth viewed his political activities very differently and as a coda to this section I want to consider why.

The *Tuft of Primroses* material Wordsworth pillaged for *The Excursion* and the *Prelude* revision of 1819 embodies two of the strongest impulses of Wordsworth's imaginative being. They are most visible, because dramatized, in *The Excursion*. On the one hand there is the longing for retreat, for seclusion, which is voiced in Book Two in the Poet's enraptured response to the 'sweet Recess' where the Solitary has retired. Here is 'peace',

> Years that pass
> Forgetfully; uncalled upon to pay
> The common penalties of mortal life,
> Sickness, or accident, or grief, or pain.   (366–9)

It is the note of longing heard in *Elegiac Stanzas . . . Peele Castle*:

> Lasting ease,
> Elysian quiet, without toil or strife;
> No motion but the moving tide, a breeze,
> Or merely silent Nature's breathing life.   (25–8)

On the other is the acknowledgement that, in the words of *Home at Grasmere*, 'Something must be done . . .' (876). The false steward is he who receives much but 'renders nothing back' (1805 *Prelude*, I, 271). In *The Excursion* the Solitary hides in retreat, a very different state from retirement. In retirement one can prepare for engagement with the world in a great work such as *The Recluse*. In retreat one is merely 'Unprofitably travelling towards the grave' (1805 *Prelude*, I, 270).

Or so Wordsworth would have it at his most confident. But the possibility that retirement and retreat are pretty much synonymous haunted Wordsworth and Coleridge. It was voiced early on in their careers by both in *Lines left upon a Seat in a Yew-Tree* and *Reflections on Having Left a Place of Retirement*, and continued to absorb Wordsworth as he re-engaged with his meditation on St Basil, St Bruno, and the Grande Chartreuse.

What the 1818 election offered was an arena in which oppositions in Wordsworth's thinking and in his sense of how he was conducting the stewardship of his gifts, could be united. If the choice before the voters was a matter of principles, with consequences for nothing less than national morality and religion, it became the duty of the philosophic poet as citizen to be involved. The *Addresses to the Freeholders* are an attempt to get the voters of Westmorland to see the 'ancient frame of society' as a value to be transmitted, not something obsolete to be rudely swept away, any more than the long-enduring monastery is. When Wordsworth revisited his earlier lines on that 'embodied dream' it was in the knowledge that he had done his utmost to stay the impious hands of those who in England, despite the evidence of the French catastrophe before their eyes, composed 'the Vanguard of a Ferocious Revolution!'.[50]

(iv)

At the same time as he and Carter were at work on the manuscripts of the autobiographical poem, Wordsworth was also putting together materials for a new volume. When it appeared in 1820, *The River Duddon* included 'Vaudracour and Julia', prefaced by a headnote: 'The following was written as an Episode in a work from which its length may perhaps exclude it. The facts are true; no invention as to these has been exercised, as none was needed.' When extracts from *The Prelude* had been published before, in *The Friend* and Wordsworth's *Poems* of 1815 (see Chapter One) independent existence had not entailed removal from the poem that was eventually published in 1850. By the time the lines beginning 'Wisdom and Spirit of the Universe' appeared in the first edition of *The Prelude* they were very familiar, having been enjoyed as 'Influence of Natural Objects' in Wordsworth's collected poetical works from 1815 on. With 'Vaudracour and Julia' the case was different. Possibly Wordsworth's 'may perhaps exclude it' did reflect genuine indecision, but whether or not, once it had been published separately, the episode was never reintegrated into *The Prelude*.[51]

By combining state and domestic tyranny in one story 'Vaudracour and Julia' depicts the *ancien régime* at its worst. Vaudracour's father is opposed to his love for the more lowly Julia, frenziedly so when she becomes pregnant. Paternal anger stretches to manipulation of the power readily available to one of his rank and even to the setting of hired ruffians on to his son. When Vaudracour kills one of them his father acquiesces in his imprisonment. Released, Vaudracour is reunited with Julia, but only briefly for he is once again arrested at his father's instigation. Eventually the pair do come together just before Julia gives birth, but there is no happy ending. Forced by her parents to give up her child, Julia enters a convent. Vaudracour flees in retreat with the baby but, either through accident or his incompetence, it dies while in his care. He goes mad and remains silent till death,

> Cut off from all intelligence with man
> And shunning even the light of common day.
> Nor could the voice of Freedom, which through France
> Soon afterwards resounded, public hope,
> Or personal memory of his own deep wrongs

Rouze him; but in those solitary shades
His days he wasted, an imbecile mind.

In the collective editions of Wordsworth's poems after 1820 'Vaudracour and Julia' was included in the group 'Poems Founded on the Affections' and it was as a moving love story that the poem found favour on its first appearance. The *Eclectic Review* thought it 'a touching and melancholy tale of unfortunate love . . . told in Mr. Wordsworth's happiest manner'; not even Shakespeare, in the view of the *European Magazine*, could have 'given a more magnificent picture of the intoxicating happiness of Love in early life'.[52] To reviewers in 1820 the poem was what it seemed, a Romance, generically not dissimilar from Keats's 'Lamia' or 'The Eve of St Agnes', published in the same year. Had they been able to read the story in its context within the autobiographical poem their responses might have been more probing.

It is many years since F. M. Todd suggested that 'Vaudracour and Julia' drew on a real life story told in Helen Maria Williams's *Letters Written in France, In the Summer 1790* (1790), and it is now generally accepted that, whether or not Wordsworth did hear of these events first-hand 'related by my patriot friend | And others who had borne a part therein', as *The Prelude*, IX, 554-5 claims, he was indebted to the work of Williams, whom he had admired since school-days.[53] But it is also generally accepted that the story is in some way autobiographical; or rather, that it stands in *The Prelude* in place of the autobiographical narrative that ought to be there, a token revelation of facts largely concealed.

The bare facts are now well known.[54] In December 1792 a daughter, Caroline, was born to Wordsworth and Annette Vallon, a Frenchwoman who was a little older than him and an ardent royalist. The pair had known each other only a matter of weeks when Annette became pregnant and before the baby was born they had been forcibly parted by Wordsworth's need to return home, where he stood the likeliest chance of raising some money. The outbreak of war in February 1793 turned a temporary severance into one with no foreseeable ending and almost certainly Wordsworth did not meet Annette again, nor the daughter he had never seen, until 1802, and by that time he was about to marry Mary Hutchinson.[55]

Links between the two stories are not difficult to make—two lovers uniting despite formidable obstacles; a child born out of wedlock; irresistible power forcing separation—and scholars have made them in increasingly sophisticated fashion as they have pondered the many questions the Vaudracour and Julia episode prompts: how far does it reflect a sense of personal guilt; what is Wordsworth saying about the relation of the private and the public spheres; what are the gender politics of the narrative and what the implications of its genre; why the tragic ending? And underlying them all is another question—why include the episode at all in the evolving *Prelude* structure of 1804–5?[56] No discussion of the thirteen-book poem can avoid speculating on some or all of these. After 1820, however, it is not the presence of the Vaudracour and Julia story that is the issue, but its absence. The question to be asked now is, why did revisiting the poem in 1819 lead Wordsworth to cut it out?

The answer, I think, is to be found in the timing of John Carter's work on a new manuscript of *The Prelude*. Whatever the reason why he undertook it—and there is no reason to challenge Reed's speculation that it was not the poet himself who initiated it—Carter began transcribing MS C and in so doing rekindled Wordsworth's interest in the poem, at a moment that with hindsight one can see as a significant turning-point in his life.

In the second half of the decade 1810–20 there is much that points to Wordsworth being aware of the end of an era in his poetic career. The two volumes of 1815—full title *Poems by William Wordsworth: Including Lyrical Ballads, and the Miscellaneous Pieces of the Author. With Additional Poems, A New Preface, and a Supplementary Essay*—were a statement: this was a Collected Poetical Works, containing, on the one hand, pieces of juvenilia, and on the other a lengthy Preface expounding the poet's mature thought on poetry and the creative imagination. Re-stating the author's aims while considering historical, generic, and theoretical issues in magisterial fashion, the Preface and the Essay Supplementary to it entirely supersede the earlier manifesto, the Preface to *Lyrical Ballads*, which, relegated to the end of the second volume and printed in smaller type, becomes a document in the poet's past history.[57]

At the same time as presenting himself as one who was drawing things together poetically, Wordsworth also began a process of tidying up. In 1815 he published a revised version of *The White Doe of Rylstone*, a poem completed in 1808 but which, with his self-confidence at low ebb after the debacle of *Poems, in Two Volumes*, he had resisted publishing then.[58] In 1819 two other pieces were disinterred, revised, and published—*The Waggoner*, dating from 1806, and *Peter Bell*, a product of the Alfoxden summer of 1798. Addressing the Poet Laureate, Robert Southey, in the Preface to the latter, Wordsworth draws attention to the poem's long gestation and the pains that have been taken 'to fit it for filling *permanently* a station, however humble, in the Literature of my Country'.[59] Wordsworth had used the word 'permanently' in a similar context before: 'Several of my Friends are anxious for the success of these Poems from a belief, that, if the views with which they were composed were indeed realized, a class of Poetry would be produced, well adapted to interest mankind permanently.' But when Wordsworth wrote that for the Preface to *Lyrical Ballads* in 1800, he was no more than yet another young poet fired with high ambition. When he italicized '*permanently*' in the dedicatory words to Southey it was with the confidence that, however slowly, he was taking his place in the 'Literature of [his] Country'.

By incorporating these poems in their revised forms into his expanding *oeuvre* Wordsworth was settling some elements in his past, making them conformable to the poetic identity he assumed as he neared fifty years of age. And this desire to draw boundaries had, I will suggest, a bearing on the decision to publish 'Vaudracour and Julia' separately in 1820. Almost certainly, however, a more directly relevant factor had been the publication of *The Excursion* in 1814.

In Book Two of *The Excursion* the Wanderer relates to the Poet the sad history of the reclusive friend they are walking to visit. In the next book he, the Solitary, gives his version of it. Both accounts are a complex amalgam of Wordsworth's own past and his more recent history; of recollection of what was mingled with representation of what might have been; and of formulations about youthful ideals and their vulnerability that could be inserted seamlessly into the French Revolution books of *The Prelude*. For example:

> Why then conceal, that, when the simply good
> In timid selfishness withdrew, I sought
> Other support, not scrupulous whence it came;
> And, by what compromise it stood, not nice?

Faced with this blind, few readers would, I suspect, be able to say with complete assurance that it (*Excursion*, III, 790–3) was not a passage from *The Prelude* Book Ten.[60]

   The Solitary has retreated to a 'recess' in the Lake District (already mentioned in the previous section of this chapter), battered by suffering from two causes. One he has no option but to bear—the loss of two children followed shortly by their mother. 'What good is given to men, | More solid than the gilded clouds of heaven?', he exclaims in 'the bitter language of the heart' (III, 437–8; 462), recalling the happiness of his married life amongst the 'sylvan combs' of Devon. Echoes in the Solitary's words of lines written in 1797–8 indicate how strongly Racedown, Alfoxden, and the *annus mirabilis* are, as ever, in Wordsworth's mind.[61] The loss of his family drives the Solitary to anguished introspection and intellectual 'toils abstruse',[62] from which he is rescued, 'reconverted to the world' by the promise of the French Revolution:

> From the depths
> Of natural passion, seemingly escaped,
> My soul diffused herself in wide embrace
> Of institutions, and the forms of things;
> As they exist, in mutable array,
> Upon life's surface. What, though in my veins
> There flowed no Gallic blood, nor had I breathed
> The air of France, not less than Gallic zeal
> Kindled and burned among the sapless twigs
> Of my exhausted heart.   (III, 736–45)

The eventual confounding of his hopes by the course of the revolution, compounded by further dispiriting experience in republican America, is the second cause of the Solitary's suffering and for this kind of pain he has found no adequate solace. Withdrawal to the Lake District is a palliative; it falls to the Wanderer to indicate sources of remedy in his homily in Book Four, 'Despondency Corrected'.

   This is a rather summary account of nearly two thousand lines of verse, but it is enough to suggest how numerous are the links between the Solitary's experiences and Wordsworth's, but also how variously they are refracted. The joy of young love is recalled in a passage that begins exactly as the story of Vaudracour and Julia does, 'O happy time . . .' (III, 550), but the pain of loss is located not in severance from a French family, but in the loss of children, a calamity that William and Mary Wordsworth had endured in 1812, when two of their children died within six months of each other. The Solitary's struggle to articulate how he went wrong as the revolution faltered, trusting to Abstractions and maintaining an intellectual strife 'Hopeless, and still more hopeless every hour' (III, 789), strikingly recalls the climactic passage in Book Ten of *The Prelude* where the poet images himself spiralling downwards, 'confounded more and more, | Misguiding and misguided' (887–8). Whereas Wordsworth in *The Prelude*, however, is 'saved', put back in touch with his 'true self', and thereby enabled to retire to his native mountains in the confident hope, as he announced to the world in 1814, that he might 'construct a literary Work that might live',[63] the Solitary hides in his mountain retreat, seeking in a life without expectation a counter-balance to the conviction burnt into him by experience, that 'Mutability is Nature's bane' (III, 458).

Books Two and Three of *The Excursion* are in large part a reprise of the French-English-Politics section of *The Prelude*; that is, a further engagement with the tumult of public and private experience, elation and dismay, that constituted Wordsworth's actual life in the first half of the 1790s. And it is striking that again Annette Vallon's role is registered only obliquely. If in *The Prelude* mother and child figure in a Romance, whose details are taken from a literary source because they can be made to serve the needs of Wordsworth's autobiographical poem for simultaneous disclosure and concealment, in *The Excursion* wife and children figure in a different narrative, whose purpose is to explain how personal anguish predisposed the sufferer to embrace the shallow promise of the revolution of 1789 with such rapture.

The fact under consideration here, though, is not what promptings may have determined how Wordsworth dealt with his time in France and its legacy, but that he did so twice, first in the autobiographical poem, *The Prelude*, and then in the dramatic one, *The Excursion*, and that he made the latter public. It would be perhaps too sweeping to say that with the publication of *The Excursion* in 1814 and its second edition in 1820 the ghost of the 1790s was laid, but it is the case that those years, the years that shaped him as man and poet, ceased to occupy Wordsworth with the imaginative intensity they had commanded for so long. *The Excursion* declares itself the harbinger of a greater work, but it is in fact, in many ways, an end. And one of the effects of publishing it is to free Wordsworth to release the Vaudracour and Julia story from the *Prelude* context in which it is embedded and which gives it its personal application and meaning. With the Solitary's tale Wordsworth has made public all he intends to say about events in the France of his youth. The Salisbury Plain poems, *The Borderers*, *The Prelude* remain under wraps: 'Vaudracour and Julia' can safely be disclosed and the act of disclosing it serves to shape a conclusion to a period of his life.

In 1820 Wordsworth also tellingly performed acts of non-literary recapitulation, merging present with past in ways that signified a conclusion. At the beginning of the summer he sought Robert Jones out and reminisced with him about their pedestrian tour thirty years earlier that had taken in the Grande Chartreuse, before setting out to go over the ground again, and for the last time. It is not difficult to imagine what Wordsworth must have felt when he realized he had found the very track that had misled him and Jones on their crossing of the Simplon Pass in 1790.

With the most significant revisiting of the 1820 tour, however, even the trusty formula of 'It is not difficult to imagine . . .' seems inadequate. At the end of September Wordsworth, with his wife and his sister, met up with Annette Vallon, their daughter Caroline, her husband, and their two children. When Wordsworth had last strolled and talked with Annette and Caroline in 1802 the occasion had been doubly momentous; he was meeting his daughter for the first time, but also announcing that he was shortly to get married—and not to her mother. In the intervening years contact had been maintained as far as the war allowed; money affairs were settled; and now they were all walking together again in the Louvre and the Jardin des Plantes. In 1792, barely out of college, Wordsworth had been a wide-eyed tourist in Paris, visiting the famous sites but in truth 'Affecting more emotion than [he] felt' (*1805*, IX, 71). Now he was a middle-aged man, with a wife and three children, one of them a daughter to whom he was devotedly attached. How did it sound to his ears, one wonders, let alone to Mary Wordsworth's, that his other surviving daughter throughout their month-long stay called him 'Father'. But what else might she have called him?

As a grace note to the larger acts of completion that took place in 1820 can be added one more that satisfyingly fulfilled an aspiration thwarted more than thirty years earlier. In 1792, primed with a letter of introduction from Charlotte Smith, Wordsworth had sought out Helen Maria Williams in Orleans, but she had just left the city. Now they came together at last. On one of their two evenings together Wordsworth performed a little act of homage by reciting from memory her sonnet *To Hope*. But as he did so he was also saluting his own earlier self, for when he had seen his verse in print for the first time, it had been with another act of homage, his 'Sonnet: On Seeing Miss Helen Maria Williams Weep at a Tale of Distress'.[64] Then he had been a 17-year-old aspirant for laurels: now he was, in the judgement of the magazine that had first published him, 'beyond all comparison the most truly sublime . . . of all the poetical spirits of the age'.[65]

Wordsworth returned home, and, buoyed up by favourable reviews of the *River Duddon* volume, oversaw the appearance of a fresh collective edition of his poems in four volumes. It was the beginning of a new era.[66] The poem on his own life was put aside, not to be re-engaged with for a decade.

4

The Prelude: 1820–1850

> There is a dark
> Invisible workmanship that reconciles
> Discordant elements, and makes them move
> In one society. Ah me, that all
> The terrors, all the early miseries,
> Regrets, vexations, lassitudes, that all
> The thoughts and feelings which have been infused
> Into my mind, should ever have made up
> The calm existence that is mine when I
> Am worthy of myself.[1]

(i)

'Father is particularly well,' Dora Wordsworth reported to a friend early in 1832, 'and busier than a *1000* Bees. Mother & he work like slaves from morning to night . . . correcting a long Poem written 30 years back.'[2] Wordsworth had returned to the autobiographical poem. Pressing his now more than 60-year-old wife into hours of service with the pen—'arduous work', Dora deemed it— Wordsworth pored over the earlier fair-copy manuscripts intent on producing a completely revised and freshly transcribed version of the whole poem.

What prompted this revisiting? In part it was a sharpened awareness of the passing of time. There was still no question of immediate publication, of course. When Dora explained to Maria Kinnaird that the work her father was engaged on was 'not to be published during his life—"the growth of his own mind"—the "ante-chapel" as he calls it to the "Recluse" ', she sounded rather as if she were repeating the official Rydal Mount line on the matter, but entering his sixties

Wordsworth was conscious that the planned posthumous publication date for the autobiographical poem might not be too far off. It needed to be made ready for eventual publication. Accordingly, great pains were taken with the preparation of the new manuscript, now known as MS D, and after numerous changes of wording and the creation of a fourteen- rather than thirteen-book structure by the division of the tenth book into two, the poem now took on pretty much the identity it was to retain until its first appearance in 1850.

Another letter of Dora's, however, gives a clue to a profounder answer to the question, 'Why now?' On 20 October 1831 Dora reported Wordsworth as promising 'that the Recluse shall be his winter employment', but ever responsive to her father's state of mind, she confessed to Maria Jane Jewsbury, 'entre nous I think his courage will fail him when winter really arrives'.[3] It did. Beth Darlington has documented how anxious Wordsworth's family had become through the 1820s at his failure to get on with *The Recluse*, and observes that the 'sparseness of Wordsworth's own comments on the poem . . . intimates that the topic was a tender one, which he preferred to avoid'.[4] At last it seemed he had returned to the task 'with good earnest',[5] but in the event all he did for *The Recluse* was revise the first book of it written long ago. As it had done from the beginning in 1798–9, when both were conceived, engagement with the autobiographical poem displaced work on the philosophical one.

There is an irony, however, to this impasse over poetical-philosophical composition. At his first mention of the plan for *The Recluse* in 1798 Wordsworth had declared that his object was 'to give pictures of Nature, Man and Society'. In the Preface to *The Excursion* in 1814 he repeated the formulation: *The Recluse* was to be 'a philosophical poem, containing views on Man, Nature and Society' and its title was chosen to indicate that its 'principal subject' would be the 'sensations and opinions of a poet living in retirement'.[6] But now it seemed that Wordsworth was doing little or nothing for *The Recluse*. In fact, to the contrary, it might be said that for years he had been doing just what he said he would, for he had been delivering views on Man, Nature, and Society with increasing firmness, not in poetry but in prose. A striking example is his long letter of 11 June 1825 to Sir Robert Inglis about the proposed Roman Catholic Relief Bill, which survives in a copy made for Lord Lonsdale, with a view possibly, Alan G. Hill surmises, to eventual publication.[7] Another is a letter of 1829 to the Cambridge luminary Hugh James Rose, a long, considered reflection on the nature of true education. Reaffirming convictions that Wordsworth had long held ('Natural history is taught in infant schools by pictures stuck up against walls, and such mummery. A moment's notice of a red-breast pecking by a winter's hearth is worth it all'), the letter broadens out to include questions about emerging ideas on schooling and the implications of them for social cohesion in the future. Such fearful concerns did not trouble Wordsworth in the late 1790s, when he and Dorothy were looking after little Basil Montagu, but they did now.[8]

The sweep outwards from consideration of a specific issue to reflections on the state of the nation characterizes all of Wordsworth's thinking in the period roughly 1815 to 1834—Waterloo to the Poor Law Amendment Act—and it was displayed most obviously at the three moments when he became absorbed to the point of obsession in politics. The first was the 1818 election in which Henry Brougham had the temerity to stand against the Lowther interest in Westmorland. The second was during the run-up to Catholic Emancipation in 1829. The third was the period of high political drama, the last act of which ended with the passing of the 1832 Reform Bill.

'A poet living in retirement', Wordsworth wrote at length on all these topics, 'delivering views on Man, Nature and Society'. Some were published—*Two Addresses to the Freeholders of Westmorland*—others were not, but could have been—letters on Catholic Emancipation, for example, addressed to the Bishop of London (3 March 1829) and Christopher Wordsworth, now Master of Trinity College, Cambridge (13 March 1829). As he considers what is immediately pressing, showing a good grasp of detail, Wordsworth moves in each case to ponder its significance. What does Brougham's intervention mean, not just as a political act with consequences for a sparsely populated region dominated by one great family, but as a pointer to nationwide disturbance in these post-war years? As had been the case with the 1809 *Convention of Cintra*, the specific event that elicited the *Two Addresses to the Freeholders of Westmorland* acts as the prompt for the revelation of a vision of how ideals and morality ought to operate in the social body. So it is with the letters on Catholic Emancipation. It may be expedient to meet Catholic demands, but what will be the impact in the longer term of conceding that the historic settlements of the previous 150 years or so have rested on injustice?

Catholic Emancipation seemed a portent—by 1831 Wordsworth was convinced he knew what it was a portent of. He was flattered that Lord Lonsdale asked his views about the Reform Bill crisis and gave them at length in a letter of 17 February 1832, but his opinions were not reserved for actors in the scene such as Lord Lonsdale— family and acquaintances were all subjected to them.[9] In 1818, detecting similarities between Brougham's attempts to dissolve established allegiances and symptoms of disorder that had presaged the revolution in France, Wordsworth had addressed the Freeholders of Westmorland as if Sansculottism was a spectre already stalking the Lake District hills. In the event, his alarm proved exaggerated. But now in 1831 all his fears returned. Ever since the general election of 1830, from which Brougham had emerged as a much strengthened figure in the movement for parliamentary reform, pressure for political action had been mounting. As reports filtered back to Rydal Mount of the manoeuvrings in London to secure the passing of what was to be the Reform Act of 1832, Wordsworth was sure that his earlier forebodings had been justified. 'I have witnessed one revolution in a foreign country', he wrote to his brother, 'and I have not courage to think of facing another in my own',[10] but daily events suggested that he might have to. What politicians in favour of reform saw as prudent measures to accommodate demands and so ease pressure for constitutional reform, Wordsworth saw as opening the way for irresistible calls for yet more radical change. Would the gaps opening up between the factions in Westminster and the King and his ministers be the fissures through which the lava of revolution could come boiling out?[11]

In 1833 Wordsworth declared that 'although he was known to the world only as a poet, he had given twelve hours thought to the conditions and prospects of society, for one to poetry',[12] and it was a comment he certainly could have made two years earlier. But although Wordsworth feared that the Muse had forsaken him, 'driven away by the villainous aspect of the Times',[13] in one respect the opposite was the case. Absorption in politics was certainly displacement activity, a way of not getting on with *The Recluse*, but it was also what returned him to the poem that in reality mattered most, *The Prelude*. For Wordsworth's agitated reflections now could not but lead him back to an earlier period of agonizing about his own and the nation's plight.

In a version of the 'Postscript' to *Yarrow Revisited* that was not published, Wordsworth confessed as much:

It has, from time to time, been the practice of the Author of this volume, since he was first interested in public Affairs, to express in verse the feelings with which he regarded them. Accordingly, it is known to all, who have read his poems, that he rejoiced in the opening of the French Revolution; & it will appear, hereafter, from his unpublished Works, how deeply he deplored the excesses into which the French people were betrayed, in its progress. . . . The lines however in the present volume, entitled 'The Warning', both by the occasion that suggested them, & the manner in which the subject is treated, show that *recent* events have intimately touched his affections, & thrown him back upon sensations akin to those he was troubled with in the early period of his life.[14]

What this confession reveals is that Wordsworth was returning in thought not just to the events of the 1790s but inevitably to the poem which both chronicles them and records his later endeavours as a poet to understand those events and his part in them. The promise that his unpublished work would hereafter reveal something of the history of his changing attitudes to France is yet another of the many references Wordsworth made in later life to the existence of *The Prelude*, and in the language of the final sentence—'touched his affections, & thrown him back upon sensations'— the cadence and diction of the poem's opening books are heard.

The Reform crisis stirred Wordsworth very deeply because he believed that much that he held dear was under threat. But it did so also because as he (supposedly a reluctant correspondent) wrote letter after letter and conversed about political issues, Wordsworth was forced to consider how his present convictions had taken shape and that meant revisiting both an old self and earlier writing. Some of this writing belonged to the period in which he was first attempting through autobiographical retrospect to recall and interpret what he had lived through and how the experience had fitted him to become a poet. Some of it, however, belonged to earlier years still, well before the autobiographical poem was conceived, and that writing survived as an unchanging reminder of an earlier passionate self, when very different convictions were no less dear.

'Incumbent o'er the surface of past time', Wordsworth had always made poetry from the struggle to 'part | The shadow from the substance',[15] and had tried and tested strategies for dealing with discomfiture. Dealing with it, in fact, was the structuring mechanism of the whole poem. Even so, in this period of revision, as the poet pored over old manuscripts that offered glimpses of a former self, he must have been more than usually aware, and not comfortably so, of 'Two consciousnesses, conscious of myself | And of some other being'.[16] The most important addition to the poem, however, would not have betrayed to its first readers anything of the turbulence that must have prompted its insertion, for it meshes very easily with verse written over a quarter of a century earlier. In the account in Book Seven of his first experiences in London, as it stood in all the versions to date, Wordsworth had recorded visiting the House of Commons in the early 1790s and being dazzled by Pitt's eloquence. Now, in 1831, he summoned Burke's presence. The addition demonstrates Wordsworth's continuing ability to sustain blank verse over the long paragraph. It cannot be excerpted and should ideally be read out loud *con brio*; the passage is, after all, about eloquence:

> Genius of Burke! forgive the pen seduced
> By specious wonders, and too slow to tell
> Of what the ingenuous, what bewildered Men
> Beginning to mistrust their boastful guides,
> And wise men, willing to grow wiser, caught,
> Rapt auditors! from thy most eloquent tongue—
> Now mute, for ever mute, in the cold grave.
> I see him, old but vigorous in age,
> Stand, like an Oak whose stag-horn branches start
> Out of its leafy brow, the more to awe
> The younger brethren of the grove. But some—
> While he forewarns, denounces, launches forth,
> Against all systems built on abstract rights,
> Keen ridicule; the majesty proclaims
> Of Institutes and Laws hallowed by Time;
> Declares the vital power of social ties
> Endeared by Custom; and with high disdain
> Exploding upstart Theory, insists
> Upon the Allegiance to which Men are born—
> Some—say at once a froward multitude—
> Murmur (for truth is hated, where not loved)
> As the winds fret within the Eolian cave,

> Galled by their Monarch's chain. The times were big
> With ominous change which, night by night, provoked
> Keen struggles, and black clouds of passion raised;
> But memorable moments intervened
> When Wisdom, like the Goddess from Jove's brain,
> Broke forth in armour of resplendent words,
> Startling the Synod. Could a Youth, and one
> In ancient story versed, whose breast had heaved
> Under the weight of classic eloquence,
> Sit, see, and hear, unthankful, uninspired?   (VII, 512–43)

The two consummate actors on 'that great stage' (491), Pitt and Burke, now confront each other in the drama of this verse episode as they did in reality.

A way in to considering where this addition—the last substantial alteration to the text of The Prelude—came from and what it meant to Wordsworth is offered by the most heartfelt observation he made during the 1831–2 Reform crisis. Shocked to discover that William Rowan Hamilton, a man he admired and liked, was 'a Reformer', Wordsworth exhorted him in a letter of 22 November 1831 to recognize the virtue of 'quiet progress in well doing'. His earnest plea concluded:

The Constitution of England which seems about to be destroyed, offers to my mind the sublimest contemplation which the History of Society and Government have ever presented to it; and for this cause especially, that its principles have the character of preconceived ideas, archetypes of the pure intellect, while they are in fact the results of humble-minded experience.

It is impossible not to hear in this profession an echo of an earlier very famous avowal, made by Charles James Fox in 1791. With Burke's Reflections on the Revolution in France in everyone's mind, Fox had assured the House of Commons that it had nothing to fear from the altered situation in France:

With regard to the change of system that had taken place in that country, Mr Fox said that he knew different opinions were entertained on that point by different men, and added that he, for one, admired the new constitution of France, taken together, as the most stupendous and glorious edifice of liberty, which had been erected on the foundation of human integrity in any time or country.[17]

All that was being enacted on the political stage in London in 1831, and almost every line of the autobiographical poem he was once more revisiting, prompted Wordsworth to remember the period when Fox and Burke were powers, to recall where he stood on the great issue of the day, and to consider what he had learnt, not just in the 1790s but in the decades that had led up to the present Reform crisis, that had brought him to the conviction, 'if this Bill passes in anything like its present shape a subversion of the Constitution and a correspondent shock to all institutions . . . is in my judgement inevitable'.[18]

Where Wordsworth did stand, in fact, on the great issues of the day in early 1791 remains hazy, but there is no lack of definition about his stance when he returned to England from France two years later: his *Letter to the Bishop of Llandaff* proclaims it. This impetuous declaration of 'a republican spirit'[19] is so injudiciously couched that it is not surprising that it did not get into print: men were soon to face trial for their lives for less.[20] What is surprising, it might seem, is that it survived. A seditious libel, unpublishable when written and long since outgrown as an expression of opinion, why risk keeping such a thing? It may be that somehow Wordsworth needed it, an unrevised reminder of his past, words enshrining a past for future restoration. What is certain is that he was in dialogue with it. Much of the *Two Addresses to the Freeholders of Westmorland* in 1818 had been shaped as if in reply to assertions in the *Letter*, about law, electoral representation, the function of monarchy and aristocracy. The major addition to the autobiographical poem in the 1831 revision constitutes a further engagement with what Wordsworth had written in 1793.

'Genius of Burke', the passage begins—to the author of the *Letter to the Bishop of Llandaff* it had seemed an evil genius. Though Wordsworth's polemic was prompted by an episcopal utterance from Richard Watson, it is the much greater figure of Edmund Burke who determines both the argument and the rhetorical coloration of the piece. Although he is mentioned directly only three times in the *Letter*, Burke is present throughout, for, as James K. Chandler observes in his indispensable study of Wordsworth and Burke, the writer of the *Letter to the Bishop of Llandaff* worked 'with a copy of *Reflections* at hand or else he had so mastered the text as to know at least its more celebrated passages by heart'.[21] In his opposition to the new social order emerging in France, Burke conjures a vision of how an organically sound community can be thought of as developing, faithful to the 'indissoluble compact' which binds the living and the dead and which gives the structure of national polity something of the character of blood relationships,

binding up the constitution of our country with our dearest domestic ties; adopting our fundamental laws into the bosom of our family affections; keeping inseparable, and cherishing with the warmth of all their combined and mutually reflected charities, our state, our hearths, our sepulchres, and our altars.[22]

Angrily resistant to the near-irresistible coerciveness of this rhetoric in 1793, Wordsworth opposes Burke's vision with a statement of realities. Britain is a country where 'laws partial and oppressive' are unjustly executed, where liberty is a chimera, where at one end of the social scale 'the unnatural monster of primogeniture' ensures the dominance of the wealthy, while at the other, the labourer cannot 'provide food for himself and his family'. This, the republican Wordsworth declares, anticipating Godwin by a year, is the state of 'Things as they Are'.[23] Only in fearless 'enquiries directed towards the nature of liberty and equality' can progress be looked for. It belongs to the republican future 'to create a race of men who, truly free, will look upon their fathers as only enfranchised'.[24]

When Burke was summoned in 1831, nearly forty years later, he was once more invested with enormous weight, but now his emblematic significance was the reverse of what it had been in 1793. In the *Letter to the Bishop of Llandaff* Wordsworth had written that the present times were 'big with the fate of the human race', and in the 1831 verse the same word was used to convey a sense of pregnant weight, 'the times were big | With ominous change'. But by this time Burke, contemned in the *Letter* as an 'infatuated moralist', was now the 'wisest of the Moderns'—as Wordsworth put it in a letter to Haydon. His formulations, in fact, had entered so deeply into the 'blood and vital juices' of Wordsworth's mind that on one occasion, becoming aware that he was just recapitulating sentiments from the *Reflections*, he had rather lamely to admit as much:

A spirit of rash innovation is every where at war with our old institutions, and the habits and sentiments that have thus far supported them; and the ardor of those who are bent upon change is exactly according to the measure of their ignorance.—Where men will not, or through want of knowledge, are unable to, look back they cannot be expected to look forward; and therefore, caring for the present only, they care for *that* merely as it affects their own importance. Hence a blind selfishness is at the bottom of all that is going forward—a remark which in other words was made by Mr Burke long ago . . .[25]

In his *Two Addresses to the Freeholders of Westmorland* Wordsworth had described the author of the *Reflections on the Revolution in France* as the 'most sagacious Politician of his age'. He cleaved to him again in 1831 because the particular quality of Burke's sagacity was what, he was convinced, had become even more needed now, in such dangerous times, than in 1818. It stemmed from a profound mistrust of 'men of theory', of concepts untested by experience, of systems not structured to meet the needs of the heart. Throughout the *Reflections* Burke exposes the false allure of the new, of the fresh start, extolling instead the virtue inherent in long-established practice and in prejudices cherished 'the longer they have lasted, and the more generally they have prevailed' (138). Ideologues envision the birth of a new Man and a new order, but 'so taken up with their theories about the rights of man . . . they have totally forgot his nature. Without opening one new avenue to the understanding, they have succeeded in stopping up those that lead to the heart' (115).

As Wordsworth in 1831 introduced Burke into the autobiographical poem, dwelling in his imagination on how the great orator had heaped ridicule on 'all systems built on abstract rights' and proclaimed the majesty of 'Institutes and Laws hallowed by Time', he clearly had the great passages from the *Reflections* in mind because they so nobly uttered what had become his own convictions. No matter that the passage of the 1832 Reform Bill was a victory for pragmatists, not ideologues, which, unlike reformist victories in France, had not demanded the sacrifice of a single life: to Wordsworth the proceedings in Westminster were threatening because they represented an attempt to model a future not based on the wisdom and strengths of the past.

Even as he reshaped the existing text of Book Seven to admit the figure of Burke, the manuscript record he was labouring over served of course to remind the elderly Wordsworth that when young he had himself welcomed just such an attempt. In the heady days of the early 1790s ('Bliss was it in that dawn to be alive, | But to be young was very heaven!'), he had shared with 'all ingenuous youth' (X, 232) the hope,

> that man should start
> Out of the worm-like state in which he is,
> And spread abroad the wings of Liberty,
> Lord of himself, in undisturbed delight.   (X, 835–8)

He had entertained with fervour the hope that 'future times' would
see 'The man to come parted as by a gulph | From him who had
been' (XI, 59–60). And with such sentiments Wordsworth would
have been firmly on the other side of the House, so to speak, from
Burke. The aspiration in the early 1790s had been 'noble' and when
Wordsworth recalled how it had possessed his younger self, as he
struggled to give an account of these years in 1804, he declared that
he still thought it noble—'A noble aspiration!—yet I feel | The aspi-
ration' (X, 839–40)—but now he declares that he is able to assess
the aspiration more wisely, 'with other thoughts | And happier'(X,
840–1). The introduction of Burke into the *Prelude* as late as 1831
serves to emphasize both that learning to make a proper valuation
of him has been essential to Wordsworth's passage to intellectual
maturity and that the poet has been learning how to arrive at it over
most of his adult life, that is, over the years in which *The Prelude* was
coming into being.

Burke was important to Wordsworth in 1831, though, not just
because he had long ago given eloquent form to views Wordsworth
had come to recognize as profound, but because he stood out as an
iconic figure of lonely heroism. He is old but vigorous, and like a
majestic oak towers above the 'younger brethren of the grove'. But
his strength, deeply rooted in experience though it is, avails nothing.
He is not heeded. In the *Two Addresses* Wordsworth had already
stressed how Burke's 'warning voice' had set him apart from his
parliamentary colleagues. Now the point is repeated. While Burke's
'most eloquent tongue' with 'high disdain | Explod[es] upstart
Theory', some, 'a froward multitude | Murmur (for truth is hated,
where not loved)'.

In the impassioned parliamentary debates, the stage for Burke's
greatest performances,

> memorable moments intervened,
> When Wisdom, like the Goddess from Jove's brain,
> Broke forth in armour of resplendent words,
> Startling the Synod.   (*1850*, VII, 537–40)

The word 'Synod' links this passage to another in the poem, in which Wordsworth's imagination is engaged by a comparable spectacle. 'Synod' is used only twice in *The Prelude*, once, here, to refer to the House of Commons of the British Parliament, and once at IX, 47, to refer to the National Convention in Paris.[26] In his account of the proceedings of both political assemblies what Wordsworth is moved by is the spectacle of the lone figure uttering a warning.

Recalling his experiences in Paris in the autumn of 1792, little more than a month after the September massacres, Wordsworth attempts to give a sense of how threatening the city seemed. Menace could be felt, but in what direction the main current of affairs flowed was difficult to discern. Loyalties were being stretched; ideals were being tested. At times, though, the underlying conflicts broke out in a fashion that made misapprehension of their significance impossible. One such, to Wordsworth at least, was the occasion on 29 October 1792 when Robespierre demanded in open session of the National Convention that anyone who had 'ill surmise' of him should speak out:

>   Whereat,
> When a dead pause ensued and no one stirred,
> In silence of all present, from his seat
> Louvet walked singly through the avenue
> And took his station in the Tribune, saying,
> 'I, Robespierre, accuse thee!' 'Tis well known
> What was the issue of that charge, and how
> Louvet was left alone without support
> Of his irresolute friends . . .   (X, 95–103)

Revision of the 1804 text—MS C stage, now confirmed for MS D—strikingly elaborates the final lines, drawing out the historical significance of the event and its universal application to political life and Mankind in general:

>   Well is known
> The inglorious issue of that charge, and how
> He, who had launched the startling thunderbolt,
> The one bold man, whose voice the attack had sounded,
> Was left without a follower to discharge
> His perilous duty, and retire lamenting
> That Heaven's best aid is wasted upon men
> Who to themselves are false.   (*1850*, X, 113–20)

Highlighting this clash between Louvet and Robespierre as a pivotal one enormously simplifies the complex and rapidly evolving struggles for mastery that characterized the National Convention in late 1792 and it exaggerates the historical significance both of Louvet and of this moment. He was not a figure of Roman virtue; he was easily out-manoeuvred by Robespierre; the challenge in the Convention merits only a sentence or two in standard histories of the French Revolution.[27] What Wordsworth's presentation of the moment does do is minister to the notion that history is shaped by the decisive interventions of men of principled courage and to the self-regarding fantasy that the poet himself might/ought to have been one of them.[28] Revolving in himself (he claims at X, 136 ff.) 'How much the destiny of man had still | Hung upon single persons', Wordsworth recalls as he chronicles that time, that he was convinced that 'the virtue of one paramount mind' could have 'quelled | Outrage and bloody power' and 'cleared a passage for just government'. Such a notion had obvious appeal in 1792, when forces were being unleashed whose power was obscure in origin, whose features were difficult to discern, and whose future was impossible to predict with any degree of optimism. In 1831-2 the struggle over the Reform Bill bore the same complexion in Wordsworth's alarmed imagination. Burke functions in the architecture of *The Prelude* in 1831 just as Louvet had in 1804. Both figures, though clearly opposed politically, serve as examples of the rightness of the heroic stand. Such rare beings, those who can perceive the truth about a historical moment however obscured it may be by the illusions of the day, must risk all.

If the 'Genius of Burke' passage is looked at from the dual perspective of Wordsworth in the 1790s and in the 1830s, the appropriateness of its inclusion in the final version of *The Prelude* becomes apparent. On the one hand it fills out the historical chronicle. Readers in 1850 were offered an account of the first twenty-eight years of the late Poet Laureate's life and that part of it dealing with Wordsworth's move to London was reliable, insofar as it was historically accurate. After a 56-line preamble to Book Seven, Wordsworth resumes his chronicle and briskly transports himself from Cambridge to London, still a 'casual dweller and at large', free to pitch his 'vagrant tent' as he pleased.

Wordsworth took his degree in January 1791 and then moved to London, where he remained until late May. During his sojourn, when he mixed in Dissenting and Radical circles, Wordsworth sought out the spectacles London had to offer and oratorical performance in Parliament was one such. In old age he recalled often seeing William Pitt 'upon the floor of the House of Commons',[29] and the 'Genius of Burke' passage suggests (although supporting evidence is lacking) that he also saw Burke. What one would like to know is, was he by chance present at one of the greatest moments of Parliamentary drama, the rupture between Burke and Charles James Fox?

Burke and Fox had been friends for nearly thirty years, but their differing attitudes to the French experiment caused an irreparable breach. Fox had uttered his encomium on the French Constitution, already quoted, on 15 April 1791. Further skirmishes in debate made a severance likely, but it did not occur until 6 May, when Burke and Fox clashed repeatedly. In mounting anger, each accused the other of extremism. Fox said he hoped the difference of opinion would not damage their friendship. Burke replied that principle must come before friendship. Both men—so contemporary report has it—stood with tears running down their faces as Burke pronounced their long association at an end.[30]

Fox does not appear in *The Prelude*, but at some point Wordsworth did make an attempt to introduce him into the scene in the House of Commons. The struggle is recorded in drafting for the 'Genius of Burke' passage in MS D, where Wordsworth's creative travail is registered in characteristic fashion in crossings out, interlineations, then separate sheets of paper pasted in with fresh copy which is itself subjected to further deletion and revision (see Figure 3). Wordsworth imagines Fox and Burke after the rift. Awaiting his turn to scatter thunder and lightning, Fox, the 'grateful pupil in the power of words', sits listening to his mentor, 'no longer near | Yet still in heart his friend'. Three versions of this scene were drafted before it was abandoned, leaving Burke splendidly unattached in the 'Genius of Burke' passage as it was eventually published in 1850.[31]

Why the lines about Fox were scrapped is not known, but it may be that the repeated attempts at drafting, followed by abandonment, reflect tensions that could not be resolved into a necessarily few lines of blank verse. If so, it would not be surprising. Wordsworth in 1831 is trying to bring into focus Fox as he had appeared to him in 1791, and as he had seemed during the period of Wordsworth's life when

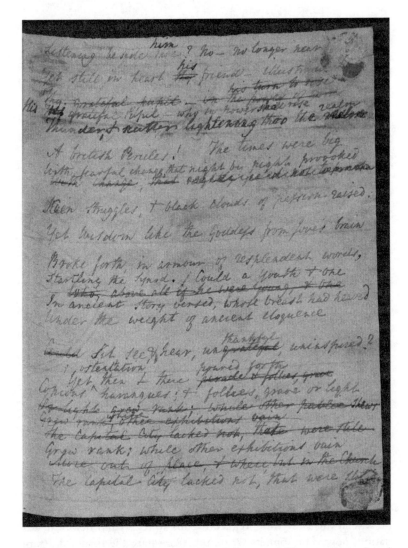

Figure 3. *The Prelude*, MS D. Dove Cottage MS 124. Reproduced courtesy of the Wordsworth Trust, Grasmere.

he first began to try to take possession of his own formative years, that is, when he began composing *The Prelude*.

The young Wordsworth, fast becoming radicalized by the Pitt government's response to events in France, shared Fox's readiness to maintain faith in the foundational ideals of the Revolution, even when their lustre had been obscured by its actual course. It was Fox's generosity of spirit towards the poor and the 'constant predominance of sensibility of heart' that moved him always to look upon men as individuals, that prompted Wordsworth to send him a copy of *Lyrical Ballads* (1800). Although Fox's love of literature was well known, it was to more than this that Wordsworth referred when he told the statesman in the accompanying letter, that he was 'dear to Poets', adding, 'if since your first entrance into public life there has been a single true poet living in England, he must have loved you'.[32]

On learning five years later that Fox was close to death, Wordsworth paid tribute in 'Loud is the Vale' to one who had been the 'glory' and the 'stay' of 'many thousands'. When published in *Poems, in Two Volumes* in 1807, this finely restrained acknowledgement that with Fox's 'dissolution' a 'Power is passing from the earth' was printed appropriately in sequence with 'Elegiac Stanzas . . . Peele Castle', Wordsworth's lament for his brother John, and the 'Ode: Intimations'. But 'Loud is the Vale' also fits appropriately with another body of work in the collection, the 'Sonnets Dedicated to Liberty'.

These poems were written during the period in which Wordsworth was brooding most intensely over what he had come to recognize as the formative years of his life and in particular over his experiences in France, in England in the immediate aftermath of the outbreak of war in 1793, and in the turbulence that followed once the French had become 'oppressors in their turn' (X, 791). *The Prelude* evolved into its thirteen-book form over 1803–5 as Wordsworth's strenuous grapple with recalcitrant material and painful memories yielded a way of understanding how he had come to the conviction that he had been called to be the poet of *The Recluse*. In the sonnets he was, at the same time, registering his anxieties and hopes for his nation, now. The sonnets written in 1802–3 are the troubled utterances of one still in the Foxite camp—hostile to Pitt, scornful of the conduct of the King's ministers, fearful for the moral health of the country, convinced, nonetheless, that 'Earth's best hopes all rest with Thee!' ('England! the time has come . . .'). The sonnets belong with 'Loud is the Vale'. The poem on Fox does not mention history or politics once, but in honouring him as one of 'the Mighty' it insists that he has been one of the beacons of the age.[33]

In the 1831 drafting Fox is presented as the 'British Pericles', but this allusion to the great Athenian law-giver is without imaginative life and remains undeveloped. Again one can see why. It was a generous attempt at rendering what Fox had once seemed, but by 1831 Wordsworth was reading the past—his and Fox's—very differently. Whereas in 1801 Wordsworth had paid tribute to Fox as one whose compassionate humanity steered him instinctively towards the right and the just, not as politician but as Man, in the 1818 *Two Addresses* Fox was already being condemned as a politician whose strength of feeling led him into errors of judgement, the more damaging because of the eloquence with which they were propounded to bedazzled followers. In a passage on the party of Opposition Wordsworth declares:

To have hoped too ardently of human nature, as they did at the commence-ment of the French Revolution, was no dishonour to them as men; but *poli-ticians* cannot be allowed to plead temptations of fancy, or impulses of feeling, in exculpation of mistakes in judgement. Grant, however, to the enthusiasm of Philanthropy as much indulgence as it may call for, it is still extraordinary that, in the minds of English Statesmen and Legislators, the naked absurdity of the means did not raise a doubt as to the attainableness of the end. Mr. Fox, captivated by the vanities of a system founded upon abstract rights, chaunted his expectations in the House of Parliament; and too many of his Friends partook of the illusion. The most sagacious Politician of his age broke out in an opposite strain.[34]

The 'Genius of Burke' addition is an imaginative enlargement of the last sentence.

When Burke had exclaimed to an astonished House, 'Fly from the French constitution', he was, in fact, an increasingly isolated figure politically.[35] As Fox's biographer, L. G. Mitchell, observes, 'In 1791 Paris was still a place to visit rather than to fear',[36] and though many were watching events across the Channel with increasing concern, the Jeremiad that was the *Reflections upon the Revolution in France* could seem unwarranted even to those who shared its assessment of the British way of doing things. But it was right. As Wordsworth put it in the *Two Addresses*, 'Time has verified his predictions'. And this is the second reason why the 'Genius of Burke' passage belongs in *The Prelude*. It reflects what Wordsworth was thinking and feeling in the run-up to the 1832 Reform Act and so constitutes a further geo-logical layer, so to speak, in the evolving formation of the poem.

England had needed Burke in the 1790s: such a figure was sorely needed now, forty years later. Extreme though it was, as we can see with hindsight, Wordsworth unhesitatingly drew the parallel between the two convulsions, the French Revolution and British Constitutional Reform. 'I resided fifteen months in France during the heats of the Revolution', he told Lord Lonsdale, 'and have some personal experience of the course these movements must take if not fearlessly resisted.'[37] But where was the Burke for the times? And would any warning voice be heeded? Wordsworth was realistic (and gloomy) enough to guess not. Reflecting on the ironies of history, moreover, would have brought home to him how astonishingly prescient Burke had been. What he had most feared had not happened, but the British Constitution had been betrayed nonetheless, not from without—the French had been defeated—but from within. And very soon, as the proponents of the New Poor Law carried all before them, it was all too apparent to Wordsworth that Burke had been right also in another of his predictions: the age of 'sophisters, oeconomists, and calculators' had arrived.[38]

(ii)

At the end of the decade Wordsworth revised the poem for the last time, labouring, according to Isabella Fenwick, 'seldom less than six or seven hours in the day, or rather one ought to say the whole day, for it seemed always in his mind—quite a possession'.[39] A fresh manuscript was copied out to the accompaniment of authorial fretting about provision 'against any unlucky accident' that might befall it.[40] Wordsworth's eagerness to ensure that the manuscript be sealed and deposited with one of his executors, John Carter, indicates that as he entered his seventieth year he wanted to be sure that the autobiographical poem was in a fit state to be published.

In July 1839, as an inscription in MS E records, Wordsworth 'Reviewed' the poem. What, one must wonder, did he make of it, for by that time the autobiographical poem had become a very strange creation.

It still had no title, but from first to last it had been the 'Poem to Coleridge'. Coleridge was in Wordsworth's mind when, snow-bound in Germany in 1798, he composed the earliest passages of the poem, and dispatched them to him in a letter. When what was begun then was first shaped into a work in two parts, it concluded with an address to Coleridge as the poet's 'brother', as 'one | The most intense of Nature's worshippers' (*1799*, II, 506–7), and was avowedly designed to enable him to 'know | With better knowledge how the heart was framed | Of him thou lovest' (*1799*, I, 457–8). Before the ailing Coleridge left the north of England for Mediterranean sunshine in 1804, Wordsworth read out to the friend he feared he might never see again 'the second Part of his divine Self-biography'.[41] Coleridge's return to England in 1807 was the occasion for a recitation of the completed poem in thirteen books. Wordsworth had longed for Coleridge's return and towards the end of the poem had fused his desire to see his friend once more with a sense that the restoration of Coleridge's presence might fill some of the vacancy left by the loss of his brother's. Against this 'private grief | Keen and enduring'—John Wordsworth's drowning two years earlier—Wordsworth placed the thought of Coleridge once more completing the domestic circle:

> a hope,
> One of the dearest which this life can give,
> Is mine: that thou art near, and wilt be soon
> Restored to us in renovated health—
> When, after the first mingling of our tears,
> 'Mong other consolations, we may find
> Some pleasure from this offering of my love. (XIII, 421–7)

In one of the many direct addresses to Coleridge, Wordsworth refers to the whole poem as a 'gift | Which I for thee design' (XIII, 411–12), and with the moving recollection of the months they spent 'on Quantock's grassy hills | Far ranging' (XIII, 393), he begins the mythologizing of 1798 and the summer of *Lyrical Ballads* as the most important period in their intertwined poetic lives. Coleridge's act of reciprocation, his poem, 'To William Wordsworth. Lines Composed, For the Greater Part on the Night on which he Finished the Recitation of his Poem (in Thirteen Books) Concerning the Growth and History of His Own Mind', is both a fulsome love-offering in return and the first ever critical response to Wordsworth's self-projection from the poem's ideal reader.

But Coleridge was now dead (25 July 1834). He had become a historical figure, to be memorialized in works such as *Early Recollections, Chiefly Relating to the Late Samuel Taylor Coleridge*, the memoir brought out in 1837 by the original publisher of *Lyrical Ballads*, Joseph Cottle. The 'late Samuel Taylor Coleridge'—it is no wonder that Isabella Fenwick found it almost too much to listen to Wordsworth reading out the autobiographical poem in 1838, so powerfully did 'the passionate feelings of his youth all come back to him'.[42] The most important figure in the shaping of the poem was now a rhetorical presence only. When at the end of Book Ten, for example, Wordsworth had invoked Coleridge setting off for the Mediterranean, he had written of his grief at their separation:

> A lonely wanderer art gone, by pain
> Compelled and sickness, at this latter day,
> This heavy time of change for all mankind.
> I feel for thee, must utter what I feel;
> The sympathies, erewhile in part discharged,
> Gather afresh, and will have vent again.   (983–8)

It was an address to the living. When Wordsworth read *The Prelude* out to Coleridge in 1807, he reminded him in Book Thirteen of the time when they had chanted to each other 'The Ancient Mariner' and 'Christabel', 'The Thorn' and 'The Idiot Boy' and declared:

> When thou dost to that summer turn thy thoughts,
> And hast before thee all which then we were,
> To thee, in memory of that happiness,
> It will be known—by thee at least, my friend,
> Felt, that the history of a poet's mind
> Is labour not unworthy of regard:
> To thee the work shall justify itself.   (404–10)

'All which then we were' had never been recovered, but until 1834 Wordsworth would have been able to cherish in these lines the knowledge that the 'memory of that happiness' was something that Coleridge could still share with him. Now Coleridge had become part of the memory: the address to 'thee at least, my friend', a figure of rhetoric merely.

Even without the added prompt of a reminder of the summer of 1798, the work would have justified itself to Coleridge, for he had been joint-begetter of the project conceived then which had brought the autobiographical poem into being—the plan for *The Recluse*— and had been involved in the creation of both works, the autobiographical and the philosophical, ever since. In 1799 Coleridge was

urging Wordsworth not to be deflected from the great work: 'I long
to see what you have been doing. O let it be the tail-piece of "The
Recluse!", for of nothing but "The Recluse" can I hear patiently.'
In 1804 Coleridge's contribution was being eagerly sought by
Wordsworth as if without it the project for the philosophic poem
might stall: 'I am very anxious to have your notes for the Recluse. I
cannot say how much importance I attach to this.'[43] By 1805,
when the retrospective impulse was, it seemed, spent, the fitting
conclusion to the autobiographical poem was re-dedication of both
poets as 'joint labourers' to the task still awaiting fulfilment:

> Prophets of Nature, we to them will speak
> A lasting inspiration, sanctified
> By reason and by truth . . .   (XII, 442–4)

Wordsworth did turn to *The Recluse*, publishing nine years later
what he had achieved so far in the struggle to turn this prophetic
aspiration into poetic fact—*The Excursion*—and here it was, as has
already been discussed in the previous chapter, that Wordsworth informed the world about the complicated relationship between this
poem, the larger philosophic project of which it was but a 'portion',
and an autobiographical work 'long finished' but not published. An
additional piece of information was that the latter was addressed to a
'dear Friend . . . to whom the Author's Intellect is deeply indebted'.
Three years later Coleridge reminded readers that the *Recluse* project
was still to be realized, when he declared in *Biographia Literaria*:

What Mr Wordsworth *will* produce, it is not for me to prophesy: but I could
pronounce with the liveliest convictions what he is capable of producing. It
is the FIRST GENUINE PHILOSOPHIC POEM.[44]

Three years later still, in his 1820 *River Duddon* collection,
Wordsworth made a further contribution to what was becoming a
somewhat bizarre public exchange of tributes, recollections, and
admonitions. Noting that 'more than twenty years ago' Mr Coleridge
outlined a 'comprehensive design' for a work to be called 'The Brook',
'of which he has given a sketch in a recent publication', Wordsworth
urged him to write it. The sketch in the recent publication, *Biographia
Literaria*, not only took readers back to the summer in which the
Recluse project was conceived, but in declaring that the poet's
intention was to give 'impassioned reflections on men, nature, and
society', it echoed the very language Wordsworth had employed

when he announced the project to his acquaintances in 1798 and to the world in 1814.

Now the friend was dead and Wordsworth could at last admit to himself and the world that the hopes for completion of the philosophic poem that originated with him were dead also: from 1836 the title-page to *The Excursion* announced it as a stand-alone poem, no longer *The Excursion, Being a Portion of The Recluse*. It was a small deletion, but one with real significance for *The Prelude*. From the outset the autobiographical exploration had served many functions, but one of them, the officially declared one, was as private precursor to a greater, public poem. It did not matter that this had always been something of a fiction, nor that it had become increasingly so as the years passed by without *The Recluse* being completed. So long as Coleridge were alive and Wordsworth still planned further work on *The Recluse*, all the moments in the autobiographical poem that touch on *the future* were gestures towards a genuine possibility: ultimately *The Prelude* would be completed and legitimated by *The Recluse*. When Wordsworth set about revising the poem again in the late 1830s, its prospective function no longer had existence in reality.

So was there any reason not to publish the poem now? Although it had been kept back, its existence was hardly a secret. Even before Wordsworth had explained in the Preface to *The Excursion* what the role of the unpublished autobiographical poem was, Coleridge had excerpted for *The Friend* passages that conveyed something of its flavour. Forty lines of meditative verse about what it felt like to be young at the dawn of the French Revolution appeared in October 1809; they were complemented in December by the whole of the skating episode, *Prelude 1805*, I, 426–89.[45] These lines were transcribed, Coleridge informed his readers, 'from an unpublished Poem on the growth and revolutions of an individual mind, by WORDSWORTH' and in 1814 they learned from the author himself that this work had been 'long finished'. The excerpts in *The Friend* were of high quality and appetites for the whole which they hinted at must have been further whetted when Coleridge published 'To William Wordsworth' in *Sibylline Leaves* (1817), even though some readers may have been daunted by the disclosure that Wordsworth's 'prophetic Lay' stretched to thirteen books. The drip-drip of allusion to the poem continued. 'Composed at Cora Linn', published 1820, was prefaced by seven lines of blank verse about Wallace, identified simply as from 'MS'. They are

Prelude 1805, I, 213–19. In 1835 Wordsworth appended a prose 'Postscript' to the *Yarrow Revisited* volume, which ranged over social changes going forward 'especially affecting the lower orders of society'.[46] It concluded with fifty-four lines of blank verse 'extracted from my MSS. written above thirty years ago'. No one who had followed the disclosures over the years could have been in any doubt which poem the passage was extracted from.

The passage (*1805*, XII, 223–7), a tribute to 'men as they are men within themselves', looks back to the moment, first publicly recorded in the Preface to *Lyrical Ballads* (1800), when Wordsworth dedicated his poetic gifts to the celebration of men and women in lowly life:

> 'Of these,' said I, 'shall be my song; of these,
> If future years mature me for the task,
> Will I record the praises . . .'

and the effect of its appearance now in 1835 is wide-ranging. It serves to convey the impression that there has been a long-spanning consistency to Wordsworth's career, such that he can quote these lines without any sense of having fallen short of the profession they made 'above thirty years ago'. Equally important, though, is the demonstration, simply by the fact of quotation itself in this context, that Wordsworth's autobiographical poem is not a fossil from the long past, but contains material relevant to the concerns of the moment.

As Wordsworth was reviewing the final MS of *The Prelude* in 1839 and parcelling it up for safe deposit with Mr Carter, a great deal about its contents was being revealed to the world by an unauthorized source. In an essay on Wordsworth for *Tait's Edinburgh Magazine*, De Quincey, though claiming his memory had not been 'refreshed by a sight of the poem for more than twenty years', gave a detailed account, with attractive quotation, of much of Book Five and Books Nine to Twelve. His expressed hope that he could write about the poem 'without any breach of confidence' is breathtakingly disingenuous, but the critique is so discerningly enthusiastic that anyone reading it might have been moved to exclaim with John Wilson, 'Christopher North', 'What right has he to keep such things from the present generation? . . . It is not fair in great authors to leave their works to be published posthumously, as if their own generation was unworthy of them.'[47] In 1844 Wordsworth himself gave a further glimpse, when he included the description of crossing the Simplon

Pass from Book Six of *The Prelude* in his letters to the *Morning Post*, afterwards reissued as the pamphlet *Kendal and Windermere Railway*. The lines were prefaced, as was now customary, by the statement that they were drawn from a MS Poem. The date appended—'1799'—made it clear that this must be the poem on Wordsworth's earlier life to which so many allusions had been made over thirty-five years.[48]

So why not publish? Two different reasons were given, both legitimate. The first was grounded in literary decorum, as Wordsworth explained to Richard Sharp in 1804. Reporting that the poem on his early life was turning out much longer than he ever dreamt of, Wordsworth added,

it seems a frightful deal to say about one's self, and of course will never be published, (during my lifetime I mean), till another work has been written and published, of sufficient importance to justify me in giving my own history to the world. I pray God to give me life to finish these works which I trust will live and do good, especially the one, to which that which I have been speaking of as so far advanced is only supplementary.[49]

In Wordsworth's vision of how he had come to be a poet—outlined most clearly in 'Tintern Abbey' but fundamental to many other poems—the crucial development was that from the intense self-absorption of childhood to hearing oftentimes the still sad music of humanity. But whenever, as in the letter to Sharp, Wordsworth expounded his vision of what his career as a poet ought to be, this trajectory was reversed. The poetry of the still sad music, dealing with the great topics of human life in their universal application, would be what counted. Once that was fully achieved, revelation of the individual life, the growth of a poet's mind, might then be justified as 'supplementary'. Since by the mid-1830s the hope of the philosophical poem had not been fulfilled, only a third part of *The Recluse* having been given to the world as *The Excursion*, fidelity to the position taken in 1804 might be thought still to embargo publication of the autobiographical one.

By this time, however, there was another persuasive reason for holding the poem back. Allying himself in 1839 with Talfourd's campaign for reform of the law of copyright, Wordsworth presented him with evidence from his own case. He had long ago written a poem on the formation of his own mind, he explained, publication of which 'has been prevented merely by the personal character of the subject'. Had it been published under existing copyright law, and when his poetic reputation was slight, the publication 'would scarcely have paid its own expenses'. Now, with the rise in its author's standing, there might be a considerable profit. Reform of the law to extend the period of copyright protection, and late, perhaps posthumous publication would ensure that the benefit to the poet's heirs would be prolonged.[50] Wordsworth was worried about his family and it was quite right that he should regard the unpublished autobiographical poem as a literary property with a financial value that was to be safeguarded for their eventual encashment.

Wordsworth's tone in the letter to Talfourd is crisp and the explanation coherent and sensible. It answers the question, why not publish now? But though the financial consideration clearly was uppermost, the temptation is strong to speculate that there may have been other reasons why Wordsworth was reluctant to release the poem he had lived and grown old with over forty years. In *Testamentary Acts*, for example, his fascinating study of the many, often devious ways in which authors have sought to control their own posthumous selves, Michael Millgate suggests that Hardy's secret composition of his own life for posthumous release can best be understood as 'a final uninterruptible and unanswerable contribution to that long dialogue between himself and his critics in which strategic and tactical advantage had always seemed to belong to the latter'. An analogous impulse may have motivated Wordsworth, Millgate speculates: 'Some such element of aggressive self-defensiveness may ultimately have entered into Wordsworth's postponement of publication of *The Prelude* until after his death, even though the poem was not written with such a destiny in view.'[51]

A further consideration might have been that so much about the autobiographical poem must have seemed belated. The London evoked in Book Seven, for example, was greatly changed. Ranelagh had vanished; Vauxhall was tottering; the Pantheon had long closed; even Bartholomew Fair was only a shadow of what it had been, soon to be closed down. The city more fabulous to the young boy than Rome or Persepolis could now be reached by train from the Lake District within the day. This new London had moreover its own young celebrant. The first series of *Sketches by Boz* appeared in 1835, the same year as *Yarrow Revisited*. Nor, of course, was it just London that had changed. In Book Thirteen of *The Prelude* (1850) Wordsworth recalls his lonely journey in 1793 traversing 'the wilds | Of Sarum's Plain', and how he had hallucinated, seeing men in wolf-skin vests with their shields and stone-axes gathering to make human sacrifice (312–49). When he and his wife revisited the West Country in the summer of 1841, making what Mary termed a *'pilgrimage'* to Alfoxden and other places with a special place in Wordsworth's memory, Salisbury Plain was a disappointment, so much changed by enclosures and modern farming methods.

Wordsworth felt out of time. He shook his head over reports from Dr Thomas Arnold that his boys at Rugby 'seemed to care for nothing but Bozzy's next Number', and, confessing himself 'quite in the dark', asked Moxon whether 'that Man's pub[lic] and others of the like kind' really were having an effect on the market for books.[52] Such a sense that he belonged not just to an earlier generation but somehow to an earlier world altogether, might well have contributed to a reluctance to issue the poem that was so richly coloured by it.

It may be, too, that Wordsworth was reluctant to publish *The Prelude* because to do so would be at some level an acknowledgement that the poem's creative evolution was over and with it, the poet's. Wordsworth liked stillness but hated fixity. He had lived with this work for forty years and each act of revision testified to its continuing life within his imagination. Holding together both the past (chronicled in the poem) and the unfolding present (registered in revision), the poem on the growth of his own mind in its development bore witness that the growth was not finished. In 1839 the latest fair-copy manuscript had been sealed and deposited, but so long as it remained unpublished the parcel could still be opened. The arduousness of revision did not daunt Wordsworth in his early seventies any more than it had fifty years before. The collection *Poems, Chiefly of Early and Late Years*, published in 1842, was the result of considerable labour over poems written in the mid-1790s. The one-volume edition of his complete poetical works, issued when Wordsworth was 75 years old, received his detailed oversight. But these were volumes which the elderly poet was presenting to his readers as the final fruits of a life's work that was drawing to a close. The title, *Poems, Chiefly of Early and Late Years*, ties up past and present, but the note is valedictory. To publish the autobiographical poem, though, rather than retain it for possible final reworking, would have been momentous—and, I think, to Wordsworth not quite conceivable. He would have been offering a completed vision of his own life, before the actual one was over.

There is, however, one further possibility. It is that by the mid-1840s the autobiographical poem had become—in a sense—one Wordsworth could not publish.

In 1839, the same year that the final manuscript of *The Prelude* was completed, Thomas Carlyle opened his investigation into the 'Condition-of-England Question' by observing, 'A feeling very generally exists that the condition and disposition of the Working Classes is a rather ominous matter at present.' *Chartism* offers no solutions to the questions it raises, but it is strong on warnings. In Chapter 5, 'Rights and Mights', Carlyle wonders what answer might working men give if they were asked whether their condition were just:

Has not broad Europe heard the question put, and answered, on the great scale; has not a FRENCH REVOLUTION been? Since the year 1789, there is now half a century complete; and a French Revolution not yet complete! Whosoever will look at that enormous Phenomenon may find many meanings in it, but this meaning as the ground of all: That it was a revolt of the oppressed lower classes against the oppressing or neglecting upper classes: not a French revolt only; no, a European one; full of stern monition to all countries of Europe. These Chartisms, Radicalisms, Reform Bill, Tithe Bill, and infinite other discrepancy and acrid argument and jargon that there is yet to be, are *our* French Revolution: God grant that we, with our better methods, may be able to transact it by argument alone![53]

Carlyle had made a name for himself as a seer a decade earlier with an essay on 'Signs of the Times' and he was always at his most disturbingly persuasive, as here, when interpreting portents.

Six years later—and it is pertinent that it should be in an essay 'On Wordsworth's Poetry'—De Quincey invoked the French Revolution even more directly and frighteningly as a historical inevitability. Like Carlyle he saw that working-class unrest was a Europe-wide upheaval, not merely a local one, and that the 1789 French Revolution had been an identity taken, not a final form of expression.

The French Revolution has not, even yet (1845) come into full action. It was the explosion of a prodigious volcano, which scattered its lava over every kingdom of every continent, every where silently manuring them for social struggles, this lava is gradually fertilising all; the revolutionary movement is moving onwards at this hour as inexorable as ever. Listen, if you have ears for such spiritual sounds, to the mighty tide even now slowly coming up from the sea to Milan, to Rome, to Naples, to Vienna. Hearken to the gentle undulations already breaking against the steps of that golden throne which stretches from St. Petersburg to Astrachan; tremble at the hurricanes which have long been mustering about the pavilions of the Ottoman Padishah. All these are long swells setting in from the French Revolution.[54]

Only three years later it looked as if percipient De Quincey had been right, when revolution swept across Europe. In 1789 the Reverend Richard Price had hailed the first French Revolution in a *Discourse on the Love of our Country*, the sermon that attracted the full fire-power of Burke's scorn in *Reflections on the Revolution in France*: 'What an eventful period this is! I am thankful that I have lived to it; and I could almost say, *Lord, now lettest thou they servant depart in peace, for mine eyes have seen thy salvation.*'[55] As news of the second French Revolution crossed the Channel, the Reverend F. W. Robertson of Brighton rejoiced in words that echoed Price's: 'The world has become a new one . . . To my mind, it is a world full of hope, even to bursting . . . I could almost say sometimes, in fulness of heart, "Now let thy servant depart in peace." '[56] But while Robertson was joyous at the apparent fulfilment of the first revolution by the second and looked to see it replicated in his own country, many throughout the 1840s were very differently mindful of French history as they watched the slide towards what surely threatened insurrection— widespread unrest in manufacturing towns; Chartism; influxes of impoverished Irish; poverty and population growth that threatened the Malthusian outcome—famine. As the Chartists marched towards London in April 1848 the Duke of Wellington oversaw the military preparations for defence of the city. It was symbolically entirely appropriate that it should have been the vanquisher of Napoleon who did so. Earlier in the century one great threat to the British Constitution had been seen off: now the Iron Duke would deal with its successor, fertilized, as De Quincey had pointed out and as it was widely believed, in the lava of the first.

Throughout 'the hungry-forties' no one could have doubted Wordsworth's steadfastness in 'Maintaining the Cause of the Poor and Simple'.[57] Why his stance was widely respected, however, was in large part at least because unlike others who maintained the same cause, such as Chartist leaders and other incendiaries, Wordsworth was no advocate of social upheaval. On the contrary.

As the prefatory verses to the 1842 collection, *Poems, Chiefly of Early and Late Years*, declare, while acknowledging how sorely 'unforeseen distress' bears down on the People, the poet hopes that some strains of his,

> Caught at propitious intervals, may win
> Listeners who not unwillingly admit
> Kindly emotion tending to console
> And reconcile . . .

The following year Wordsworth became Poet Laureate.

When preparing the *Yarrow Revisited* collection for publication in 1835, Wordsworth had thought to give an account in a 'Postscript' of his political journey since the 1790s. In one version of it, referring to himself as 'the Author of this volume', Wordsworth observed that, 'It is known to all who have read his poems, that he rejoiced in the opening of the French Revolution',[58] and he followed this statement with a promise that readers would find out 'hereafter, from his unpublished Works, how deeply he deplored the excesses into which the French people were betrayed, in its progress'.[59] As has been mentioned earlier, this version of the 'Postscript' did not reach print. This further authorial hint about the interest of the unpublished poem, however, is by far the most teasing of the many such hints dropped over the years. Had *The Prelude* been available in the 1840s, when many were quick to follow Carlyle in reading in contemporary social conditions portents of a convulsion similar to the French Revolution, Wordsworth's readers would have found in the poem an account of history, and of the poet's history, that was nothing like as straightforward as this remark suggests.

It was known that Victoria's Laureate, when young, had 'rejoiced in the opening of the French Revolution', but not that he had prayed for French victories. No one had been in any doubt about the patriotism of the author of lines such as,

> We must be free or die, who speak the tongue
> That Shakespeare spake; the faith and morals hold
> Which Milton held . . .[60]

and *The Prelude* certainly does deplore the 'excesses into which the French people were betrayed', but the poem also grittily retained its author's judgement on the government that in the 1790s suspended Habeas Corpus, staged the Treason Trials, passed the Gagging Acts, transported political activists, and set up a network of spies and *agents provocateurs*, one of whose number had been sent in 1797 to investigate the activities of Wordsworth and Coleridge at Alfoxden:

> Our Shepherds, this say merely, at that time
> Acted, or seemed at least to act, like men
> Thirsting to make the guardian crook of law
> A tool of murder; they who ruled the State,
> Though with such awful proof before their eyes
> That he, who would sow death, reaps death, or worse,
> And can reap nothing better, child-like longed
> To imitate, not wise enough to avoid;
> Or left (by mere timidity betrayed)
> The plain straight road, for one no better chosen
> Than if their wish had been to undermine
> Justice, and make an end of Liberty.   (*1850*, XI, 62–73)

This is much softened from what it had been in 1804–5, when Pitt and his ministers were said to have 'Thirsted to make the guardian crook of law | A tool of murder', and were likened to vermin, leaguing 'Their strength perfidiously to undermine | Justice, and make an end of liberty'. But though its force is weakened, the tone of the *Letter to the Bishop of Llandaff* is echoed in an argument that survives revision intact: Britain 'in those days' was governed in such a way as 'To turn *all* judgements out of their right course', not just those of idealists led into 'juvenile errors' (*1850*, XI, 54–6).

And most telling of all is that at the core of the political books of the poem remained the passage that highlights a moment of dedication. In Book Four the young man's joy in 'all the sweetness of a common dawn' is presented as a moment of avowal—'vows | Were then made for me . . .' (IV, 341–2). Book Nine offers a deliberate parallel in the recollection of another dedication moment, when the poet's commitment to the French cause was confirmed. Wordsworth and his mentor, Beaupuis, chance

> One day to meet a hunger-bitten Girl
> Who crept along, fitting her languid self
> Unto a Heifer's motion, by a cord
> Tied to her arm, and picking thus from the lane
> Its sustenance, while the Girl with her two hands
> Was busy knitting, in a heartless mood
> Of solitude.   (IX, 512–18)

At the sight Beaupuis exclaims, ' 'Tis against *that* which we are fight-ing.' It is a sight and a declaration against which there can be no argument:

> I with him believed
> That a benignant spirit was abroad
> Which might not be withstood, that poverty
> Abject as this would in a little time
> Be found no more, that we should see the earth
> Unthwarted in her wish to recompense
> The meek, the lowly, patient child of toil.   (*1850*, IX, 518–24)

Nothing in the poem blunts the force of this; nothing softens or repudiates the urgency of the young man's fired-up conviction that things must change. And nothing challenges the connection made so uncomplicatedly here between poverty and the justice of radical action. It is cause and effect, problem and remedy.

Had the autobiographical poem been published at any point in the 1840s a cursory glance at the hunger-bitten girl passage would per-haps have placed it as only one more dramatically rendered emblem of human distress, in a decade of many such—Oliver Twist asking for more, for example, or the Irish widow, dying of typhus, who proves her sisterhood by fatally infecting seventeen others.[61] A closer reading of the whole poem, though, would have surely raised eyebrows. Dickens and Carlyle were young turks, determined to make themselves heard as voices of and for their era, but the elderly Wordsworth was Victoria's Poet Laureate, respected and honoured as one of the ornaments of the social order. What was locked away in his autobiographical poem, however, was the material for construction of a figure with a much less comfortable make-up than that now generally supposed to characterize the Sage of Rydal Mount and a presentation of the politics of the past that had dismaying implications for the present. On the question of poverty, for instance: had Britain made any real progress since the 1790s? Was the earth any nearer fulfilment of her wish 'to recompense | The meek, the lowly patient child of toil'? Had any lessons been learned from the French experience? or, rather, had the right ones?

When John Keble was about to dedicate the collection of his Oxford poetry lectures to Wordsworth, he wavered for a moment on hearing a rumour that the poet had 'begun life as a Radical'. 'Radi-cal' was strong language in 1844. In 1850, when the autobiographical poem was at last open to scrutiny, the great Whig historian, Thomas Babington Macaulay used still more opprobrious terms. If Wordsworth had begun life as a Radical, it seemed shockingly clear to Macaulay that he had remained one. 'The poem is to the last degree Jacobinical, indeed Socialist', he declared, adding, 'I understand perfectly why Wordsworth did not choose to publish it in his life-time.' Yawning over the 'endless wildernesses of dull, flat, prosaic twaddle', Macaulay could not take seriously the poet's 'flimsy philosophy . . . the old crazy, mystical metaphysics', but he was alert to politics and in this judgement on the politics of *The Prelude* he was, it seems to me, right.[62]

5

Where Once We Stood
Rejoicing

'Imagination almost always transcends reality.'[1]

(i)

'Musings Near Aquapendente. April 1837' purports to record ideas that arose in Wordsworth's mind as he rested on the road between Siena and Rome during the European tour he and Henry Crabb Robinson undertook in 1837. The poem concludes with the aged traveller stirring himself to move on: 'Let us now | Rise, and tomorrow greet magnificent Rome'. It is a fine ending, conveying a sense of excited anticipation of entry into the fabled imperial city—but in actuality Wordsworth was in Rydal Mount when he wrote these words and it was 1841.

There was, of course, nothing unusual in this time lapse between experience and lyric composition. Wordsworth met the Leech Gatherer in 1800, but the old man was not called into poetic service until 1802. Nor was the creation of an illusion of spontaneous utterance an uncommon manoeuvre. The woman may have said, 'What! you are stepping westward?' to the Highland travellers in 1803, but it was two years before 'Stepping Westward', the poem that begins with her words, was written. 'Behold her single in the field'—the inward eye of the reader tracks across fields to the solitary reaper, but what had prompted the poet's to do so had been not a woman in a field but words on a page.[2] Scribbling a reproof on the margin of his copy of Wordsworth's 1815 *Poems*, Blake exclaimed, 'Imagination has nothing to do with Memory': 'Musings Near Aquapendente' might be seen as almost the last demonstration by the poet he was reproving of exactly the opposite point of view.[3] Composed as Wordsworth entered his seventies and neared the end of his writing life, 'Musings Near Aquapendente' is even for Wordsworth a more than usually retrospective poem and when it was published in 1842 in his last collection of original poetry, the overall title of the volume, *Poems, Chiefly of Early and Late Years*, might have been formulated expressly for it: 'Musings Near Aquap-endente' is, fascinatingly, a product both of early and late years.

At 372 lines 'Musings' is quite long and feels so, not least because the blank verse, compared for example with that of *The Prelude* or 'Tintern Abbey', is rather stiff. The movement of the poem as a whole, on the other hand, is relaxed, meandering through rumina-tions about history, faith, and power suggested by high-spots of the Italian tour, such as the Campo Santo at Pisa or boating in the bay of Genoa. Only at one point do the musings come really alive. The poet presents himself as taking refuge from the 'noon-tide's sultry heat' in the shade of chestnut trees on a slope of the Apennines. He is pleased by the varied scene, but passive, until a 'Broom in flower' prompts him to fly to her sisters, 'soon like her to be attired | With golden blossoms opening at the feet | Of my own Fairfield' (26–30). Time and distance dissolve into the familiar landscape of the Lake District, as 'the local Genius' hurries Wordsworth aloft over the hills and mountains to the east of the vale of Grasmere, over Seat Sandal, over Fairfield, transporting him finally to 'Helvellyn's top, | There to alight upon crisp moss and range, | Obtaining ampler boon, at every step, | Of visual sovereignty' (34–40). From his aerial survey point the poet reveals a dweller's, not a traveller's intimacy with this landscape by noting particular features of it that affect the shepherd in his daily task, before his eye sweeps still further east towards Ulls-water. A long quotation rather than a paraphrase is necessary if the vigour of the verse is to be felt:

> Onward thence
> And downward by the skirt of Greenside fell,
> And by Glenridding-screes, and low Glencoign,
> Places forsaken now, but loving still
> The muses, as they loved them in the days
> Of the old minstrels and the border bards.—
> But here I am fast bound;—and let it pass,
> The simple rapture;—who that travels far

To feed his mind with watchful eyes could share
Or wish to share it?—One there surely was,
'The Wizard of the North,' with anxious hope
Brought to this genial climate, when disease
Preyed upon body and mind—yet not the less
Had his sunk eye kindled at those dear words
That spake of bards and minstrels; and his spirit
Had flown with mine to old Helvellyn's brow,
Where once together, in his day of strength,
We stood rejoicing, as if earth were free
From sorrow, like the sky above our heads.

    Years followed years, and when, upon the eve
Of his last going from Tweed-side, thought turned,
Or by another's sympathy was led,
To this bright land, Hope was for him no friend,
Knowledge no help; Imagination shaped
No promise. Still, in more than ear-deep seats,
Survives for me, and cannot but survive
The tone of voice which wedded borrowed words
To sadness not their own, when, with faint smile
Forced by intent to take from speech its edge,
He said, 'When I am there, although 'tis fair,
'Twill be another Yarrow.'   (47–77)

Unknown to the first readers of 'Musings Near Aquapendente', whatever the poet may actually have thought as he rested on 25 April 1837, when he came to recall it in verse he returned to material he had written over forty years earlier. The lines about Seat Sandal and the view from the top of Helvellyn that precede and introduce the passage above (ll. 36–45) and the first five lines of the quotation itself are to be found in a manuscript that preserves work not incorporated into 'Michael' and an early version of what was to become 'The Matron's Tale' in Book Eight of *The Prelude*.[4] They belong to 1800 and the earliest years of Wordsworth's life home at Grasmere. The inclusion of this old but never published material in 'Musings Near Aquapendente' is an astonishing act of poetic husbandry. It marks the climax of one creatively rich strand of revisiting in Wordsworth's later years and demonstrates once more the subtle way in which his imagination creates through, or in conjunction with, memories of people, events, places—and of poems.

(ii)

Throughout Wordsworth's sixties—the 1830s—a great many factors had made for retrospection. In 'Musings Near Aquapendente' tributary streams converge.

Wordsworth's resting place under the chestnut trees of the Apennines is the place from which to start tracking back. In 1837 Wordsworth was himself at last in Italy on what had been a long-awaited and long-hoped-for tour. He thought that he had left it too late, that his imagination could no longer respond to travel and sights with the vigour that it once had and he also lamented that he grew tired easily, that he was not capable any longer of the pedestrian feats that took him and Robert Jones nearly two thousand miles in 1790. Wordsworth nonetheless gained an enormous boost from this visit and pursued an itinerary that would have daunted many people half his age.[5] It was such a contrast to what had transpired for Sir Walter Scott on his Italian venture.

When Wordsworth had last visited Abbotsford in September 1831, the ailing Scott was about to set off to the Mediterranean in search of better health, just as Coleridge had done nearly thirty years before. Seeing just how enfeebled his old friend was, Wordsworth realized that in all likelihood they were saying farewell. For once profound emotion did not need to be recalled in tranquillity to generate poetic creation of the highest order. Returning from an excursion that included Newark Tower, Wordsworth recalled, 'we had to cross the Tweed directly opposite Abbotsford. The wheels of our carriage grated upon the pebbles in the bed of the stream, that there flows somewhat rapidly; a rich but sad light of rather a purple than a golden hue was spread over the Eildon hills at that moment; and, thinking it probable that it might be the last time Sir Walter would cross the stream, I was not a little moved . . .'. Within days, while still at Abbotsford, Wordsworth had composed one of the most assured of his late poems. The year before, on hearing of the onset of Scott's illness, Wordsworth had written to Samuel Rogers, 'Your account of his seizure grieved us all much. Coleridge had a dangerous attack a few weeks ago; Davy is gone. Surely these are men of power, not to be replaced should they disappear.'[6] Now, in 'On the Departure of Sir Walter Scott from Abbotsford, for Naples',

Wordsworth took up the idea of 'men of power' to figure Scott as a 'wondrous Potentate':

> A trouble, not of clouds, or weeping rain,
> Nor of the setting sun's pathetic light
> Engendered, hangs o'er Eildon's triple height:
> Spirits of Power, assembled there, complain
> For kindred Power departing from their sight;
> While Tweed, best pleased in chanting a blithe strain,
> Saddens his voice again, and yet again.
> Lift up your hearts, ye Mourners! for the might
> Of the whole world's good wishes with him goes;
> Blessings and prayers in nobler retinue
> Than sceptred King or laurelled Conqueror knows,
> Follow this wondrous Potentate. Be true,
> Ye winds of ocean, and the midland sea,
> Wafting your Charge to soft Parthenope!

In depicting Nature as mourning her loss, one of the strongest conventions of elegy is revised, for the elements are lamenting the loss not of the dead but of the living power whose local attachment animates them. The effect is elegiac, nonetheless, a mood that is strengthened by a suggestion of an echo of 'Lycidas' in the final line ('And O ye dolphins waft the hapless youth') and by the beautiful movement from real to ideal. The topographically exact reference to 'Eildon's triple height' opens the poem in the rainy border country that is Scott's domain, the world of 'real' pastoral. By the end, as he approaches 'Parthenope', Virgil's magical name for Naples, the sick man is being enfolded into the world of classical pastoral, an ideal realm that exists only in imagination and art.[7]

But 'Musings' also reaches further back—to August 1805, when Scott first visited Wordsworth on his home ground. Having passed an uncomfortable night at the inn in Patterdale, Wordsworth, Scott, and Humphry Davy set off for Grasmere, taking in Helvellyn on their way.[8] Scott, Wordsworth was later to recall, 'healthy, gay, and hopeful', scrambled along Striding Edge towards the summit with a vigour which Wordsworth 'could not but admire', and which forcefully returned to him as he conjured up the two men on 'old Helvellyn's brow, | Where once together, in his day of strength, | We stood rejoicing, as if earth were free | From sorrow, like the sky above our heads'. He also recalled that Scott beguiled the time and their necessarily slow progress by 'telling many stories and

amusing anecdotes as was his custom', but that Davy eventually became irritated and left the other two for a quicker descent.[9] Coming
down via Grisedale Tarn, it seems unlikely that Wordsworth did
not indicate the spot where he and Dorothy had said farewell to
John Wordsworth in September 1800, not knowing that they would
never see him again, for it was a sacred place. In the Fenwick Note
to 'Elegiac Verses' Wordsworth located it exactly—'The point is 2 or
3 yards below the outlet of Grisedale Tarn on a foot-road by which
a horse may pass to Patterdale—a ridge of Helvelyn [sic] on the left,
and the summit of Fairfield on the right'—where he and Dorothy
had stood, waving to their brother as he hurried down the track.
After John drowned in shipwreck in February 1805 Wordsworth
had been unable to face going to Grisedale Tarn and it had become
important to repopulate the place with happy memories. Scott became part of that process. As they stood on the summit of Helvellyn
surveying the 'prospect right below of deep coves shaped | By
skeleton arms' and as they picked their way down to Grisedale Tarn,
Wordsworth countered Scott's invocation of his special country by
reciting his own lines about Greenside fell, Glenridding-screes, and
low Glencoign, 'Places forsaken now, but loving still | The muses, as
they loved them in the days | Of the old minstrels and the border
bards'. Thirty-six years later, as he shaped his recollection of how
Scott's 'sunk eye kindled at those dear words | That spake of bards
and border minstrels', Wordsworth summoned from their hiding-
place the lines he had written in 1800 and quoted to Scott in
1805. The passage pays tribute to the 'Wizard of the North' as he
was in his day of strength, but it is also an embodiment of what
Wordsworth was when at the height of his powers and at the most
hopeful moment of his poetic career.

'Musings Near Aquapendente' harks even further back, however.
In the lines quoted from 'Musings' the reference to 'Yarrow Unvisited' takes the poem back to 1803 and to Wordsworth's first acquaintance with Scott. It began as William and Dorothy came towards
the end of their tour of what Wordsworth called 'the most
poetical Country I ever travelled in'—Scotland.[10] They met Scott on
17 September and the following day explored the banks of the
Tweed. A visit to the river Yarrow was mooted, but not followed up.
'Yarrow Unvisited' memorializes the day by recording, purportedly,
an exchange between the poet and his female companion, in which

her desire to 'turn aside, | And see the Braes of Yarrow' is countered
not only by his refusal to do so, but by his insistence that not to see
the Yarrow will leave them 'a vision of their own'. Actually to go
there would destroy the vision: 'For when we're there, although 'tis
fair, | 'Twill be another Yarrow!' It seems likely that the tourists
confessed to Scott that they had wondered about visiting one of his
favourite spots but decided against it, but certain that as one poet
to another, Wordsworth will have expected Scott to appreciate the
subtle ways in which 'Yarrow Unvisited' interweaves elements of
'real-life' and poetry. It was written, he told Scott when he sent him
a copy in January 1805, 'not without a view of pleasing you'.[11] One
can see why.

   In 1803 Scott was hard at work on an additional volume for
the *Minstrelsy of the Scottish Border* published in two volumes the previous year and in the early stages of composition of the *Lay of the Last
Minstrel*, which he recited to his visitors. Scott struck them as a man
of intense 'local attachments'—the phrase is Dorothy Wordsworth's,
who reported to Lady Beaumont that 'his whole heart and soul seem
to be devoted to the Scottish Streams Yarrow and Tweed, Tiviot and
the rest of them of which we hear in the Border Ballads'[12]—and there
can be no doubt that this devotion to the locality was impressed
upon them not only by the enthusiasm with which Scott acted as
tour guide but by his association of every spot with a ballad or a tale.
'Yarrow Unvisited', a poem rooted in the soil of the minstrelsy of
the Scottish border, honours Scott's passion and his labours on the
Minstrelsy by offering him a sort of collage of everything he loved.

   When published as the final lyric in the section 'Poems Written
during a Tour in Scotland' in the 1807 *Poems, in Two Volumes* collection, the poem was prefaced by a deft textual manoeuvre:

YARROW UNVISITED
(See the various Poems the scene of which is laid upon the Banks of the
Yarrow; in particular, the exquisite Ballad of Hamilton, beginning

> 'Busk ye, busk ye my bonny, bonny Bride,
> Busk ye, busk ye my winsome Marrow!')

A poem about not going to the Yarrow begins by reference to
numerous other poems which are about the river. As Michael Baron
points out, the 'cult of the Yarrow grew quite remarkably during
the ballad revival of the eighteenth century', so that Wordsworth's

expansive 'various Poems' may have been filled out differently by
different readers, depending on which of the most popular collections of ballads they favoured—Ramsay's *Tea-Table Miscellany*, Percy's
Reliques of Ancient English Poetry, Herd's *Scottish Songs*, or Scott's
Minstrelsy of the Scottish Border.[13] From all the currently familiar
Yarrow ballads, Wordsworth singles out one for quotation in his
headnote and in the first stanza of 'Yarrow Unvisited', William
Hamilton's *The Braes of Yarrow*, and in so doing he reaches out
to Scott. This 'exquisite ballad' is one which Scott makes special
mention of in the *Minstrelsy*, when introducing 'The Dowie Dens
of Yarrow'. This latter Scott declares to be a 'very great favourite
among the inhabitants of Ettrick Forest' and one of ancient descent,
'although the language has been gradually modernized, in the course
of its transmission to us, through the inaccurate channel of oral
tradition'. In fact, its editor concedes, 'It will be, with many readers,
the greatest recommendation of these verses, that they are supposed
to have suggested to Mr Hamilton of Bangour, the modern ballad,
beginning, "Busk ye, busk ye, my bonny bonny bride."'[14]

But Wordsworth gestures still further to Scott's loves. The third
stanza of 'Yarrow Unvisited' begins,

> There's Galla-water, Leader haughs,
> Both lying right before us;

Leader water, not far from Melrose Abbey, one of the favourite
spots to which Scott took the Wordsworths, is the subject of another
Yarrow poem, 'Leader Haughs and Yarrow', supposed to be by Nicol
Burne of Selkirkshire. The subject and its setting endeared this poem
to Scott so strongly that he said, 'from early youth [it] has given my
bosom a thrill when sung or repeated'.[15] He had been tracking down
manuscripts of it in 1803 and many years later in 1819, as Lockhart
recalled, he recited stanzas of it as he looked over the panorama of
the Tweed and discoursed to him about its beauty and history. The
'pretty stanzas', were, so Lockhart understood, 'ascribed to the last of
the real wandering minstrels of this district'.[16] And, as Wordsworth
pointed out to Scott in his letter of January 1805, it was the metre of
'Leader Haughs' which he drew on for 'Yarrow Unvisited'.

Wordsworth's first poem on the Yarrow was sent as a gift to Scott
in 1805 and elicited a warm response from the poetic guardian of the
region: 'I am very much flattered by your choosing Yarrow for a

subject of the verses sent me . . . At the same time I by no means admit your apology however ingeniously & artfully stated for not visiting the bonny holms of Yarrow & certainly will not rest till I have prevailed upon you to compare the ideal with the real stream.'[17] The comparison ought to have been made the following year, when the two men planned an excursion through the border region in the summer.[18] In creative potential this tour might have been at least as rich as the expedition to the Valley of Stones mounted by Coleridge and Wordsworth late in 1797, but it did not take place; nor did Wordsworth actually see the Yarrow until many years later.

(iii)

On 1 September 1814 Wordsworth visited the Yarrow in the company of his wife and her sister, Sara Hutchinson, James Hogg, and the editor of the *British Poets* volumes, Dr Robert Anderson. Wordsworth memorialized his visit almost at once and published the poem, 'Yarrow Visited', as a companion piece to 'Yarrow Unvisited' in his collected *Poems* the following year. Its structure is very characteristically Wordsworthian: a recognition of loss compensated for by an assertion of gain or at least a more tempered joy. In the silence of the vale the poet's heart is filled with sadness, partly by thoughts that arise from the melancholy stories that are attached to the spot through the many Yarrow poems, but also because the 'waking dream' of Yarrow that his imagination has cherished for so many years has perished, eliminated by sight of the actual stream. But, as counter-balance, the poetry that sings the 'unconquerable strength of love' is 'delicious' and the vale itself 'in the light of day' is so beautiful that it rivals imagination's 'delicate creation'. The poet concludes by declaring that he has not won Yarrow by sight alone, that fancy's sunshine still plays upon the river, and so wherever he goes, he will take with him its 'genuine image' to heighten joy and cheer his mind in sorrow. It is the fundamental structure of 'Tintern Abbey', the 'Ode: Intimations of Immortality', 'Elegiac Stanzas . . . Peele Castle', and, of course, the whole of *The Prelude*. In 'Yarrow Visited', though, a sense of melancholy and loss dominates the attempts to draw consolation from the beauty of the river and its surrounding landscape features.

One might account for this in a number of ways. Biographical considerations have a place. Dorothy Wordsworth was not of the party in 1814, an absence Wordsworth regretted, as the Fenwick Note to the poem reveals: '. . . she would have had so much delight in recalling the time when, travelling together in Scotland, we declined going in search of this celebrated stream, not altogether, I will frankly confess, for the reasons assigned in the poem on the occasion.'[19] It is as if Wordsworth yearns to have by his side the 'winsome marrow', who was involved in the earlier real-life situation and complicit in the poetic fiction it gave rise to, so as to complete both in the actual visit to the Yarrow.

The Fenwick Note also reveals, though, another, profounder source of sadness. In it Wordsworth pays 'a tribute of gratitude' to Robert Anderson, observing that it was through the volumes of his *British Poets* that 'I became first familiar with Chaucer, and so little money had I then to spare for books that, in all probability, but for this same work, I should have known little of Drayton, Daniel, and other distinguished poets of the Elizabethan age and their immediate successors till a much later period of my life.' As the old man's recollections also make clear, however, this pleasurable memory was inextricable from ever-fresh painful ones. Meeting Dr Anderson, Wordsworth expressed his obligation to him for 'his collection, which had been my brother John's companion in more than one voyage to India, & which he gave me before his departure from Grasmere never to return'. John Wordsworth had believed in his brother's vocation and his final, fatal voyage was undertaken in part in the hope of securing the future financially for himself and the Dove Cottage family. In one lament written shortly after John's death, Wordsworth dwells with anguish on the fact that the manuscript book in which he is writing was intended to accompany his brother on his voyages. It did not go with him, but the poet will continue to enter verses into it,

> Making a kind of secret chain
> If so I may, betwixt us twain
> In memory of the past.

The volumes of the *British Poets* that stayed behind in Grasmere served as another covenant between Wordsworth and the brother he always thought of as 'a silent poet'.[20]

Whatever the historical-biographical causes of the melancholy undertone of 'Yarrow Visited', the poetic realization of them is particularly striking at two moments. The first is where Wordsworth evokes not just his own Yarrow poem, 'Yarrow Unvisited', nor even just Hamilton's 'Braes of Yarrow', but yet another, 'The Braes of Yarrow', a ballad by John Logan (1748–88). It is a very sad tale of loss and sudden death. On the eve of her wedding, Logan's young mourner tells how her beloved, 'the flower of Yarrow', went to his 'watery grave' and how the water-wraith ascended thrice with a 'doleful groan' to tell her that he was drowning. In the fourth stanza of 'Yarrow Visited' her vision is recalled as the poet asks,

> Where was it that the famous Flower
> Of Yarrow Vale lay bleeding?
> His bed perchance was yon smooth mound
> On which the herd is feeding:
> And haply from this crystal pool,
> Now peaceful as the morning,
> The Water-wraith ascended thrice—
> And gave his doleful warning.

We know that Logan's poem meant a great deal to Wordsworth. Late in life he declared that it 'always brings tears to my eyes; its melancholy is so intense and indescribable', and he drew on it for the opening to 'Extempore Effusion Upon the Death of James Hogg'.[21] To which one might add that with Logan's 'The Braes of Yarrow' Wordsworth was prompted to melancholy by not just the poem, but its author. In June 1802 William and Dorothy Wordsworth had read together 'the Life & some of the writings of poor Logan. . . . "And everlasting Longings for the lost." It is an affecting line. There are many affecting lines & passages in his poems.'[22] What they found in volume eleven of Anderson's British Poets was not just Logan's 'Ode: Written on a Visit to the Country in Autumn', from which the affecting line comes, 'Song: The Braes of Yarrow', and 'Ode to the Cuckoo', but, in the biographical memoir prefacing the poems, an account of one whose volatile spirit was crushed by 'the failure of his schemes of literary ambition' and who died early, his constitution in part wrecked by 'that temporary relief which the bottle supplies'. As I have argued elsewhere, in 1802 Logan joined in Wordsworth's fearful imagination with Burns, and with the Coleridge of 'Dejection:

An Ode': 'We Poets in our youth begin in gladness; | But thereof
comes in the end despondency and madness.'[23]

The second reason for detecting the presence of insistent melancholy in the poem is that at a crucial moment there emerges an
echo of Wordsworth's own earlier self and writing. The last two
stanzas read:

> I see—but not by sight alone,
> Lov'd Yarrow, have I won thee;
> A ray of Fancy still survives—
> Her sunshine plays upon thee!
> Thy ever-youthful waters keep
> A course of lively pleasure;
> And gladsome notes my lips can breathe,
> Accordant to the measure.
>
> The vapours linger round the Heights,
> They melt—and soon must vanish;
> One hour is theirs, nor more is mine—
> Sad thought, which I would banish,
> But that I know, where'er I go,
> Thy genuine image, Yarrow,
> Will dwell with me—to heighten joy,
> And cheer my mind in sorrow.

It is impossible not to be returned to the opening stanzas of the
'Ode: Intimations of Immortality', in which waters and sunshine are
both invoked and declared beautiful, only for the counter-certainty
to be uttered:

> But yet I know, where'er I go,
> That there hath passed away a glory from the earth.

When Wordsworth published 'Ode: Composed upon an Evening of
Extraordinary Splendor and Beauty' in 1820, he made sure readers
linked this ode to the earlier one by appending a note pointing out
the connection. With an echo as insistent as this in 'Yarrow Visited'
he did not need to.

(iv)

In his memorial to his first visit to the vale of Yarrow, it is as if
Wordsworth cannot but think of the region without wanting Scott

there, for he beckons to him when he gestures to 'The ruined front of Newark's Towers, | Renowned in Border story'—but more recently renowned, of course, through *The Lay of the Last Minstrel*. Old and infirm, Scott's minstrel—the 'last of all the bards was he | Who sung of Border chivalry'—gains refuge in 'Newark's stately tower', where he sings his Lay. Having been at work on the poem when he and Wordsworth first met in 1803, when they climbed Helvellyn together in 1805, Scott had just published it to immediate acclaim. Poetically, Scott had claimed Newark's stately tower and its setting as firmly as Wordsworth had claimed Greenhead Ghyll and Grasmere in 'Michael', though if sales figures are proof of a poetic region conquered, Scott had done so much more successfully.[24] But Scott was unable to be one of the party that visited in 1814 'where Newark's stately tower | Looks out from Yarrow's birchen bower'. That much-planned and long-wished-for combination—the place, the two friends, and the poetry—had to wait until Wordsworth's penultimate visit to Scotland.

Wordsworth had been pressed to make a visit by Scott's insistence that 'if [he] did not come soon to see him it might be too late'[25] and it was with this melancholy injunction preying on him that he journeyed to Abbotsford in September 1831. Many things made this sojourn memorable, such as the carriage ride to the ruin of Newark Castle, or the evening when Scott's daughter, Sophia (Mrs Lockhart) chanted old ballads to her harp, but a sense that things were being done for the last time coloured every gathering and two valedictory moments in particular ensured that this final visit to Scott and his domain would be burnt into Wordsworth's memory. On the last morning of the visit, Sir Walter made a faltering entry in Dora Wordsworth's autograph album, saying to her, 'I should not have done anything of this kind but for your Father's sake; they are probably the last verses I shall ever write.'[26] Knowing Wordsworth's devotion to his daughter, Scott could hardly have done or said anything more likely to move his guest, but he did:

> when, upon the eve
> Of his last going from Tweed-side, thought turned,
> Or by another's sympathy was led,
> To this bright land, Hope was for him no friend,
> Knowledge no help; Imagination shaped
> No promise. Still, in more than ear-deep seats,

> Survives for me, and cannot but survive
> The tone of voice which wedded borrowed words
> To sadness not their own, when, with faint smile
> Forced by intent to take from speech its edge,
> He said, 'When I am there, although 'tis fair,
> 'Twill be another Yarrow.'

This was a beautifully judged act of poetic courtesy and it moved Wordsworth very deeply. By reaching back to their first meeting and alluding to the poem which cemented their friendship, Scott demonstrated how fully and instinctively he shared with Wordsworth the retrospective impulse to bring the past into vital conjunction with the present.

In a passage of verse that was eventually not used for 'Michael' Wordsworth writes of the crucial importance of agencies by which,

> still paramount to every change
> Which years can bring into the human heart
> Our feelings are indissolubly bound
> Together, and affinities preserved
> Between all the stages of the life of man.

These lines have already been quoted in the introduction to this book, but they bear repetition for they go to the very heart of Wordsworth's deepest compulsions. What is of special interest here is that they are to be found in the same manuscript as the lines with which this chapter started that were incorporated forty-one years later into 'Musings Near Aquapendente'. Were they in Wordsworth's mind as he pondered the moment when Scott quoted 'Yarrow Unvisited' back to him in 1831? I think so: 'affinities preserved between all the stages of the life of man'.

Wordsworth hastened back home and in a very short time had written 'Yarrow Revisited' and sent it to catch Scott before he embarked. The title, of course, chose itself, but it is nonetheless splendidly apt, for the poem registers a threefold revisitation by Wordsworth—to the river, to his own poetry of 1805 and 1814, and thus to his own earlier self and to one of the important friendships of Wordsworth's life. 'Dear Sir Walter! I love that Man . . .', he declared simply in 1830—not the kind of public testimony he was much given to making.[27] It is a wonderful title, too, for this poem of friendship, which, as the opening suggests, is really throughout a tribute to Scott and his domain.

YARROW REVISITED

(The following Stanzas are a memorial of a day passed with Sir Walter Scott, and other Friends visiting the Banks of the Yarrow under his guidance, immediately before his departure from Abbotsford, for Naples.

The title *Yarrow Revisited* will stand in no need of explanation, for Readers acquainted with the Author's previous poems suggested by that celebrated Stream.)

> The gallant Youth, who may have gained,
>   Or seeks, a "Winsome Marrow,"
> Was but an infant in the lap
>   When first I looked on Yarrow;
> Once more, by Newark's Castle-gate
>   Long left without a Warder,
> I stood, looked, listened, and with Thee,
>   Great Minstrel of the Border!

Hamilton's 'The Braes of Yarrow' (1803) and 'Yarrow Unvisited' (1814) and 'Yarrow Visited' (1831) and Sir Walter Scott and *The Lay of the Last Minstrel*—all gathered in another poem about the Braes of Yarrow. Or rather, not really about the Braes of Yarrow so much as about what Yarrow has meant to the two poets in their morn of youth, then at the moment when Wordsworth first had sight of the river, and now, as two middle-aged men 'made a day of happy hours | Our happy days recalling'.[28]

Recall of the sequence of events and of poems they gave rise to colours the opening of Wordsworth's great dirge, his Lament for the Makers, which was prompted by the loss of one more contemporary in 1835. 'Extempore Effusion Upon the Death of James Hogg' begins with allusions to the 1814 visit to the Yarrow, to the 1831 revisit with 'the border minstrel', and to Hogg, dead 'upon the braes of Yarrow'. It closes by bringing together, as all Wordsworth's Yarrow poems do, the actual and the poetic imaginary:

> No more of old romantic sorrows,
> For slaughtered Youth or love-lorn Maid!
> With sharper grief is Yarrow smitten,
> And Ettrick mourns with her their Poet dead.

This might sound as if Yarrow were played out for Wordsworth— 'No more of old romantic sorrows'—but it was not the case. As he rested on the slope of the Apennines two years later he thought of Scott and the Braes of Yarrow and, in Wordsworth's own splendid phrase, 'interrogated his memory'.[29] The result was 'Musings Near Aquapendente', his last great lament for his friend.

(v)

One moment in 'Yarrow Revisited' is of special significance. It is where Wordsworth plays with the conceit that though Scott must leave the Tweed for other slopes and other rivers, the hope must be that 'classic Fancy' will link with 'native Fancy' to preserve the sick man's spirits from sinking:

> For thee, O Scott! compelled to change
> Green Eildon-hill and Cheviot
> For warm Vesuvio's vine-clad slopes;
> And leave thy Tweed and Teviot
> For mild Sorento's breezy waves;
> May classic Fancy, linking
> With native Fancy her fresh aid,
> Preserve thy heart from sinking!
>
> O! while they minister to thee,
> Each vying with the other,
> May Health return to mellow Age,
> With Strength, her venturous brother;
> And Tiber, and each brook and rill
> Renowned in song and story,
> With unimagined beauty shine,
> Nor lose one ray of glory!
>
> For Thou, upon a hundred streams,
> By tales of love and sorrow,
> Of faithful love, undaunted truth,
> Hast shed the power of Yarrow;
> And streams unknown, hills yet unseen,
> Where'er thy path invite thee,
> At parent Nature's grateful call,
> With gladness must requite Thee.

The reference to the Tiber is important for it brings into the picture the other poet whose life and death were very much in Wordsworth's thoughts at this moment: Robert Burns.

In one of the most engaging poems of his *Poems, Chiefly in the Scottish Dialect* (1786), 'To William Simpson, Ochiltree', Burns exhorts his friend and brother bard to rise to the challenge of celebrating their own locality, and in particular its rivers:

> Th' Illissus, Tiber, Thames an' Seine,
> Glide sweet in monie a tunefu' line;
> But Willie set your fit to mine,
>   An' cock your crest,
> We'll gar our streams an' burnies shine
>   Up wi' the best.

Wordsworth read this epistle as soon as it appeared and it clearly spoke to him over his whole lifetime. He signalled the borrowing of a phrase from it in an early manuscript of *The Ruined Cottage*; he quoted from it again twenty years later in the curious Postscript to the *River Duddon* collection, in which he claims that Coleridge had chosen four lines from the poem in 1798 as a motto for his projected rural poem, *The Brook*; and finally, as a very old man, he turned to Burns's poem once again for quotation to bolster his argument against the Kendal and Windermere Railway scheme.[30]

Burns, in fact, had long been vital to Wordsworth's imagination, and the creative poetic connection began just when the connection with Scott did—in 1803. The previous year Wordsworth had invoked 'Him who walked in glory and in joy | Behind his plough, upon the mountain-side' in 'Resolution and Independence' and by the time that poem was published in 1807 it was accompanied by an 'Address to the Sons of Burns' which had arisen from a visit to Burns's grave during the Wordsworths' tour of Scotland in 1803. None of this needs rehearsing.[31]

What is less familiar is that Burns re-enters Wordsworth's poetry with force exactly thirty years later.

In the summer of 1833 Wordsworth made a short tour of Western Scotland. The return journey took him through places associated with Burns and across rivers which, he remarked to Allan Cunningham, 'naebody sung till he [Burns] named them in immortal verse'. 'The Banks of the Nith', he went on, 'I *had* seen before, and was glad to renew my acquaintance with them, for Burns's sake; and let me add, without flattery, for yours.'[32] At one moment a fellow-passenger on the top of the coach gestured to Mossgiel farm, where the Burns family had moved to in 1783. It was the kind of incident that Wordsworth had always fed off poetically—a place, words, a gesture—but this one was particularly rich in commemorative possibilities. The result was:

'There!' said a Stripling, pointing with meet pride
Towards a low roof with green trees half concealed,
'Is Mossgiel farm; and that's the very field
Where Burns ploughed up the Daisy.' Far and wide
A plain below stretched sea-ward, while descried
Above sea-clouds, the Peaks of Arran rose;
And by that simple notice, the repose
Of earth, sky, sea, and air, was vivified.
Beneath 'the random *bield* of clod or stone'
Myriads of Daisies have shone forth in flower
Near the lark's nest, and in their natural hour
Have passed away, less happy than the One
That by the unwilling ploughshare died to prove
The tender charm of Poetry and Love.

This is an elegant piece that from such an accomplished practitioner in this genre might look like a poetical five-finger exercise,
but it taps into the deepest places of Wordsworth's being. The sonnet
plays on and quotes from Burns's 'To a Mountain Daisy'. This poem
was one of Wordsworth's favourites, something he shared with
Dorothy, who singled it out for special commendation when she first
read Burns.[33] When Wordsworth visited Scotland in 1803 it was in
her company. They visited Burns's grave together and together saw
Ellisland, Burns's farm in Dumfriesshire. But the 'dear, dear Sister'
of 'Tintern Abbey', the Dorothy who in 1803 could match William
step for step on any walk, no matter how taxing, was slipping into
dementia and rarely left her room. Twice already the family at Rydal
Mount had thought she was dying and now in 1833, Wordsworth's
companion on the tour, Crabb Robinson, wrote that after saying
farewell to Dorothy at Rydal Mount he deemed it 'very improbable
that I shall see her again'.[34]

The voice that once was 'like a hidden Bird that sang' was now
often querulous.[35] Wordsworth's distress at his sister's inexorable
decline was immeasurable and it did not diminish with time. Years
later when he made a final visit to Alfoxden and other haunts of
the *annus mirabilis*, the 'only painful feeling that moved in his mind',
Isabella Fenwick reported, was the 'thought of what his sister, who
had been his companion here, was then and now is'.[36] But this loss
was only the worst of many losses. On 14 January 1834 Wordsworth
wrote to Rogers that, 'No less than 14 of our Relatives, friends, or
valued acquaintance have been removed by death within the last 3 or

4 months.' Coleridge died in July, and grief at the state of Dorothy Wordsworth's health fused with the profound sense of loss at the passing of the 'heaven-eyed creature'. And then Charles Lamb, the other companion from the 1790s, died too in December 1834. What happened next brings Burns back into the picture.

In late 1835 Wordsworth was struggling to compose an epitaph for Lamb and during negotiations with Lamb's sister, Mary, Wordsworth revealed to Moxon, his London conduit in the matter, the imaginative turbulence the task had brought about:

The verses upon dear Lamb, threw my mind into that train of melancholy reflexion which produced several things in some respects of the same character, such as those lines upon Hogg and some others brought forth with more reflexion and pains—for on turning over an old vol: of Mss, I met with some verses that expressed my feelings at the Grave of Burns 32 years ago. These I was tempted to retouch, and not only added to them, but threw off another piece which is a record of what passed in my mind when I was in sight of his residence on the banks of the Nith, at the same period.[37]

The remark about 'those lines upon Hogg' confirms what any reader of the 'Extempore Effusion Upon the Death of James Hogg' suspects, namely, that extempore though it might be, the effusion had been gathering force for some time in 'train[s] of melancholy reflexion' started primarily by the death of Coleridge in 1834.[38]

More intriguing, though, is the revelation that Wordsworth retouched a poem about his feelings thirty-two years earlier, added to it, and then wrote a companion piece. Not yet fully privy to the working practices of the poet he had recently taken on, Moxon could have been forgiven for being confused as to quite what this burst of new composition from old amounted to, but it would have seemed to come clear as he received copy for Wordsworth's next collection in 1842, *Poems, Chiefly of Early and Late Years*. 'At the Grave of Burns. 1803', he would see, must have been the first poem mentioned in Wordsworth's letter, and it is followed by 'Thoughts | Suggested the Day Following on the Banks of the Nith, Near the Poet's Residence', clearly the other piece thrown off. In fact, the story is rather more complicated.

Wordsworth and his sister visited Burns's grave on 18 August 1803. In her journal of the tour Dorothy Wordsworth records that their overwhelming sense of melancholy was mixed up with anxious thoughts about their own future survival. The dejection of her brother's 'Resolution and Independence' written the previous year was not simply a rhetorical feint. The recognition that 'there may come another day to me | Solitude, pain of heart, distress, and poverty', had been uttered with intense and justifiable seriousness by a poet whose collected *oeuvre* by 1802 had barely cleared 500 copies.[39] Whatever Wordsworth's feelings were on that occasion, however, there is no evidence that he tried to make a poem of them until two or more years later, when he composed 'Ejaculation at the Grave of Burns'.[40] This striking poem is almost completely unknown because, for whatever reason, it was omitted from the cluster of memorials of the Scottish Tour in *Poems, in Two Volumes* (1807) and from all manuscripts of Dorothy Wordsworth's *Recollections of a Tour Made in Scotland*, despite the inclusion of other lyrics written after the tour, such as 'The Solitary Reaper'. The chief reason for the unfamiliarity of the poem, however, is that when Wordsworth happened upon it thirty or so years later, the poem was not so much retouched as transformed.

The 'Ejaculation' reads:

> I shiver, Spirit fierce and bold,
> At thought of what I now behold!
> As vapours breath'd from dungeon cold
>   Strike pleasure dead;
> So sadness comes out of the mold
>   Where Burns is laid!
>
> And have I, then, thy bones so near?
> And thou forbidden to appear!
> As if it were Thyself that's here
>   I shrink with pain;
> And both my wishes and my fear
>   Alike are vain.
>
> But wherefore tremble? 'tis no place
> Of pain and sorrow, but of grace;
> Of shelter, and of silent peace,
>   And 'friendly aid':
> Grasp'd is he now in that embrace
>   For which he pray'd![41]

The poem works in part by unsettling expectations. There is nothing in the opening of the repose of Gray's churchyard—here are vapours, cold, bones, and fear—but little either of traditional consolation at the close. Burns rests in the embrace of the power—Death—to which in his ode 'To Ruin' he had offered up 'a wretch's prayer' for 'friendly aid'.

'At the Grave of Burns' expands the three 'Ejaculation' stanzas into fourteen. The acknowledgement that 'both my wishes and my fear | Alike are vain' is put aside in transition to an extended reflection on what the two poets might have meant to one another, had Burns lived.

> Well might I mourn that He was gone
> Whose light I hailed when first it shone,
> When breaking forth as nature's own,
>   It showed my youth
> How Verse may build a princely throne
>   On humble truth.
>
> Alas! where'er the current tends,
> Regret pursues and with it blends,—
> Huge Criffel's hoary top ascends
>   By Skiddaw seen,—
> Neighbours we were, and loving friends
>   We might have been.

These lines reach back over thirty years to the moment in 1803 when Wordsworth and Dorothy, about to make progress on their tour of Scotland, caught their last look of the Cumberland mountains within half a mile of Ellisland. 'We talked on Burns', Dorothy Wordsworth recorded, 'and of the prospect he must have had, perhaps from his own door, of Skiddaw and his companions, indulging ourselves in the fancy that we *might* have been personally known to each other.'[42]

The poem further marks itself as a revisiting through a series of allusions to poems long known and called on. The early favourite, 'To a Mountain Daisy', offers a suggestive analogy for the freshness of Burns's own genius (ll. 19–20). A phrase from 'A Bard's Epitaph' (l. 50) recalls the sober lines brother and sister had repeated to each other over Burns's grave in 1803, 'with melancholy and painful reflections':

> Is there a man whose judgment clear
> Can others teach the course to steer,
> Yet runs himself life's mad career

> Wild as the wave?—
> Here let him pause, and through a tear
> Survey this grave.
>
> The poor Inhabitant below
> Was quick to learn, and wise to know,
> And keenly felt the friendly glow
> And softer flame;
> But thoughtless follies laid him low
> And stain'd his name.[43]

In 1803 Burns's title, 'A Bard's Epitaph', would have called to mind Wordsworth's own attempt in the genre, 'A Poet's Epitaph', which had been published in *Lyrical Ballads* in 1800. That poem's declaration about 'the Poet' that, 'you must love him, ere to you | He will seem worthy of your love', must have returned to William and Dorothy as they gazed at the resting-place of 'the poor Inhabitant below'. But now, in 1835, Wordsworth's sense of what it meant to write a bard's epitaph was sharpened by the loss of so many friends who were also bards.[44] Almost at the close of the poem the consolation of 'To Ruin' is entertained, as it was in 'Ejaculation', namely, that the grave can be for such as Burns's innocent son, lying beside him, 'a quiet bed'. The last two stanzas, however, demonstrate the limitation of this kind of consolatory conceit by framing it within the larger certainty of Christian hope. The poems closes with the

> Music that sorrow comes not near,
> A ritual hymn,
> Chaunted in love that casts out fear
> By Seraphim.[45]

What is of particular interest here is not the fact of a poem's composition about an experience of the long past, a common enough occurrence in Wordsworth. Nor is it the nature of the composition itself, though 'At the Grave of Burns' would reward more detailed analysis as a fine example of Wordsworth's late lyric style. It is rather what Wordsworth says about the composition of 'At the Grave of Burns' and its complement, 'Thoughts Suggested the Day Following'. What is in fact the transformation of the 'Ejaculation' stanzas is referred to as if it is the continuation of the original creative impulse, as if the lapse of thirty years was of no moment. Remarks about 'Thoughts Suggested' make the point even more unequivocally. On

11 December 1835 Wordsworth repeated the claim he had made the day before to Moxon, when he told David Laing that the poem, though 'written only a few days ago', was 'a faithful record of my feelings when in the Summer of 1803 I passed near Ellisland'.[46] Four years later he admitted tinkering with the poem to the extent of adding a new concluding stanza. 'Thoughts Suggested' is a poem of 1835 and 1839. In the Fenwick Notes of 1843 Wordsworth nonetheless had no hesitation in declaring it a poem of 1803 because, though 'not composed till many years after', it was '*felt* at the time'.[47]

This is a very revealing remark, as such off-the-cuff formulations tend to be. The poem 'Thoughts Suggested' has existed, Wordsworth avers, since 1803; it just hasn't been written down. The feelings which gave rise to it were felt in 1803 and would have been recorded then, had the poem taken form. As it was, formal realization had to wait more than thirty years.

Wordsworth's comment is disingenuous. The opening stanzas of 'At the Grave of Burns' undoubtedly capture the intensity of his response in 1803, 'I shiver, Spirit, fierce and bold | At thought of what I now behold', but what gives the two later poems their power is that quickened memory of the past is shaped by one who is very conscious of the present moment. They are poems of 1803 but also poems of 1835. The warm tributes embody both the feelings of the young Wordsworth, who had stood at Burns's grave in 1803 only too aware that at 33 he was already within a year or two of the age at which the 'poor Inhabitant below' had died, and the reflections of a poet in his mid-sixties, whose career path was now laid out and who was conscious of how much he owed to the one who had shown him, when he was just starting out, 'How Verse may build a princely throne | On humble truth'.

Beneath the disingenuousness, however, are two elements that deserve highlighting. The first accounts for the vehemence of Wordsworth's hostility to the presentation of his poems in order of composition. Learning that Lamb favoured chronological arrangement, Wordsworth thundered, 'Lamb's order of time is the very worst that could be followed' (Letter, 27 April 1826). Accordingly, when published in 1842, 'At the Grave of Burns' had the date '1803' in its title-line. Nothing indicated that 'Thoughts Suggested the Day Following' belonged to any other time. And as soon as publication of the next freshly-set collected edition permitted, in 1845, both poems were folded into the section, 'Memorials of a Tour in Scotland', alongside such pieces as 'Address to the Sons of Burns', 'Rob Roy's Grave', 'The Solitary Reaper', and the other poems which had constituted this category since *Poems, in Two Volumes* in 1807.

The second is that not only is there clearly no element of intentional duplicity here, but also, it would seem, no misgiving in Wordsworth's remarks about the poems. In revisiting the work and experience of the long past on this occasion, Wordsworth was treating both as he always did, as if work and life were essentially of the same substance—integrated, interdependent, indissoluble— and equally subject to re-inspection.

6

On Sarum's Plain

'These were farewell visits for life.'

(i)

The opening pages of *Yarrow Revisited, and Other Poems* strike the keynote of the collection itself and the era in Wordsworth's creative life to which it belonged—retrospection. An epigraph on the title-page from Akenside's *The Pleasures of the Imagination* highlights an indebtedness that dates from as far back as school-days in Hawkshead and although its message is positive—'Poets . . . dwell on earth | To clothe whate'er the soul admires and loves | With language and with numbers'—there is an air of belatedness about it. By 1835 it was late in the day to be invoking Akenside.[1] The following page is given over entirely to a dedication 'To Samuel Rogers, Esq. as a Testimony of Friendship, and an Acknowledgment of Intellectual Obligations'. Wordsworth read *The Pleasures of Memory* as soon as it was published in 1792 and with such a title it does not need explanation why, as Wu puts it, he 'should have found Rogers' poem interesting'.[2] What intellectual obligation Wordsworth felt he owed to the author of *The Voyage of Columbus* (1814) and *Italy* (1822–8) would not be easy to identify and his letters to Rogers demonstrate that he found it a struggle to be honest and yet complimentary when called upon to make a judgement on his poetic achievement.[3] But Rogers, the elder by seven years, was a survivor, one of the few who could still share memories of the heady 1790s, and by 1835 Wordsworth was naturally drawn to the dwindling number of his acquaintance who were. In 1829 William Calvert had died and the following years saw the deaths of Scott (1832), James Losh (1833), Coleridge (1834), Lamb (1834), Sara Hutchinson (1835), John Fleming (1835), Richard Sharp (1835), Robert Jones (1835), Raisley Calvert (1838). Given such loss of friends, when Wordsworth reminded Rogers that several of his poems were 'among my oldest and dearest acquaintance in the Literature of our day', he might have added that their author too was increasingly valued simply for the longevity of their connection.[4]

There were other prompts to the exercise of memory in the years following *Yarrow Revisited*. In 1836, as already noted in Chapter One, Wordsworth issued a completely revised edition of his collected poetical works in six volumes. Looked at from one point of view, this venture could be regarded as forward-looking, for, making a significant break with his past, Wordsworth transferred his business from Longmans to Edward Moxon. But the truth is that the 1836 edition was the product of a sustained backward look. At 66 years old Wordsworth was consciously shaping the 'Wordsworth' he wanted to go down to posterity and that meant close attention to everything he had been prepared to make public from school-days onwards. The self-inflicted labour of revision was enormous and necessarily most taxing when the elderly poet worked on 'the revisal of so many of the old Poems, to the re-modelling, and often re-writing whole Paragraphs'.[5]

Even public recognition, though welcome, could not but direct the glance backward. When Wordsworth was awarded an honorary degree by Oxford University in 1839 it was in recognition of past achievement. To dwell, as Keble did at the presentation ceremony, on how over his poetic lifetime Wordsworth had explored that 'secret and harmonious intimacy which exists between honourable Poverty, and the severer Muses, sublime Philosophy, yea, even our most holy Religion', was to affirm the coherence of all that he had done since *Lyrical Ballads* but inevitably with the note of summation. To the young Arnold and Clough, both in the audience in the Sheldonian Theatre, the white-haired 69-year-old honorand was a figure from history, fascinating, perhaps grand, but one whose richest experiences must have taken place before they were born.[6]

A return to the past was also called for when Wordsworth was approached late in the same year by Thomas Powell, who was angling for a contribution to his proposed *Poems of Geoffrey Chaucer, Modernized*.[7] Though wary—rightly—of the oleaginous Powell and equally so of his co-worker Richard Hengist Horne, Wordsworth was ready to furnish material for the sake of fostering readership of the 'mighty Genius', Chaucer, but first he had to find it.[8] Wordsworth had worked on translating *The Manciple's Tale* and *The Prioress's Tale* over the turn of the year 1801–2, but nothing had been published. As he and his growing family had moved from Dove Cottage to Allan Bank to the Grasmere vicarage and finally to Rydal Mount in the space of only a few years, however, it was not to be expected that his poetic archive would be sorted even if complete. 'With great diligence have Mrs Wordsworth and I looked in vain among my papers for the Mss which contains the Manciple's Tale, and if I am not mistaken a small portion of Troilus and Cressida', Wordsworth reported to Powell on 18 January 1840, adding that the manuscript, he recalled, contained 'also, by the bye, a Translation of two Books of Ariosto's Orlando, and this and other of its contents, I should be sorry to lose altogether'. Any 70-year-old rummaging through relics of forty years earlier would be assailed by memories and for Wordsworth on this occasion they must have been particularly poignant, for in so many respects 1802 was a turning-point year in his poetic life. Triggered by the search through old manuscripts, memories would have returned of the last months of intimacy with Dorothy in Dove Cottage, recorded in the journal of the beloved sister now mostly confined to her room; memories of his renewed determination to get on with *The Recluse*, the grand project, which he had recently had to acknowledge, finally and painfully, as abandoned; memories of all the signs that indicated with increasing certainty that the *annus mirabilis* with Coleridge in the Quantocks would not be replicated in the Lakes.

The elusive manuscripts for Powell's collection were found and so were many other fugitives, discoveries which prompted Wordsworth to one last effort at poetic husbandry, resulting in 1842 in the publication of his final discrete collection—*Poems, Chiefly of Early and Late Years*. In this collection a number of poems, readers could infer from their subject matter, had been products of the 'early' years of the title. Examples—and some of these have already been touched on in earlier chapters—might be 'Address to the Scholars of the Village School', origin 1798–9; 'At the Grave of Burns', origin 1803; 'Elegiac Verses', origin 1805; 'At Applethwaite', origin 1803–4; 'Lines on the Expected Invasion', origin 1803; 'Epistle to Sir G. H.

Beaumont', origin 1811. All of these poems, to a greater or lesser degree, were the result of revisiting old unpublished work. But it was the poem that opened the collection, *Guilt and Sorrow; or, Incidents Upon Salisbury Plain*, that embodied the most astonishing act of revisiting. It was one which spanned a greater period of time than any other revisiting Wordsworth dared to make.

That the poem belonged to a much earlier time Wordsworth revealed in a prefatory 'Advertisement', in which he dated it 'before the close of the year 1794'. It had its origins, he also revealed, in 'two days . . . wandering on foot over Salisbury Plain'.[9] What he did not tell his readers was that he had just made the journey again.

In May 1841 William and Mary Wordsworth travelled south for their daughter's wedding in Bath. Acknowledging that at his advanced age these 'were farewell visits for life', Wordsworth planned an itinerary almost guaranteed to stir depths of memory and emotion. A visit to the Wye Valley and Tintern was followed by what Mary Wordsworth called a 'Pilgrimage' to the Quantocks and Alfoxden, where, Isabella Fenwick reported, the poet 'was delighted to see again those scenes . . . where he had thought and felt so much'. It seems likely that a visit to Racedown was fitted in before, continuing to reverse the chronological movement of Wordsworth's actual life—1798–1795–1793—they crossed Salisbury Plain. Having a sense of the place as she did only through her husband's accounts of it, Mary Wordsworth was mildly disappointed to find that 'cultivation going on in many parts of the Plain takes sadly from the poetical feelings we had so *elaborately* attached to that region'.[10] What Wordsworth thought and felt as he looked across at Stonehenge from the highroad to Salisbury is not recorded.

(ii)

Whatever his feelings were on that day in May 1841, they had been stirring for some time. In 1837 Joseph Cottle had published his *Early Recollections, Chiefly Relating to the Late Samuel Taylor Coleridge*, in which, while giving an account of the negotiations that led to the publication of *Lyrical Ballads* in 1798, he had divulged the existence of the unpublished 'Salisbury Plain', with the additional comment that it 'was always with me a great favourite, and, with the exception of the "Excursion," the poem of all others, on which I thought Mr. Wordsworth might most advantageously rest his fame as a poet'.[11] When news had reached them in 1836 that Cottle was planning to include material disclosing the existence of *The Borderers*, there was anxiety in the Rydal Mount circle that Wordsworth might decide to destroy the tragedy.[12] Though Wordsworth certainly thought Cottle's venture lamentable, both in conception and execution, there is no evidence that Wordsworth entertained such a thought about *Salisbury Plain* and it is not inconceivable that when he eventually did read the critically ludicrous, but nonetheless flattering footnote about the poem he was not wholly displeased by it.

A year later, in 1838, John Kenyon, a friend known for nearly twenty years, had sent Wordsworth a copy of his collection, *Poems: For the Most Part Occasional*.[13] It was dedicated to Thomas Poole, who had died the previous year. For Kenyon, memories of Poole brought back his twenties, when he had lived near him over the years 1802–12 at Woodlands, between Alfoxden and Nether Stowey. With Wordsworth, though, memories of Poole reached back a decade earlier. It was Poole who had arranged for the Wordsworths to take a lease on Alfoxden House and who, after they had come to be regarded as dangerous undesirables, had vainly fought to help them retain it. It was Poole who had unobtrusively but vitally supported Coleridge, and Poole who through conversation and hospitality had been one of the strongest of the agents bonding the poetical inhabitants of Alfoxden and Nether Stowey. Memories of the tenor of his discourse must surely have been prompted by one poem in particular in Kenyon's collection: 'Inscription for a Vase', footnoted as 'Belonging to my late friend, Thomas Poole, Esq., and which enclosed a lock of Washington's hair'.[14] The glow of youthful radicalism had cooled since 1798, but Wordsworth's regard for this embodiment of intellectual liberalism had not diminished, not least because Poole was inextricable from memories of Coleridge. 'Your neighbourhood is very dear to me,' Wordsworth told him in 1836, 'the more so since poor Coleridge is gone.'[15]

Another poem in Kenyon's collection, however, was a doorway to memories that reached back even earlier than Alfoxden. 'Moonlight' consists of blank verse recollections mostly of childhood, a long way away in quality from the opening books of *The Prelude*, but not dissimilar in tone. It progresses through meditations on what the moon

meant to the poet, both through first-hand experience and as medi-
ated through books. One passage of heightened intensity concerns
Stonehenge. Once he was led, the narrator claims,

> To where the mighty mystery of Stonehenge
> Broods o'er the silent plain, and with mute power
> Rules the vast circuit of its sea-like space,
> As Thou dost rule the sky.[16]

What is Stonehenge? What does it represent? What era does it belong
to?—the monument prompts all the expected but unanswerable
questions, reinforcing the sense that this indecipherable monument is
indeed a 'mighty mystery'.

Wordsworth worked conscientiously through Kenyon's collection—'entertained by parts . . . and instructed also', he was, he
declared, 'not a little moved and pleased by others'. In particular, as
his thank-you letter makes clear, 'Moonlight' stirred Wordsworth
deeply with memories of his own journey on foot across Salisbury
Plain in 1793. 'I fall in exactly with your train of thinking and feeling
in your Moonlight', he told Kenyon. 'Stonehenge has given you at
your *advanced* years just such a feeling as he [*sic*] gave me when in my
23rd year, I passed a couple of days rambling about Salisbury Plain,
the solitude and solemnities of which prompted me to write a Poem
of some length in the Spenserian stanza.'[17] But what was that feeling?
When touching on his own history in his letters Wordsworth tended
to veer towards the studiedly unsensational. He had done so a year
before in a magnificent brush-off to Samuel Carter Hall: 'nothing
could be more bare of entertainment or interest than a biographical
notice of me must prove, if true . . . my life . . . has been so retired
and uniform.'[18] He did so again now in the letter to Kenyon, bringing
his little narrative to a close on a light-hearted note: 'Overcome with
heat and fatigue I took my Siesta among the Pillars of Stonehenge;
but was not visited by the Muse in my Slumbers.'

As has already been outlined in Chapter Three, however, the
other record of that time in *The Prelude*, Book XII, 312–53, tells a
very different story. In this account three, not two, days of solitude
induce hallucinatory reveries in which the traveller

> Saw multitudes of men, and here and there
> A single Briton in his wolf-skin vest,
> With shield and stone ax stride across the Wold;

> The voice of spears was heard, the rattling spear
> Shaken by arms of mighty bone, in strength
> Long moulder'd of barbaric majesty.
> I call'd upon the darkness; and it too,
> A midnight darkness seem'd to come and take
> All objects from my sight; and lo! again
> The desart visible by dismal flames!
> It is the sacrificial Altar, fed
> With living men—how deep the groans! the voice
> Of those in the gigantic wicker thrills
> Throughout the region far and near, pervades
> The monumental hillocks; and the pomp
> Is for both worlds, the living and the dead.

Did anything like this actually happen? I think it did and that recollections of it fused with others as factors impelling Wordsworth towards the creation of *Guilt and Sorrow; or, Incidents Upon Salisbury Plain*.

Wordsworth's 'a couple of days rambling' makes his traverse of Salisbury Plain in 1793 sound like a pleasant summer jaunt, when in fact it must have been an ordeal. What Dorothy Wordsworth called her brother's 'firm Friends, a pair of stout legs',[19] had performed astonishing feats day after day in France three years earlier, but that expedition had been planned and Wordsworth had enjoyed the support of his companion, Robert Jones. This pedestrian tour had not been planned; Wordsworth was alone; he had no money; and Salisbury Plain was inhospitable terrain. Where did he sleep? What did he eat and drink? How was he dressed and shod? Wordsworth was in a highly over-wrought state before he began what must have been a physically exhausting journey. It is not at all improbable that something momentous, some experience of imaginative intensity took place.

A further reason for believing that a 'spot of time' did occur is simply that *The Prelude* says it did. When experience is reported as being known at second-hand—the tale of Vaudracour and Julia, for example, or The Matron's Tale—it is presented as such, but otherwise *The Prelude* offers an account of what Wordsworth declares actually happened to him, not chronologically exact, maybe, but potentially verifiable. While one's willingness to credit the account at any given point is fostered by specificity—the hedgehog on the ascent of Snowdon, for example—it is not important whether such

details can be verified or not; but it would be quite fatal to the poem
were it to be proved that Wordsworth never did climb Snowdon or
ever rowed a boat out into Ullswater at night. As he folded the crossing of Salisbury Plain into the *Prelude*'s narrative more than ten years
after it took place, Wordsworth recalled the experience as including
moments of hallucinatory vision. Kenyon's 'Moonlight' brought
these recollections from their hiding-places a quarter of a century
deep and within months they were refreshed again as the final revision of *The Prelude* got under way.

What Kenyon's poem also stirred in Wordsworth, of course, was
memories of how crossing Salisbury Plain in 1793 had stirred him
poetically, that is, both what composition it inspired and what it—
the crossing and the composition—contributed to his sense (if any)
of himself as 'a poet'.

(iii)

To say that what Wordsworth was remembering was one of the most
turbulent periods of his life is so uncontentious an observation that
it calls for only the briefest recapitulation of the evidence for making
it. At barely 23 years of age, unemployed and without prospects but
having fathered a child on a woman in France, Wordsworth returned
to England to seek means of supporting himself and his family only
to break irretrievably with relatives who might have helped. War
was declared between the old enemies, France and Great Britain,
and Wordsworth, who was already nursing, justifiably, a sense of
personal injustice because of the Lonsdale debt, now discovered that
he was at odds with not only the government, the aristocracy, and
the institutions of his country, but also the rank and file of its people.
The mood music about Liberty and Reform that was still being
played when he had left England to live in France had given way
to more martial tunes by 1793 and Wordsworth was unprepared
for such a change. That the situation induced the torment both of
internal conflict and of intense loneliness is caught wonderfully in
the passage highlighted earlier in this book (*Prelude*, X, 227–74), in
which the young man, seething with suppressed anger and feeding
'on the day of vengeance, yet to come', sits in a village church among
the worshippers, 'like an uninvited Guest'.

A month's stay on the Isle of Wight in July 1793 did nothing to alleviate the burden of anxiety. What Wordsworth recalled in the 1842 'Advertisement' preceding *Guilt and Sorrow* was that, as he and William Calvert watched the fleet 'which was then preparing for sea off Portsmouth at the commencement of the war', he was filled with 'melancholy forebodings' that the struggle then beginning 'would be of long continuance, and productive of distress and misery beyond all possible calculation'.[20] The language of *Prelude*, X, 249–53 very strikingly conveys that what Wordsworth remembered most clearly about the pain of being torn by competing loyalties and affections was that it felt *unnatural*:

> I felt
> The ravage of this most unnatural strife
> In my own heart: there lay it like a weight,
> At enmity with all the tenderest springs
> Of my enjoyments.

Something of the same sense of unnaturalness, of the natural order being out of kilter, is caught in an uncompleted poem of 1793 that belongs to the Isle of Wight sojourn. Wordsworth looks out over the sea at twilight as Nature passes tranquilly from light to darkness:

> But hark from yon proud fleet in peal profound
> Thunders the sunset cannon; at the sound
> The star of life appears to set in blood
> Old ocean shudders in offended mood
> Deepening with moral gloom his angry flood.[21]

Quite what happened next remains unclear. In late July or early August Wordsworth and Calvert, it seems, returned to the mainland to resume their tour but decided to abandon it after an accident with their conveyance. They also, for whatever reason, decided to part company. When Wordsworth began the long haul across Salisbury Plain he was alone, shaken from an accident, and highly overwrought. It is not surprising that his mind worked with a sense of unknown modes of being. Whatever did happen on the Plain, it is certain that it was brought back to Wordsworth by perusal of Kenyon's 'Moonlight': 'My ramble over many parts of Salisbury plain . . . left upon my mind imaginative impressions the force of wh[ich] I have felt to this day.'[22] And that remark was made fifty years after the 'ramble' took place.

As Wordsworth's letter to Kenyon in the summer of 1838 makes clear, however, 'Moonlight' also stirred memories of how he had used his experience on Salisbury Plain poetically. The disclosure that he had written 'a Poem of some length in the Spenserian stanza' gave little away, but the preliminary 'Advertisement' to *Guilt and Sorrow* three years later was apparently more forthcoming. 'The Female Vagrant' had been known since its appearance in *Lyrical Ballads*, 1798, but actually, Wordsworth now revealed, it was an 'extract' from the longer poem being presented for the first time and 'it was necessary to restore it to its original position, or the rest would have been unintelligible'.[23] In the Fenwick Note to *Guilt and Sorrow* Wordsworth again commented on 'The Female Vagrant' as the earliest composition towards 'this Poem'. Nothing here is strictly speaking mendacious, but as he looked back from the secured position of having completed and published *Guilt and Sorrow; or, Incidents Upon Salisbury Plain*, Wordsworth tidied up the history of an imaginative project which had demanded not one but numerous revisitings.

(iv)

As Wordsworth sifted his recent experiences during composition of a new poem over 1793 to 1794 the site of the most intense of them seemed to provide the most suitable title for it: *Salisbury Plain*. That he was uneasy about the title is suggested by the jocoseness with which he answered an enquiry from William Mathews: 'You inquired after the name of one of my poetical bantlings, children of this species ought to be named after their characters, and here I am at a loss, as my offspring seems to have no character at all. I have however christened it by the appellation of Salisbury Plain, though A night on Salisbury plain, were it not so insufferably awkward, might better suit the thing itself.'[24]

Wordsworth's play on 'character' was not meant to be taken too seriously, but it is in fact apt for the poem. *Salisbury Plain*, though for the most part a narrative poem, consists of figures, not characters. A traveller—no name, age, or occupation—trudges westward over 'Sarum's plain'.[25] Late in the poem we learn that he 'had withered young in sorrow's deadly blight', but nothing more about his past. As if in a nightmare, he hears voices warning him that he is trespassing on a 'baleful place' that belongs to 'hell's most cursed sprites', who will torment him to madness unless he carries on through the gathering storm. Exhausted to the point of 'wishing the repose | Of death', he eventually stumbles on a ruin that provides some shelter. It is already occupied by 'a female wanderer'—no name—who tells of her encounter with an old man—no name—carrying a rusty gun. In sun and shower this feeble bird-scarer remains completely alone, save for his famished dog; his tottering step indicates that he too is barely clinging to life. Though familiar with the wide fields of corn, the old man knows that the plain is also a place of mystery and he tells the woman 'Much of the wonders of that boundless heath', speaking of fires lighting the night sky, sacrificial altars with living victims, huge crowds, and the Druids in ritual ceremonials. The Female Vagrant explains how she comes to be wandering alone across Salisbury Plain, but tells her story without revealing her name or her wronged father's or her dead husband's. Morning breaks, bringing some comfort as the 'friendless hope-forsaken pair' reach a cottage in a valley. Here they will be revived with a simple meal, but this is not a fade-out on a happy ending. 'Friendless'—the word is repeated in successive lines—the two must take their several roads.

Salisbury Plain is a poem of encounters, but it is unlike the later encounter poems which are amongst Wordsworth's finest work, in that the figures in *Salisbury Plain* are anonymous emblems, unrealized by names or occupations or idiosyncrasies, and in that the poet himself does not participate in the encounter. How different *Salisbury Plain* would be, if the Woman were named, as Margaret is in *The Ruined Cottage*, if she referred to her lost husband as Robert, or if it were the poet-speaker who hears her story, as he hears that of the shepherd in 'The Last of the Flock'. In *Salisbury Plain* the human beings are figures in a tableau framed by the poet's observations on them as emblems of contemporary life. The narrative ends with a rhetorical salute:

> Adieu ye friendless hope-forsaken pair!
> Yet friendless ere ye take your several road,
> Enter that lowly cot and ye shall share
> Comforts by prouder mansions unbestowed.
> For you yon milkmaid bears her brimming load,
> For you the board is piled with homely bread,
> And think that life is like this desert broad,

> Where all the happiest find is but a shed
> And a green spot 'mid wastes interminably spread.

But though the narrative has ended, the poem has not. It began with four stanzas of homiletic declamation and ends with thirteen more, which frame the story of the two vagrants as evidence that many thousands such as these are weeping now, 'Beset with foes more fierce than e'er assail | The savage without home in winter's keenest gale'.

Wordsworth's observation that his poetic offspring 'seems to have no character at all' is worth examining, however, from a different point of view. It might be as accurate to say that on the contrary *Salisbury Plain* has too clearly identifiable a character, none of the elements of which are unique to it. Since the publication in 1975 of a complete and easily readable text of the poem, evidence of its allegiances and indebtednesses has accumulated.[26] The pathos of the Female Vagrant's tale has been seen to link her to comparable suffering figures in Goldsmith, Langhorne, and Shenstone—the latter two being poets praised by Wordsworth for bringing 'the Muse into the Company of common life'.[27] Echoes of Thomson and Chatterton have been identified. The overwhelming influence, of course, is Spenser, or rather, Spenser-through-James-Beattie. In *Salisbury Plain* Wordsworth recalls many phrases from *The Minstrel* (1771–4), a poem he had loved since Hawkshead school-days and which—although perhaps he never knew this—provided Dorothy Wordsworth with a way of understanding her brother—'the whole character of Edwin resembles much what William was when I first knew him after my leaving Halifax.'[28]

The didactic thrust of the poem is similarly highly characterized, but not at all individual. Rousseau and Paine stand out amongst others as ideological progenitors. The sacrificial altars of the Druids owe as much, it seems, to what Wordsworth has absorbed from traditional and contemporary interpretations of Stonehenge as from his imaginative response to the monument itself. Salisbury Cathedral and its ancient clock, Old Sarum, the topography of the plain, even the emblem of the 'smoking cottage' that welcomes the vagrants— all these elements of the poem bring with them established meanings from other contemporary discourses, meanings which—consciously or unconsciously—Wordsworth exploits in *Salisbury Plain*. Philip

Shaw, for example, has highlighted how pervasive is the 'image of the destitute and grieving widow in war poetry of the 1790s'. Stephen Behrendt notes how often 'British writing of the war years' voices the 'bitter and largely inconsolable grief' of the bereaved, especially women such as the Female Vagrant. John Barrell's observation that the cottage 'as the site of an idealized, private, domestic life, was far more widely invoked in the 1790s than in the 1770s or 1780s' is directly apposite to the Female Vagrant's account of her birth-place cottage and the description of the 'lowly cot' to which she walks in stanza 46 of *Salisbury Plain*. Reading the poem as 'an engagement with the antiquarian strains of British radicalism in the early 1790s', Tom Dugget demonstrates how the plain itself and Stonehenge have long figured in competing histories of British 'Liberty'.[29]

Many more indebtednesses, echoes, and analogues could be paraded. In short, *Salisbury Plain*, just like the *Letter to the Bishop of Llandaff*, is an identikit protest polemic of the early 1790s. In both the poem and the prose tract there is nothing factitious about either the generalized anger and bitterness that fuels them or about the denunciation of specific outrages, but the commanding structure of ideas consists essentially of radical commonplaces. In a world dominated by the tyranny of unjust power, the poor fare worse than the hungry savage; he at least shares his suffering with 'men who all of his hard lot partake' and together with them can subdue the evils he faces by the strength of his own arm. How unlike the lot of the Female Vagrant whose young life has been blighted by injustice, economic necessity, careless cruelty, and finally the loss of husband and children through the ravages of war. But hers is the common and inevitable lot of the powerless, whose rulers export 'Injury and Strife, | Outrage and deadly Hate', straining for empire, while denying 'Justice and the kindly train | Of Peace and Truth' in their own countries, whose peoples 'crushed by their own fetters helpless sink, | Move their galled limbs in fear and eye each silent link'. Richard Gravil tartly but justifiably describes the stanzas in which these propositions are advanced as a 'digest of Price and Priestley'.[30]

The author of *Salisbury Plain* may be marching under the same banner as Price and Priestley, but invoking them here serves to emphasize not similarity but a significant difference between them. In *A Discourse on the Love of our Country*, delivered in November 1789 in the Meeting-House in the Old Jewry, Richard Price rapturously welcomed the new era in which he saw 'the dominion of kings changed for the dominion of laws, and the dominion of priests giving way to the dominion of reason and conscience', a vision which was broadcast to a far greater audience the following year when Burke assailed him in *Reflections on the Revolution in France*.[31] That Joseph Priestley, another Dissenter, had a public face and reputation was demonstrated unequivocally when a Birmingham mob burnt his house down in 1791. Both of these Friends of Liberty made a public impact through their writings and personal profile. *Salisbury Plain* made no impact outside its author's small circle. Discussion of the poem's merits as political protest, with citation of analogues from other contemporary verse featuring vagrants and bereaved women, ought always to register that its merits were unknown, its contemporaneity unnoticed, its impact nil, because it was not published.[32]

Why it was not published, or apparently not even offered for publication, remains an unsettled question. There were very good reasons for being cautious, as the Pitt government moved on to a war footing and began to clamp down on sedition in all its guises.[33] It may be that Wordsworth was dissatisfied artistically and that even as Dorothy was completing the fair-copy manuscript of *Salisbury Plain* in 1794 he knew that the poem was not adequate. But whatever the cause of the non-appearance of the poem, the young radical, who forcefully spelt out his republican principles to William Mathews in 1794—'I am of that odious class of men called democrats'—cannot but have been aware that the rhetoric of his poem, voiced but not heard, was impotent.[34]

> Heroes of Truth pursue your march, up tear
> Th'Oppressor's dungeon from its deepest base;
> High o'er the towers of Pride undaunted rear
> Resistless in your might the herculean mace
> Of Reason; let foul Error's monster race
> Dragged from their dens start at the light with pain
> And die; pursue your toils, till not a trace
> Be left on earth of Superstition's reign,
> Save that eternal pile which frowns on Sarum's plain.

Richard Price similarly addressed comrades in arms: 'Be encouraged, all ye friends of freedom, and writers in its defence! The times are auspicious. Your labours have not been in vain. Behold kingdoms, admonished by you, starting from sleep, breaking their fetters, and claiming justice from their oppressors!'[35] Price, though, knew he had an audience and had ample evidence that his chosen means of reaching it—a prose sermon—had caused a stir, that it was a contribution to public debate. As Wordsworth looked over *Salisbury Plain* in 1794, the Treason Trials were opening in London. At this moment of high tension—what Godwin in his literally life-saving intervention called, 'the most important crisis in the history of English liberty, that the world ever saw'[36]— Wordsworth must have pondered whether the voice of poetry could make itself heard in the current ideological cacophony and how any work of his might hope to be adequate in the cause of human liberty.[37]

He perhaps also wondered about the form he had chosen. As a poetic model and resource Spenser-through-Beattie was not without problems, or at least potential problems. Emphasizing Beattie's significance for the Spenserian renaissance at the turn of the eighteenth century, Greg Kucich rightly points out that, 'What made *The Minstrel* so attractive was its elaborate drama about a maturing poet's division between imaginative beauty and intellectual truth.'[38] To which one might add that *The Minstrel*, especially Book One, offered Wordsworth a model of the Spenserian stanza deployed with great skill and it must have been immensely heartening to the young Beattie admirer that he proved just as capable himself of handling it. But, as Kucich encapsulates in his formulation 'division between imaginative beauty and intellectual truth', by the time Wordsworth chose to use it, the Spenserian stanza was firmly fixed in an interpretative discourse that, playing off moralizing against the creation of beauty, determined to some extent the artistic freedoms available to any given poetic project. And so, at the all-important technical level, did the structure of the stanza itself. When Wordsworth commented on it at some length many years later, what he emphasized were the technical challenges of an 'almost insurmountably difficult' form. Solemnly passing on considered judgements to a fellow practitioner, it was perhaps with some ruefulness that Wordsworth recalled his own struggles with the stanza thirty and more years before. The Spenserian stanza, though 'a fine structure of verse', was, he advised Catherine Grace Godwin, 'ill adapted to conflicting passion', 'unfit for narrative' and, 'for circumstantial narrative', impossible to succeed in, because of 'the poverty of our language in rhymes'.[39]

(v)

At five hundred and forty-nine lines in a challenging verse form *Salisbury Plain* was a substantial achievement. A considerable amount of labour went into the composition of it; the imaginative organization of the disparate elements of the whole is impressive. Nonetheless, within a year of completing a fair-copy of it, Wordsworth was taking it apart and in so doing he confirmed the pattern of work he was to follow for the rest of his life. In 1793 he had published *An Evening Walk*. Less than a year later he greatly revised it.[40] A year after that he returned to *Salisbury Plain*. By November 1795 he was referring to that poem as a 'first draught' to which, he told Francis Wrangham, he had 'made alterations and additions so material as that it may be looked on almost as another work'.[41] 'Almost' is quite telling. Wordsworth always revisited his work boldly, willing to engage in recasting to almost any extent, but the originating germ always remained in whatever form a poem might eventually take. So it was with *Salisbury Plain*. The Female Vagrant's tale survived as a major element in the poem's attempt to awaken humane sympathies through representative human stories, but what was added to it was so substantial that the next version could indeed be 'looked on almost as another work'.

Adventures on Salisbury Plain opens directly with a human encounter. Gone are the declamatory stanzas that opened *Salisbury Plain*, replaced by a meeting between a sick old man, once a soldier, now barely able to totter along the skirt of Salisbury Plain, and a discharged sailor. Having assisted the old man, the sailor presses on and eventually meets the vagrant woman. His story has been related by the narrator—press-ganged, discharged, denied his just reward, the sailor has killed a traveller in a botched robbery and is now on the run—but the woman tells her own tale of comparable suffering. A soldier's widow, she too is destitute. The two vagrants find comfort in one another's company and share the same sense of sympathetic grief when they encounter another poor family, whose head has just beaten his infant son to the ground. But worse is to come. A further chance encounter brings the sailor face to face with his wife and he learns that she has been driven out of her home by suspicion that her husband was the killer of the stranger lying dead by her door. Homeless, and denied relief by unfeeling overseers, she dies, but not before her husband has revealed himself to her and begged forgiveness. Kindly cottagers ensure that the sailor's widow is properly buried, but it becomes clear to them that her husband is the guilty man. Now resolute, the sailor turns himself over to the authorities and 'Justice' is done. The poem ends with his gibbeted body swinging in the wind.

When Wordsworth told Wrangham about his recent composition late in 1795, he defined it through its social and ideological context: '. . . almost as another work. Its object is partly to expose the vices of the penal law and the calamities of war as they affect individuals.' It is fully understandable why he should have thought of the poem in terms of its historical moment, for it was coming into being at a particularly bad one for reformers of every hue. The government's failure to obtain guilty verdicts in the 1794 Treason Trials did not, as an exultant Wordsworth declared it would, 'abate the insolence and presumption of the aristocracy by shewing it that neither the violence, nor the art, of power can crush even an unfriended individual, though engaged in the propagation of doctrines confessedly unpalatable to privilege'.[42] On the contrary, the Treasonable Practices Bill and the Seditious Meetings Bill, both passed in November 1795, together with the continued suspension of Habeas Corpus, ensured that the propagation of such doctrines became increasingly difficult and risky. Had Thelwall, Tooke, Hardy, Holcroft, and the other defendants been found guilty, their lives would most probably have been gruesomely forfeited, but one did not need to engage in High Treason to end up on the gallows. In his *Letter to the Bishop of Llandaff* Wordsworth had inveighed against 'laws partial and oppressive' and a penal code 'crowded with disproportioned penalties and indiscriminate severity'.[43] When he returned to such language in his November 1795 letter to Wrangham—'the vices of the penal law'— there were over two hundred offences for which a guilty verdict could mean death.[44]

For those among the poor who avoided the gallows, the recruiting sergeant, and the press-gang, conditions in general worsened dramatically in 1795 as a result of bad harvest and the economic impact of funding a war.[45] Evidence of poverty and distress, such as that which in this year prompted the creation of the Speenhamland system, was very obvious to the Wordsworths when they moved to Racedown.[46] 'The country people here are wretchedly poor', Wordsworth reported to Mathews. Dorothy wrote in similar terms: 'The peasants are miserably poor; their cottages are shapeless structures (I may almost say) of wood and clay—indeed they are not at all beyond what might be expected in savage life.'[47] They could not know that historians would later characterize it without exaggeration as 'a year of near-famine'. At the beginning of the year Sheridan had made play in the House of Commons on the contrast between ministers 'scrambling for places and pensions' and the poor struggling to afford bread and coal.[48] Just how justified this rhetorical flourish was the Wordsworths knew from personal experience by the end of the winter 1795–6, for coal had become prohibitively expensive: 'You would be surprized', Dorothy told Jane Marshall, 'to see what a small cart full we get for three or four and twenty shillings.'[49]

Wordsworth was keenly alive to the distresses of this dark time, but he was not alone in that. Where he was alone was in the struggle to find a voice and a role. To him as young would-be poet the duty to speak out on social issues necessarily presented itself in the form of artistic difficulties to be identified and surmounted.

The revised version of *Salisbury Plain* was intended, Wordsworth told Wrangham, 'partly to expose the vices of the penal law and the calamities of war as they affect individuals'.[50] As the synopsis just given has indicated, *Adventures on Salisbury Plain* is peopled with suffering figures whose history and present condition testify to the calamities of war—the sick and poor old soldier; the discharged sailor, who has been twice robbed, of his liberty by the press-gang and of his just reward for service by the 'slaves of Office'; his destitute wife, harried by unfeeling Poor Law overseers; the traveller whom in desperation he robbed and killed; the impoverished labouring family with the violent father; the female vagrant, a soldier's widow who has lost everything. That these are the stock figures of radical protest poetry, soon to be parodied in the *Anti-Jacobin*, does not reduce their representative weight—such figures really could be encountered as the war took its course. But successful depiction of how the calamities of war affect individuals requires something denser, more varied, and more interesting than just a parade of specimen figures in tableaux. In its revised version the poem works through a structure in which declamation has been replaced by narrative and dramatic interplay. Some of the life-histories are only cursorily sketched in, such as that of the old soldier who opens the poem skirting Salisbury Plain. The two important ones are presented more fully. How and why the sailor and the soldier's widow are in their present situation is accounted for in some detail, as is the desperate plight of the sailor's wife.

In its deployment of these narratives the poem anticipates the story-telling poet of *The Excursion* and via that poem the author of *Adam Bede* and *Silas Marner*. That people's lives are interconnected adventitiously is brought out clearly enough, but what is also emphasized is the moral dimension linking past and present acts and encounters and its relation to the irresistible force of Law and Power. It is chance that confronts the sailor with his wretched wife, but it is something more than chance that makes him realize his responsibility for her suffering and his guilt as a murderer. It is also important that most of the figures in *Adventures on Salisbury Plain* are at the bottom of the social pile and all of them are lowly. 'Nature's unambitious underwood', the Pastor in *The Excursion* would later call them in a phrase that spoke to George Eliot at the very beginning of her career.[51] The soldier's widow is a Vagrant, a social category firmly recognized in the 1790s as a growing nuisance; the sailor's widow is every Poor Law ratepayer's nightmare, an out-of-parish dependant; the sailor is a fugitive thief and murderer; even the kindly housewife and her husband in the cottage can only offer the comforts of 'a rustic Inn'.[52] Each one of these figures, however, turns instinctively, open-heartedly, to their own like. When Wordsworth introduced 'Michael' and 'The Brothers' to Fox in 1801 he was commending much finer poems than *Adventures on Salisbury Plain*, but the terms of his commendation can be applied to the earlier as well as the later work: this is poetry 'written with a view to shew that men who do not wear fine cloaths can feel deeply'.[53]

Viewed in the light of Wordsworth's whole body of work *Adventures on Salisbury Plain* dwindles in stature, but it was important to Wordsworth, because it offered him further evidence of the depth of his own poetic resources and—as one may infer from what happened next—because with it Wordsworth reached the point of knowing that he wanted to be something more than a closet intellectual radical who wrote verses. He wanted an actual, not a notional audience. At the beginning of 1796 he was confident enough to promise Joseph Cottle an early glimpse of his Salisbury Plain manuscript. A copy was dispatched to Bristol and in March he was contemplating publication by subscription. Coleridge was immensely taken with the poem; Lamb hurried through it 'not without delight'; in April its appearance within a few weeks seemed certain. But the hopes of the early summer came to nothing.[54] The second version of the Salisbury Plain poem circulated in a wider circle than the first, but it too remained unpublished, admired by a coterie but otherwise unknown.

(vi)

The poem that had emerged from Wordsworth's experiences on Salisbury Plain was losing its hold as an imaginative possibility. Sometime in 1796, perhaps even while the mirage of publication was still beckoning, Wordsworth seems to have worked on verse related to the landscape of the plain and the woman's story, but by October he was 'ardent in the composition of a tragedy' and for the moment *Adventures on Salisbury Plain* ceased to engage him.[55] Before long, however, the poem was again under consideration in reopened negotiations with Cottle: 'I say nothing of the Salisbury plain 'till I see you, I am determined to finish it, and equally so that You shall publish.'[56] It is a revealing declaration. No matter how much Wordsworth had done to the poem since moving into Racedown, he could not, characteristically, regard it as final, and though he may have thought he was 'determined to finish it', whatever he had in mind did not come into being.

The next step in the history of the poem's revisiting entailed a lot more than tinkering: it was dismembered altogether. In the summer of 1798 the woman's tale was excerpted under the title 'The Female Vagrant', an excision which helped bulk out the *Lyrical Ballads* collection which Wordsworth, Coleridge, and Cottle had finally agreed on, but which crippled the poem. Either substantial fresh composition was required for a narrative of specifically female sufferings to balance the sailor's story, or the structure of the whole poem had to be reshaped. Neither happened.

The raw material for a human drama with a local setting was given to Wordsworth and Coleridge by Tom Poole and it has been plausibly suggested that what Wordsworth worked up from it was for a while conceived as being integrated into *Adventures on Salisbury Plain*.[57] The story concerns a Quantocks charcoal-burner called John Walford, who, though promised to a certain Ann Rice, is forced to marry a half-witted girl he has made pregnant. Eventually the misery of his marriage is such that he is driven to murder her. At his execution, which he makes no attempt to avoid, Walford is reconciled to his beloved Ann and he dies asking for the world's and God's forgiveness for a crime he never intended to commit.

Whether Wordsworth composed *A Somersetshire Tragedy* with the needs of *Adventures on Salisbury Plain* in mind or whether the poem was already written and he just saw the possibility of using it in the creation of a new version of the now mutilated *Adventures* cannot be determined from what little manuscript evidence has survived,[58] but what is clear is that there are at least two grounds for thinking that the Walford story did not seem an artistic possibility for very long. The first is simply that Wordsworth needed a story that brought out a woman's sufferings, whereas the focus of sympathy in *A Somersetshire Tragedy* must be the man's. Ann (apparently Agnes in Wordsworth's poem) does suffer, but she survives. The murdered woman is not presented in extant accounts as someone who could be dramatized as anything other than a sad victim of her sex and mental incapacity. But Walford is an essentially good man brought low, who goes to the gallows in the same spirit as the sailor in *Adventures on Salisbury Plain*.

The second ground is that from what little Wordsworth says about it, it sounds as if he had lost interest in, or patience with, the whole poetic venture. Towards the end of a very long catching-up letter to Coleridge early in 1799 Wordsworth vouchsafed:

I also took courage to devote two days (O Wonder) to the Salisbury Plain. I am resolved to discard Robert Walford and invent a new story for the woman. The poem is finished all but her tale. Now by way of a pretty moving accident and to bind together in palpable knots the story of the piece I have resolved to make her the widow or sister or daughter of the man whom the poor Tar murdered. So much for the vulgar. Further the Poets invention goeth not. This is by way of giving a physical totality to the piece, which I regard as finish'd minus 24 stanzas the utmost tether allowed to the poor Lady.[59]

The substance of this declaration is interesting—the details of plotting changes help date and explain surviving manuscript materials, as does the assertion that the poem is 'finished' though admittedly up to twenty-four stanzas have yet to be written; the mention of Walford confirms some link between the poem and *A Somersetshire Tragedy*.[60] What is altogether more revealing than the substance of this declaration, however, is its tone. The jocularity, the drop into archaism, above all the reference to the Female Vagrant as a 'poor Lady' who is to be allowed a certain 'tether', all indicate how far Wordsworth had travelled since the 'vices of the penal law' letter to Wrangham of November 1795. Then the emerging *Adventures on Salisbury Plain* was at the centre of Wordsworth's creative endeavour: now he is barely taking the poem seriously.

The main reason why is suggested by one phrase in the progress report to Coleridge—'pretty moving accident'. Wordsworth was to use it again only months later, when the narrator's profession that 'The moving accident is not my trade' in 'Hart-Leap Well' was a significant element in the artistic manifesto embodied in the Preface to *Lyrical Ballads* 1800 and the poems in the second volume.[61] It emerged from events and the pursuit of ideas that confirmed the direction of Wordsworth's life and the nature of his identity as a poet which had been taking shape over the *annus mirabilis*. At the beginning of the period, 1797–8, *Adventures on Salisbury Plain* was already moribund, displaced by *The Borderers* and *The Ruined Cottage*. Its demise as a current project became inevitable when Wordsworth took stock over 1798 to 1799 and made his choice of life. Many factors coalesced. With Napoleon's subjugation of the Swiss, it was farewell to those aspects of the earlier self that had identified with the French cause. Recognition of what obligations were entailed in acknowledging a vocation as the philosophic poet of *The Recluse* generated as much anxiety about the future as excitement, as did the courageous, if not foolhardy decision to return to a remote part of northern England in the hope of there 'being enabled to construct a literary Work that might live'. All these factors were important, but the chief one in relation to *Adventures on Salisbury Plain* was that Wordsworth's choice of life was inseparable from a new and confident sense of artistic direction.

Over the winter of 1798–9 Wordsworth had begun to theorize what was voiced in a variety of dramatic ways in the lyrics of the summer of 1798, namely, that 'Poetry is passion: it is the history or science of feelings' and that it was to be valued according to the degree to which it either generated them afresh or called them from their hidden recesses. When he read Bürger, Wordsworth told Coleridge, he had no 'recollection of delicate or minute feelings which he has either communicated to me, or taught me to recognise', a shortcoming which was ascribed fundamentally to reliance on 'incidents'.[62] These, Wordsworth declared, 'are among the lowest allurements of poetry', preparing the ground for the most important claim in the 1800 Preface to *Lyrical Ballads*, namely, that in these poems 'the feeling therein developed gives importance to the action and situation, and not the action and situation to the feeling'.[63] By the time of writing to Coleridge in February 1799 Wordsworth's thinking about the manner in which poetry might offer stimulation, but not 'outrageous stimulation',[64] and about the relation in any tale between story and incidents, was not yet fully developed, but it was firm enough in essentials for it to be clear that *Adventures on Salisbury Plain* belonged to the past. The 'poor Lady' was not to get the twenty-four new stanzas allowed her and quite soon Wordsworth's judgement of the poem and the genre to which it belonged had hardened. By 1801 overt protest poetry had come to seem suspect as verging on 'jacobinical pathos'. Reporting Coleridge's 'severest reprehension' of 'those writers who seem to estimate their power of exciting sorrow for suffering humanity, by the quantity of hatred and revenge which they are able to pour into the hearts of their Readers', Wordsworth declared his own conviction that 'the human heart can never be moved to any salutary purposes in this way'. And on the same day, in a separate letter to the sister of the recipient of the one just quoted, Wordsworth revealed how far he had left the Salisbury Plain poems behind. Commenting on 'The Female Vagrant' to Anne Taylor, he observed that 'the diction of that Poem is often vicious and the descriptions are often false, giving proofs of a mind inattentive to the true nature of the subject on which it was employed'.[65] This was self-criticism as pointed as it could be. In the Preface to *Lyrical Ballads* the year before, Wordsworth (identified by name for the first time in this edition) had written, 'I do not know how . . . I can give my Reader a more exact notion of the style in which I wished these poems to be written than by informing him that I have at all times endeavoured to look steadily at my subject . . .'.[66]

Wordsworth's comments to Anne Taylor in 1801 quickened, not unexpectedly, the impulse to revision. It was not enough to make a generalized point about what was wrong with 'The Female Vagrant': the opportunity was taken to make 'a few corrections of this poem in which I have endeavoured to bring the language nearer to truth'. In fact 'a few corrections' amounted to radical surgery. Whole stanzas were deleted, others completely remodelled. As an admirer of *Lyrical Ballads*, Anne Taylor must have been astonished by the poet's readiness to declare, 'Omit the first stanza entirely . . . omit the 3rd and 4th stanzas' and was perhaps left wondering how she was supposed to enter new readings into her volume by the unintentionally comical statement, 'Page 70 the line "His little range of water was denied" must have another substituted for it which I have not written.' By the time of the third edition of *Lyrical Ballads* in 1802 the line had been written and the other corrections had been incorporated, which notably softened the social protest element of the poem. As Basil Willey long ago pointed out,[67] the description of soldiers as 'the brood | That lap (their very nourishment!) their brother's blood', for example, was excised. For the 1815 collective *Poems* the process was taken still further. Classed under 'Juvenile Pieces', 'The Female Vagrant' was now reduced to such a severely truncated form (thirteen full stanzas only), with the abandonment of the accounts of how injustice destroyed her father and how her husband was driven to become a soldier, that an introductory sentence was required if readers were to make sense of what was left of the woman's story: 'Having described her own Situation with her Husband, serving in America during the War, she proceeds'. Then follows 'All perished— all, in one remorseless year . . .'.

The full version of 'The Female Vagrant' was restored for the next collective edition in 1820, but though the restoration indicated some continuing attention to the poem, Wordsworth's creative engagement with the Salisbury Plain project had lapsed.

(vii)

Stirred by the various promptings discussed earlier in this chapter, Wordsworth returned to it in 1841. The manuscript version abandoned in 1799 was looked out and heavily worked over; a new manuscript was prepared, largely by Mary Wordsworth, which was also revised. It was substantial labour and, as always, very pernickety. In some passages in the new manuscript, for example, Wordsworth revised the fair-copy so intensively that it became illegible. Recognizing that no printer could be expected to set type from such a mess, Wordsworth transferred the new readings to other slips of paper which were stuck on to the original with sealing wax. On occasion, though, even these versions were subjected to further crossings out and revision. Inevitably tinkering did not stop with the beginning of the production process. Both first and second proof stages enabled further scrutiny of the text. The result was a new poem and a new title. In every previous version the poem's title had advertised its setting—*Salisbury Plain*; *A Night on Salisbury Plain*; *Adventures on Salisbury Plain*— now it did so only as a secondary consideration. *Guilt and Sorrow; or, Incidents Upon Salisbury Plain* was its title when after such long gestation this poem finally appeared in *Poems, Chiefly of Early and Late Years* (1842).

The historicizing note of the volume's title was picked up by the 'Advertisement' that preceded *Guilt and Sorrow*. Declaring that 'the whole [poem] was written before the close of the year 1794', Wordsworth explained the relation of 'The Female Vagrant' to it before offering, 'rather as a matter of literary biography than for any other reason' an account of 'the circumstances under which it was produced'. The main portion of it reads:

During the latter part of the summer of 1793, having passed a month in the Isle of Wight, in view of the fleet which was then preparing for sea off Portsmouth at the commencement of the war, I left the place with melancholy forebodings. The American war was still fresh in memory. The struggle which was beginning, and which many thought would be brought to a speedy close by the irresistible arms of Great Britain being added to those of the allies, I was assured in my own mind would be of long continuance, and productive of distress and misery beyond all possible calculation. This conviction was pressed upon me by having been a witness, during a long residence in revolutionary France, of the spirit which prevailed in that country. After leaving the Isle of Wight, I spent two days in wandering on foot over Salisbury Plain . . . .

The monuments and traces of antiquity, scattered in abundance over that region, led me unavoidably to compare what we know or guess of those remote times with certain aspects of modern society, and with calamities, principally those consequent upon war, to which, more than other classes of men, the poor are subject.

Readers in 1842 would have needed to be intimate with Wordsworth's particular way of conceiving the life of his poems— essentially the subject of this book—to have been able to register in what sense to understand the mendacious assertion that the whole of this newly-published poem was written before the end of 1794; and they might have been intrigued to probe further into the claims of the 'Advertisement' had they known that in drafting it Wordsworth had originally given a different date of composition—1795—and had declared, 'How it came to be so long suppressed is of no importance to the Reader.' 'Suppressed' has a power quite lost in the more anodyne, 'I will detail, rather as a matter of literary biography, the circumstances under which it was produced'.[68] In fact there was nothing here to agitate either Wordsworth's loyal following or younger readers new to his work. Neither the 'Advertisement' to *Guilt and Sorrow* nor the poem itself need have shaken anyone's sense of what kind of poet Wordsworth was. The 'Advertisement' declares that when the poem was composed the horrors of war were fresh in mind from the American campaigns—true; that Wordsworth had seen enough of the French to judge that a war with them would be bound to be of long duration—true; and that the inevitable suffering entailed in such a war would bear more hardly on the poor than on any other class—true. What the 'Advertisement' implicitly confirms is the complete congruence between the opinions of the young poet of the 1790s and those of his later self, the author of sonnets on National Independence and Liberty.

There was, moreover, almost nothing in the public domain to suggest anything else. None of the evidence which now informs scholarly treatments of Wordsworth's radical years was available. The *Letter to the Bishop of Llandaff*, Wordsworth's long letters to William Mathews in 1794 avowing his 'odious' democratic alle- giances, the unequivocal revelations of Books Nine and Ten of *The Prelude*—all remained private.[69] When Coleridge had assured Joseph Cottle in 1798 that whereas his name stank, 'Wordsworth's name is nothing', he was right.[70] Of course something of the complexion of the young Wordsworth's politics could be gleaned from *Biographia Literaria* (1817), from Hazlitt in *The Spirit of the Age* (1825), from Cottle's *Early Recollections, Chiefly Relating to the late Samuel Taylor Coleridge* (1837), and most recently from De Quincey's unwelcome memoirs in *Tait's Edinburgh Magazine* (1839). Nothing at all in any of these retrospective pieces, however, would suggest for a moment that Wordsworth had been anything other than an English patriot.[71] Perhaps the knowledge that Byron and Shelley were amongst those who regarded Wordsworth as a one-time radical turncoat might have caused some readers to wonder whether the revelation provided in the 'Advertisement' of the circumstances in which *Guilt and Sorrow* was produced was all that might be said on the subject. But it was not very likely. And the most important reason why was simply that nothing in the poem that appeared for the first time in 1842 as *Guilt and Sorrow; or, Incidents Upon Salisbury Plain* need have given rise to questions about the political orientation of the young man who, roaming across Salisbury Plain, had been led 'unavoidably to compare what we know or guess of those remote times with certain aspects of modern society . . .'.

In the substantial recasting that resulted in the version of 1842 the earlier poems had been changed in matters of detail in such a way that aspects of their historical significance were disguised or even eliminated. Overall the narrative was tightened by reducing the number of dramatis personae, by excising some of the Gothic heightening, such as the sailor's trance in stanzas 45–6 of *Adventures on Salisbury Plain*, and by cutting out the episode in which the good cottagers wrestle with their feelings on learning of the sailor's guilt. These changes, it could be argued, make *Guilt and Sorrow* a better poem rhetorically than *Adventures on Salisbury Plain* without really altering its impact as a whole. The apparently smaller, more local changes do.[72] In the last version of the poem most of the painful details about the soldier's past at the beginning of *Adventures* have been cut. The 'ruffian press gang dire' becomes a body of seamen who themselves have been victims and who act only reluctantly, ' 'Gainst all that in *his* heart, or theirs perhaps, said nay' (l. 54). When the sailor returns to England he is denied his just reward by 'fraud' rather than 'the slaves of office'. Details of why the Female Vagrant's father 'fails' are spared. The earlier description of soldiers as 'the brood | That lap (their very nourishment!) their brother's blood' is removed, as is the evocation of the Rape and Murder of Mother and Child as fixed features of War (*Adventures*, ll. 445–7). In earlier-stage revision to *Salisbury Plain* the sailor tries to cheer the woman by talk of 'social Order's care', but it is made clear that this is 'delusion fond' invoked solely from his concern at her fragile psychological state. In *Guilt and Sorrow*, a quite different sense is conveyed—there is reason to trust in an ultimately benevolent order. At the end of the Female Vagrant's account of her sufferings, stanza 51 takes up the narrative:

> True sympathy the Sailor's looks expressed,
> His looks—for pondering he was mute the while.
> Of Social Order's care for wretchedness,
> Of Time's sure help to calm and reconcile,
> Joy's second spring and Hope's long-treasured smile,
> 'Twas not for *him* to speak—a man so tried.
> Yet to relieve her heart, in friendly style
> Proverbial words of comfort he applied,
> And not in vain, while they went pacing side by side.[73]

Cumulatively these changes tend to diminish the presence of malign agency, be it state or individual tyranny, in the life of the poor. What oppresses them is simply the law of life, which changes its forms from era to era but is always the same—the law of unending struggle. As the sailor puts it in his summation declaration, 'Bad is the world, and hard the world's law . . .' (stanza 57).

If changes in detail have obscured the origins of *Guilt and Sorrow* in poems of protest at the historical realities of the 1790s, however, it does not mean that this final version has been depoliticized or that Wordsworth's introductory note about its history would have seemed at odds with readers' experience of it in 1842. To put it simply, *Guilt and Sorrow* is quite as historically located a protest poem as *Adventures on Salisbury Plain*, but, as Richard Gravil has finely put it, its historical moment is not 'the hungry 90s' but 'the newly hungry 40s'.[74] And the reason why the introductory note on the poem's history would not have raised any eyebrows is that nothing in it jars with anything that readers had come to expect of the poet who in almost his earliest defence of his work explained why he had chosen as subject matter 'Low and rustic life'.

By the time Keble reminded the assembled Oxford audience in 1839 that Wordsworth was being honoured in part for having exhibited 'the manners, the pursuits, and the feelings, religious and traditional, of the poor', the tribute was already familiar.[75] Evidence of its appositeness had of course existed from the beginning of his career in poems such 'Simon Lee', 'Goody Blake and Harry Gill', and 'The Old Cumberland Beggar', but it had been strikingly confirmed more recently in the 'Postscript' to the collection *Yarrow Revisited* in 1835. With links to the Prefaces to *Lyrical Ballads* and to Wordsworth's manifesto letters to Charles James Fox (14 January 1801) and John Wilson (7 June 1802), this prose 'Postscript' testifies to continuities of bearing between his earlier and later work.[76] In a response to changes 'especially affecting the lower orders of society', primarily the result of the 1834 Poor Law Amendment Act, this generously humanitarian discussion insists that in framing legislation 'the prudence of the head' must never 'supplant the wisdom of the heart'. Declaring it a principle that '*all* persons who cannot find employment, or procure wages sufficient to support the body in health and strength, are entitled to maintenance by law', Wordsworth acutely observes that the framing of the Act 'proceeds too much upon the presumption that it is a labouring man's own fault if he be not, as the phrase is, beforehand with the world'. In one passage the lot of 'the famished Northern Indian' and the 'savage Islander' is compared with that of those in the present day, who are reduced to 'wandering about as strangers in streets and ways, with the hope of succour from casual charity'. Wretchedness of this kind is frequently endured 'in civilised society', it is timeless and universal: 'multitudes, in all ages, have known it, of whom may be said:—

> Homeless, near a thousand homes they stood,
> And near a thousand tables pined, and wanted food.'

A quotation from 'The Female Vagrant'—there could not be surer evidence that on this topic Wordsworth's imagination is working exactly as it did long ago in *Salisbury Plain*. Further evidence of continuities was offered when Wordsworth concluded the 'Postscript' with a long passage 'extracted from my MSS. written above thirty years ago' (*The Prelude*, 1805, XII, 223–77), because 'it turns upon the individual dignity which humbleness of social condition does not preclude, but frequently promotes'.

Nor did his anxiety about the New Poor Law evaporate. When further development of the Act was being debated in 1842, Wordsworth set out his disquiet very bluntly. In a letter to the eminent physician Robert Ferguson he stressed his dislike of the attitudes to the poor being embodied in the legislation, deeming them inconsistent 'with the dictates of humanity'. It seemed, he observed, that the labouring poor were to be punished to set an

example 'for the benefit of the generation to come—Nay more . . .
to be punished also for the faults of the preceding ones.'[77]

Such an emphasis on the rights, as well as the needs, of the labouring poor allies the Wordsworth of *Guilt and Sorrow* squarely with the
Dickens of *Oliver Twist* (1836–9), the Carlyle of *Chartism* (1840) and
Past and Present (1843), and the Gaskell of *Mary Barton* (1848). Whatever the differences between these works—and the differences in
analysis and prognosis are considerable—each registers the impact of
the mountingly severe conditions that prevailed as the 1830s became
the 'hungry-forties' by telling stories about those whose lives are
invariably the most affected by economic decline. The sufferings of
the female vagrant and the sailor on Salisbury Plain may have begun
before war against the French had even started, but the account of
them is as apposite in 1842 as it would have been in the 1790s. The
woman's hunger 'near a thousand tables' is the same as Oliver Twist's
when he asks for more. There is a kinship between the sailor who is
driven to murder by injustice and wretchedness and the good man,
John Barton—whose pitiable story is set in the year of the publication of *Guilt and Sorrow*, 1842. And as an introduction to the poem,
the opening sentences of *Past and Present* could serve as text: 'The
condition of England, on which many pamphlets are now in the
course of publication, and many thoughts unpublished are going
on in every reflective head, is justly regarded as one of the most
ominous, and withal one of the strangest, ever seen in this world.
England is full of wealth, of multifarious produce, supply for human
want of every kind; yet England is dying of inanition.'[78]

Guilt and Sorrow belongs to the hungry-forties, the era of Chartism
when, as the 'Prelude' to *Poems, Chiefly of Early and Late Years* puts it,
'unforeseen distress spreads far and wide | Among a People mourn-
fully cast down'. But there is another context also in which the
poem's appearance in 1842 might have been regarded as timely.

Guilt and Sorrow tells essentially the same story as *Adventures on
Salisbury Plain*. The guilt and sorrow highlighted in the newly
sombre title burdens the sailor figure in both poems. Though in a
desperate plight and justifiably angered by the fraud that robs him of
his expected reward for serving his country, what he does when he
robs another hapless victim of his life is murder. But can it be
extenuated? Ought it to be? And if the judgment is inexorable that
the law must take its course, what ought that course properly to be?

In the earlier poem such questions are sifted in a thoroughly God-winian, rationalist manner in which the anger and scorn vented in the *Letter to the Bishop of Llandaff* are heard again. The sailor is a victim of the state; an essentially good man, he is driven to crime by want; to condemn such a one to death violates the name of 'Justice'; to let his corpse swing on the gibbet is a barbarity that shames a so-called civilized society. In the later poem, although, as has been indicated, the indictment of the apparatus of the state has been softened, it remains the case that the sailor is a victim, whose plight must raise the question in the mind of every compassionate and Christian reader, what is condign punishment for such a crime committed by such a man?

When *Poems, Chiefly of Early and Late Years* was published these questions were matters of intense Parliamentary debate and wider public concern. Throughout the 1830s, especially following the report of a Royal Commission in 1837, legislation greatly reduced the severity of the penal law relating to capital punishment and there was powerful agitation for abolition of the death penalty altogether.[79]

That the poet was engaged by the capital punishment debate had become became public knowledge in 1841, when in the course of a substantial article on Wordsworth's collected sonnets in the *Quarterly Review*, Henry Taylor gave an account of the as yet unpublished sequence 'Sonnets Upon the Punishment of Death'. After a review of earlier measures to reduce greatly the number of capital offences, Taylor refers to the recent agitation for further reform and declares:

Thus the broad question which is left for the country to look at, in respect to the punishment by death, is in effect its *abolition*. It is to this question that Mr. Wordsworth's Sonnets refer; and the general drift of the sentiments which they express is that there is a deeper charity and a more enlarged view of religious obligations than that which would dictate such a measure in this country in the present state of society.[80]

Dismissing the notion that the topic might not be suitable for poetry, Taylor commends Wordsworth's treatment of it with the reverence which many of his younger admirers adopted the nearer he approached the end of his life:

the main subject, being a subject for deep feelings, large views, and high argumentation, is essentially a subject for poetry, and especially so in the hands of one who has been accustomed, during a life which has now reached to threescore years and ten, to consider the sentiments and judgments which he utters in poetry with as deep a solicitude as to their justness as if they were delivered from the bench or pulpit.

The sonnet sequence was published very shortly afterwards in *Poems, Chiefly of Early and Late Years.*

Taylor's reference to the 'pulpit' is apt, for complementing each other, the 'Sonnets Upon the Punishment of Death' and *Guilt and Sorrow* make an avowedly Christian intervention in the debate about capital punishment, placing the poem firmly within the discourse of the Anglican revival of the 1830s and 1840s. In Sonnet XI the case is made that compared with life imprisonment in a dungeon cell or 'life-long exile on a savage coast', the penalty that the law demands for murder is actually merciful, in that it transfers the guilty one to a higher and more merciful judge,

> Leaving the final issue in *His* hands
> Whose goodness knows no change, whose love is sure,
> Who sees, foresees; who cannot judge amiss,
> And wafts at will the contrite soul to bliss.

The Sailor's last words in *Guilt and Sorrow* even more explicitly invoke the Redeemer:

> 'O welcome sentence which will end though late,'
> He said, 'the pangs that to my conscience came
> Out of that deed. My trust, Saviour! is in thy name!'

Such an appeal to the 'Saviour' is paralleled by Margaret's gaze on the Cross in the late revision to Book One of *The Excursion* discussed in Chapter Two.[81]

In *Adventures on Salisbury Plain* the Sailor's execution, the final horror he experiences, is inflicted by those 'who of Justice bear'st the violated name', and it closes a miserable life. But the execution itself is not Authority's last act of violence against him: the Sailor's body is gibbeted, 'hung on high in iron case'. The 'swinging corpse' is supposed to act as a salutary warning to the 'unthinking and untaught', but is actually unheeded by the dissolute who have been hardened by such sights. The ending of *Guilt and Sorrow* could not be more different:

> His fate was pitied. Him in iron case
> (Reader, forgive the intolerable thought)
> They hung not:—no one on *his* form or face

> Could gaze, as on a show by idlers sought;
> No kindred sufferer, to his death-place brought
> By lawless curiosity of chance,
> When into storm the evening sky is wrought,
> Upon his swinging corse an eye can glance,
> And drop, as he once dropped, in miserable trance.

At first glance this seems an odd way to end the poem. The poet rejects thoughts that readers would not have entertained had he not introduced them, denying rather insistently (though unknown to readers in 1842) his own imaginative vision of over forty years before. Might it not have been better simply to close the poem with the Sailor's heartfelt committal of himself to the mercy of God?

Perhaps, but the stanza does in fact chime with other declarations in the collection *Poems, Chiefly of Early and Late Years*, which are unexpected from the poet whose life, as Henry Taylor solemnly put it, had reached threescore years and ten. Wordsworth's gloom around the time of the 1832 reformed Parliament was so comically awful that in biographical treatments it tends to overshadow the presentation of Wordsworth's outlook in his last decade. What needs to be emphasized is that although he remained very susceptible to local anxieties occasioned by political and social change, Wordsworth recovered a larger sense of the possibilities for human progress. In the 'Prelude' to the volume, lines already quoted in part in Chapter Four express the poet's hope that in these difficult times his new work may serve to 'console and reconcile' and

> both with young and old
> Exalt the sense of thoughtful gratitude
> For benefits that still survive, by faith
> In progress, under laws divine, maintained.[82]

Sonnet XIII in the 'Upon the Punishment of Death' sequence likewise adverts to 'hopeful signs' of progress:

> The social rights of man breathe purer air;
> Religion deepens her preventive care;

In time—and 'Oh, speed the blessed hour, Almighty God!' the poet exclaims—the 'awful rod' of capital punishment will drop from 'Law's firm hand' from 'lack of use'. Gibbeting was prohibited in 1834. To remind readers in 1842 that not long ago the Sailor's corpse would have swung in chains would have served justifiably as a pointer that faith in progress 'under laws divine' was justified. That his most recent collection so firmly embodied this conviction is one of many reasons why Queen Victoria could have been assured that the choice of her next Poet Laureate in 1843 was a sound one. Of course, despite the 'Advertisement' to *Guilt and Sorrow; or, Incidents on Salisbury Plain*, neither she nor her advisers knew anything about the Salisbury Plain poems from which it had evolved, nor that its author, as he completed the first of them, had once declared, 'I am of that odious class of men called democrats'.[83]

Appendix

The following passage came into being in 1798 as a declaration from the Pedlar in *The Ruined Cottage*. See Butler, *The Ruined Cottage*, pp. 261–75. Lines 1–18 were inserted by Coleridge in a letter of 10 March 1798 to his brother George, reinforcing the pronouncement he had just made: 'I love fields & woods & mountains with almost a visionary fondness—and because I have found benevolence & quietness growing within me as that fondness [has] increased, therefore I should wish to be the means of implanting it in others—& to destroy the bad passions not by combating them, but by keeping them in inaction' (*STCL*, I, 397–8). The lines were first published, in slightly revised form, in *The Excursion* in 1814 where they serve as the climax (ll. 1201–71) to the Wanderer's discourse in Book Four, 'Despondency Corrected'. See *The Excursion*, ed. Sally Bushell, James A. Butler, and Michael C. Jaye (Ithaca and London: Cornell University Press, 2007), 163–5.

> Not useless do I deem
> These quiet sympathies with things that hold
> An inarticulate language, for the man
> Once taught to love such objects as excite
> No morbid passions, no disquietude,
> No vengeance and no hatred, needs must feel
> The joy of that pure principle of love
> So deeply that, unsatisfied with aught
> Less pure and exquisite, he cannot choose
> But seek for objects of a kindred love   10
> In fellow-natures, and a kindred joy.
> Accordingly he by degrees perceives
> His feelings of aversion softened down,
> A holy tenderness pervade his frame,
> His sanity of reason not impaired,
> Say rather all his thoughts now flowing clear
> —From a clear fountain flowing—he looks round,

He seeks for good and finds the good he seeks;
Till execration and contempt are things
He only knows by name, and if he hears   20
From other mouths the language which they speak
He is compassionate, and has no thought,
No feeling, which can overcome his love.
And further, by contemplating these forms
In the relations which they bear to man
We shall discover what a power is theirs
To stimulate our minds, and multiply
The spiritual presences of absent things.
Then weariness will cease—We shall acquire
The [   ] habit by which sense is made   30
Subservient still to moral purposes,
A vital essence and a saving power;
Nor shall we meet an object but may read
Some sweet and tender lesson to our minds
Of human suffering or of human joy.
All things shall speak of man, and we shall read
Our duties in all forms, and general laws
And local accidents shall tend alike
To quicken and to rouze, and give the will
And power by which a [   ] chain of good   40
Shall link us to our kind. No naked hearts,
No naked minds, shall then be left to mourn
The burthen of existence. Science then
Shall be a precious visitant; and then
And only then, be worthy of her name.
For then her heart shall kindle, her dull eye,
Dull and inanimate, no more shall hang
Chained to its object in brute slavery,
But better taught and mindful of its use
Legitimate, and its peculiar power,   50
While with a patient interest it shall watch
The processes of things, and serve the cause
Of order and distinctness; not for this
Shall it forget that its most noble end,
Its most illustrious province, must be found
In ministering to the excursive power
Of Intellect and thought. So build we up
The being that we are. For was it meant
That we should pore, and dwindle as we pore,
Forever dimly pore on things minute,   60
On solitary objects, still beheld

In disconnection, dead and spiritless,
And still dividing, and dividing still,
Break down all grandeur, still unsatisfied
With our unnatural toil, while littleness
May yet become more little, waging thus
An impious warfare with the very life
Of our own souls? Or was it ever meant
That this majestic imagery, the clouds,
The ocean, and the firmament of heaven,   70
Should be a barren picture on the mind?
Never for ends of vanity and pain
And sickly wretchedness were we endued
Amid this world of feeling and of life
With apprehension, reason, will and thought,
Affections, organs, passions. Let us rise
From this oblivious sleep, these fretful dreams
Of feverish nothingness. Thus disciplined
All things shall live in us, and we shall live
In all things that surround us. This I deem   80
Our tendency, and thus shall every day
Enlarge our sphere of pleasure and of pain.
For thus the senses and the intellect
Shall each to each supply a mutual aid,
Invigorate and sharpen and refine
Each other with a power that knows no bound,
And forms and feelings acting thus, and thus
Reacting, they shall each acquire
A living spirit and a character
Till then unfelt, and each be multiplied,   90
With a variety that knows no end.
Thus deeply drinking in the soul of things
We shall be wise perforce, and we shall move
From strict necessity along the path
Of order and of good. Whate'er we see,
Whate'er we feel, by agency direct
Or indirect, shall tend to feed and nurse
Our faculties and raise to loftier heights
Our intellectual soul.

Notes

INTRODUCTION

1. *Home at Grasmere*, MS B, 620–2. Darlington, *Home at Grasmere*, 76.
2. Butler and Green, *Lyrical Ballads*, 328. I first considered this passage many years ago in '"Affinities Preserved": Poetic Self-Reference in Wordsworth', *Studies in Romanticism*, 24 (1985), 531–49.
3. Preface to *Lyrical Ballads* (1802). *Prose*, I, 141.
4. MW and WW to Henry Crabb Robinson, 21 June [1845]. *WL*, VII, 679.
5. Curtis, *Last Poems*, 397.
6. *Kendal and Windermere Railway*. *Prose*, III, 352. The sonnets are 'On the Projected Kendal and Windermere Railway' and 'Proud were ye, Mountains, when, in times of old'. Curtis, *Last Poems*, 389–90.
7. Curtis, *Last Poems*, 350. Curtis notes, p. 487, that WW recorded that the poem was 'Retouched, or rather rewritten August 25th 1843'.
8. In 1874 Ruskin was awarded the Gold Medal of the Royal Institute of British Architects. Causing much astonishment and dismay he refused to accept it and gave as one of his reasons the complicity of British Architects as a profession in acts of vandalism, such as that at Furness, where 'The railway . . . is carried so near the Abbey that the ruins vibrate at the passing of every luggage train; and the buildings connected with the station block the window over the altar of the Abbot's Chapel; so that nothing else can be seen through it' (letter, 20 May 1874). *The Works of John Ruskin*, ed. E. T. Cook and Alexander Wedderburn, 39 vols. (London: George Allen, 1903–12), XXXIV, 513–16. Jack Simmons's indispensable *The Victorian Railway* (London: Thames and Hudson, 1991), 162–3 put me on track here.
9. Quotation from 'Proud were ye, Mountains, when, in times of old', as also the following quotation, 'the passion of a just disdain.'
10. Final words of 'Proud were, ye, Mountains, when in times of old'. Curtis, *Last Poems*, 390.
11. This bird returns in Wordsworth's beautiful tribute to his sister, Dorothy, in *Home at Grasmere*, 109–13: 'Where'er my footsteps turned, | Her voice was like a hidden Bird that sang; | The thought of her was like a flash of light | Or an unseen companionship, a breath | Of fragrance independent of the wind.'

12. The summer is recalled at the opening of 'Elegiac Stanzas . . . Peele Castle'. 'So pure the sky, so quiet was the air!', Wordsworth had written in 1806, recalling 1794. By the time of Wordsworth's death the spot where he had once gazed across the 'glassy sea' at Piel Castle had become the coastal terminus of the Furness Railway line. The line officially opened for traffic 12 August 1846. See W. McGowan Gradon, *Furness Railway: Its Rise and Development 1846–1923* (privately printed, 1946).

13. Howard Erskine-Hill, *Poetry of Opposition and Revolution: Dryden to Wordsworth* (Oxford: Clarendon Press, 1996), 250. The Furness Abbey poetry is acutely discussed throughout chapters 6 and 7 of this fine book. When he divided Book Ten into two, Wordsworth chose to end the new Book Ten dramatically with this line, a clear case I think where the 1850 text is artistically superior to that of 1805.

14. In *The Lake District* (London: Eyre Methuen, 1970; rev. edn. 1974), Roy Millward and Adrian Robinson give a good account of the railway age in the region. The map on p. 243 shows the perimeter of the Lake District entirely joined up by the 1860s, with penetration into its heart at Coniston and two points on Windermere.

15. *Home at Grasmere*, 162–3.

16. Closing lines of 'The world is too much with us', published 1807. In the *Kendal and Windermere Railway* letters Wordsworth writes of the enmity towards 'moral sentiments and intellectual pleasures of a high order' displayed by ' "Utilitarianism," serving as a mask for cupidity . . .'. *Prose*, III, 352.

17. 1843 note to 'The Old Cumberland Beggar'. Curtis, *Fenwick Notes*, 56.

18. See the 'Postscript' to *Yarrow Revisited* (1835). *Prose*, III, 240–59.

19. See Stephen Gill, *Wordsworth and the Victorians* (Oxford: Clarendon Press, 1998), 274, n. 73 for full wording.

20. WW to Henry Crabb Robinson [*c*.27 April 1835]. *WL*, VI, 44.

21. Quotations from Hardy's 'At Castle Boterel' and Wordsworth's 'Ode: Intimations of Immortality'.

CHAPTER ONE

1. WW to R. P. Gillies, 22 December 1814. *WL*, III, 179.

2. Quillinan's diary is in the Wordsworth Library, Grasmere. This entry is quoted by Eric Birdsall in the introduction to his Cornell edition of *Descriptive Sketches* (1984), 19. It is striking that Housman should have used Wordsworth's own term when he wrote to Grant Richards on 24 July 1898, 'I think it best not to make any alterations, even the slightest, after one has printed a thing. It was Shelley's plan, and is much wiser than Wordsworth's perpetual tinkering . . .'. *The Letters of A. E. Housman*, ed. Archie Burnett, 2 vols. (Oxford: Clarendon Press, 2007),

I, 109. It is worth noting that W thought tinkers led a happy life—see his poem 'The Tinker'.

3. The 1827 set was sold at Sothebys, 17 December 2003. The 1836 set is in Wellesley College Library. See Jared Curtis, 'The Wellesley Copy of Wordsworth's *Poetical Works, 1832'*, *Harvard Library Bulletin*, 28 (1980), 5–15.

4. W W to Nathaniel Biggs [19 December 1800]. *WL*, I, 311.

5. The phrase 'great moral triumph' comes from the prefatory 'Advertisement' to *Thanksgiving Ode, January 18, 1816* (1816), p. iii.

6. Just to be balanced, it is worth noting that Wordsworth's friend Henry Crabb Robinson admired the whole section of the poem, remarking that one line of it, 267, 'deserves to pass into a proverb'. See Ketcham, *Shorter Poems*, 537.

7. 'You know what importance I attach to following strictly the last copy of the text of an author.' W W to Alexander Dyce [*c.*19 April 1830]. *WL*, V, 236. In 1843 W W was agonizing over the inscription for the memorial to Robert Southey to be placed in Crosthwaite Church. At a very late stage he made an alteration which meant that the already carved wording on the monument had to be erased in favour of the new line. See *WL*, VII, 520, n. 4.

8. W W to Edward Moxon [late December 1836]. *WL*, VI, 337.

9. I have given a brief account of Wordsworth's Chaucer work and Powell in *The Oxford Companion to Chaucer*, ed. Douglas Gray (Oxford: Oxford University Press, 2003), 497–8.

10. W W to Thomas Powell, 18 January 1840. *WL*, VII, 8. Just one further example from many: on 26 October 1842 W thanked Elizabeth Barrett profusely for her sonnet inspired by Haydon's *Wordsworth on Helvellyn*, but could not resist proposing a revision to make a line less liable to misreading, 'The verse as I take it, would be somewhat clearer thus, if you could tolerate the redundant syllable . . .'. W W was, moreover, on this occasion, right. *WL*, VII, 384–5.

11. By this date Quillinan recognized both the compulsiveness and the risk of W W's revisionary practice. On 19 March he wrote to Henry Crabb Robinson about W W's work on *The Excursion*: 'to mend it without losing more in the freshness and the force of expression than he will gain in variety of cadence is in most cases I believe impracticable . . .'. *WL*, VII, 542.

12. For a detailed and scrupulous assessment of the evidence about Wordsworth's composition on-the-hoof, see Andrew Bennett, *Wordsworth Writing* (Cambridge: Cambridge University Press, 2007), esp. ch. 1.

13. The manuscript record of this encounter is in the Berg Collection of the New York Public Library. The word Elizabeth Barrett noted as pronounced in a northern fashion was 'livelong'. In August 1787 the young Dorothy Wordsworth told Jane Pollard that Hayley's poems were among the books given to her by her brothers. *WL*, I, 8.

14. WW to Alexander Dyce, 22 June [1830]. *WL*, V, 292.
15. Jackson, *Sonnet Series*, 197.
16. Osborn, *The Borderers*, 752.
17. Ketcham, *Shorter Poems*, 243-4; 251-5. ' "Lycoris" was the Latin poet C. Cornelius Gallus' pseudonym for the beautiful freedwoman Cytheris' (ibid. 544).
18. See Eric C. Walker, *Marriage, Writing and Romanticism* (Stanford: Stanford University Press, 2009), 111-28 for a discussion, including a detailed chart of the development of the poem(s). See also Douglass H. Thomson, ' "Sport of Transmutations": The Evolution of Wordsworth's "To Lycoris" ', *Studies in English Literature*, 27 (1987), 581-93.
19. DW to Lady Beaumont, 4 May 1805. *WL*, I, 598.
20. *Ode: To Lycoris*, 53. Ketcham, *Shorter Poems*, 244.
21. Curtis, *P2V*, 611-14.
22. Butler and Green, *Lyrical Ballads*, 807. Appendix VI, pp. 807-19 documents the 'Development of Mathew Elegies in *Address to the Scholars of the Village School of* —. (1842 Text)'.
23. Landon and Curtis, *Early Poems*, 452.
24. To be exact: there was a collected edition in seven volumes in 1846, re-issued in 1849. The six-volume set of 1849-50 is mentioned here as it was the final authorized edition.
25. This and the preceding quotation are from WW to David Laing, 11 December 1835. *WL*, VI, 136-9.
26. For a narrative of the critical reception see Stephen Gill, *William Wordsworth: A Life* (Oxford: Clarendon Press, 1989), 266-71; and for the reviews themselves see Robert Woof's *William Wordsworth: The Critical Heritage. Vol. I: 1793-1820* (London and New York: Routledge, 2001), 169-231.
27. See Gill, *Life*, 149-50.
28. All these quotations are from the note appended in 1842. See Osborn, *The Borderers*, 813.
29. The 'Advertisement' preceding *Guilt and Sorrow* in 1842. See Gill, *SPP*, 215-17.
30. WW to William Mathews, 23 May 1794. *WL*, I, 119.
31. WW to James Webbe Tobin, 6 March [1798]. *WL*, I, 211.
32. WW's IF note to *Epistle to Sir George Howland Beaumont, Bart.* Curtis, *Fenwick Notes*, 66.
33. Barron Field to WW, 10 April 1828. Quoted *WL*, IV, 600-1. This letter, and a comparably detailed one of 28 April 1828, are included in Barron Field's *Memoirs of Wordsworth*, ed. Geoffrey Little, Australian Academy of the Humanities Monograph 3 (Sydney: Sydney University Press, 1975), 132-42. Alongside Field's comment might be put Mary Wordsworth's admission some years later that her husband's 'alterations' convince her 'understanding and judgment . . . but . . . not

always my *feelings* . . .'. MW to Jane Marshall, 24 December 1836. *WL*, VI, 332.

34. WW to Barron Field, 24 October 1828. *WL*, IV, 645. See also the previous letter of 16 April 1828.

35. Curtis, *P2V*, 408.

36. W uses the term 'discarded poem' in the IF note to *Lament of Mary Queen of Scots*, cited Butler and Green, *Lyrical Ballads*, 357.

37. For a discussion of the theory and practice that have led to the dislodging of the poet's authorized text and its arrangement, see Zachary Leader, *Revision and Romantic Authorship* (Oxford: Clarendon Press, 1996), 19–77.

38. WW to Sir George Beaumont, 3 June 1805. *WL*, I, 594.

39. There is ample evidence that WW was thinking earlier about grouping poems for collective effect, such as his observation, 21 May 1807, that the sonnets in *Poems, in Two Volumes*, 'while they each fix the attention upon some important sentiment separately considered, do at the same time collectively make a Poem on the subject of civil Liberty and independence'. *WL*, II, 147. On the other hand, he was introducing a new category, 'Evening Voluntaries', as late as 1835. See Curtis, *Last Poems*, 235–6. For a succinct but authoritative account of Wordsworth's categorizing, see Ketcham, *Shorter Poems*, 19–32.

40. *Poems*, 2 vols. (London: Longman, Hurst, Rees, Orme, and Brown, 1815), I, p. xiii.

41. In view of the poor sales of the 1807 poems, one might wonder who Wordsworth imagined himself to be addressing in the note. For discussion of his growing anxiety about readership see Lucy Newlyn, *Reading, Writing, and Romanticism: The Anxiety of Reception* (Oxford: Oxford University Press, 2000), 91–133.

42. *The Works of Jonathan Swift*, ed. Walter Scott, 19 vols. (Edinburgh: Archibald Constable, 1814), I, 89. Grateful thanks to David Womersley for locating this quotation for me.

43. 'I have not ventured to call this Poem an Ode; but it was written with a hope that in the transitions, and in the impassioned music of the versification would be found the principal requisites of that species of composition.' Note in 1800 edition of *Lyrical Ballads* only.

44. Ketcham, *Shorter Poems*, 78–95; Curtis, *Last Poems*, 365. In *Poems, Chiefly of Early and Late Years* (1842) the two poems are, of course, printed straightforwardly in sequence.

45. DW journal entry for 29 April 1802. See Mary Moorman, *William Wordsworth: A Biography. The Early Years 1770–1803* (Oxford: Clarendon Press, 1957), 532–4.

46. WW to Robert Southey [24 June 1835]. *WL*, VI, 66.

47. For the complicated textual history of 'Beggars' see Curtis, *P2V*, 113–16; ibid. 206–7 for 'Written in March' and 100–1 for 'To H.C. Six Years

Old'. On the education of Basil Montagu, see DW's letter of 19 March [1797]. *WL*, I, 180.

48. Jackson, *Sonnet Series*, 384–7.

49. Curtis, *Fenwick Notes*, 26.

50. Ibid. 6.

51. Ibid. 23.

CHAPTER TWO

1. For some account of the marketing of Wordsworth after his death in 1850 see my *Wordsworth and the Victorians* (Oxford: Clarendon Press, 1998), ch. 3.

2. Coleridge's comment is recorded under 21 July 1832 in *Specimens of the Table Talk of the Late Samuel Taylor Coleridge* (1835). See *Table Talk*, ed. Carl Woodring, 2 vols. (London: Routledge, and Princeton: Princeton University Press, 1990), II, 176–7.

3. WW to Alexander Dyce [*c.*19 April 1830]. *WL*, V, 236.

4. All quotations are taken from Butler, *The Ruined Cottage* and will only be noted separately if the reader will have difficulty finding the passage quoted without a page reference. Where it is likely to be useful, page references are inserted in the text.

5. This version constitutes Butler's MS B Reading Text, *The Ruined Cottage*, 41–72.

6. This version constitutes Butler's MS D Reading Text, *The Ruined Cottage*, 43–75.

7. This version constitutes Butler's MS E Reading Text, *The Ruined Cottage*, 382–448.

8. This version constitutes Butler's MS M transcription, *The Ruined Cottage*, 383–449.

9. WW to Sir George Beaumont, 25 December 1804. *WL*, I, 518.

10. See the Cornell Wordsworth series, *The Excursion*, ed. Sally Bushell, James A. Butler, and Michael C. Jaye (Ithaca and London: Cornell University Press, 2007), 48–76.

11. In March 1798 the eventual publisher of *Lyrical Ballads*, Joseph Cottle, was being offered a two-volume possibility that would include Wordsworth's 'Tale of a Woman'. In 1800 Coleridge entertained the idea of a joint publication of his 'Christabel' and Wordsworth's 'The Pedlar'. See Butler, *The Ruined Cottage*, 22–4. It is unclear what texts are really under consideration here or how serious the possibility of publication was in either case.

12. *The Poetical Works of William Wordsworth*, ed. Ernest de Selincourt and Helen Darbishire, 5 vols. (Oxford, 1940–9), V, 376–404.

13. Jonathan Wordsworth, *The Music of Humanity* (London: Thomas Nelson and Sons, 1969), pp. xiii, 22. Further page references in text.

14. In 'Framing *The Ruined Cottage*', in *Wordsworth's Counterrevolutionary Turn: Community, Virtues, and Vision in the 1790s* (Newark: University of Delaware Press, 1997), John Rieder echoes Jonathan Wordsworth's critical judgement when he refers to 'Wordsworth's obsessive and ultimately suffocating revisions of *The Ruined Cottage*' (p. 147).

15. In 1799 lines about the Pedlar not used in MS D of *The Ruined Cottage* were fair-copied elsewhere in the manuscript notebook. They are untitled. Jonathan Wordsworth presented an edited text of them in *The Music of Humanity* (1969), *The Borders of Vision* (1982), and the student edition, *The Pedlar, Tintern Abbey, The Two-Part Prelude* (1985) and 'chiefly for convenience' (*Music of Humanity*, 157) called the lines *The Pedlar*. His decision to use the name was unwarranted and continues to cause confusion. As Butler demonstrates (*The Ruined Cottage*, 24–5) the title 'the Pedlar' was in use among the Wordsworths in 1801–2 and can legitimately be given to composition from that period that incorporated and developed the lines from the 1799 copy, even though Dorothy Wordsworth's references to 'the Pedlar' in her journal are occasionally puzzling. By 1804, however, there was no longer any ambiguity. As Butler observes, *The Pedlar* was 'the title the Wordsworths now assigned to the combined stories of Margaret and the Pedlar' (p. 378). This is the only version of the poem that can properly be so called.

16. I am not, of course, implying that Butler thinks MS E 'final'. As one of the editors of the Cornell *Excursion* he is better placed than anyone to know the later history of Wordsworth's engagement with the story of the Pedlar and Margaret.

17. WW to Sir George Beaumont, 12 March 1805. *WL*, I, 556.

18. The fullest and most probing treatment to date of Wordsworth's larger concerns for his philosophic project, which this chapter touches on only in part, remains Kenneth R. Johnston's *Wordsworth and The Recluse* (New Haven and London: Yale University Press, 1984).

19. STC to George Coleridge, 10 March 1798. *STCL*, I, 397–8.

20. [*Essay on Morals*], *Prose*, I, 99–107. The title is editorial. In the chapter 'Returning to the Ruined Cottage', David Fairer discusses the importance of this *Essay* as demonstrating that 'Wordsworth was coming to understand how human beings should be judged not by Idea, but by their own inner grain, their settled habits . . .'. *Organising Poetry: The Coleridge Circle, 1790–1798* (Oxford: Oxford University Press, 2009), 268.

21. Quotations from 'Expostulation and Reply' and 'The Tables Turned'. See also 'Lines. Written at a Small Distance from my House' ('It is the first mild day of March'), in which Wordsworth fuses mind and body in the declaration:

> One moment now may give us more
> Than fifty years of reason;

> Our minds shall drink at every pore
> The spirit of the season.

22. Preface to *Lyrical Ballads* (1802). *Prose*, I, 139.

23. For a thought-provoking scrutiny of the Pedlar, see Jonathan Barron and Kenneth R. Johnston, '"A Power to Virtue Friendly": The Pedlar's Guilt in Wordsworth's "Ruined Cottage"', in Robert Brinkley and Keith Hanley (eds.), *Romantic Revisions* (Cambridge: Cambridge University Press, 1992), 64–86.

24. Matthew 13: 54–5. *Edinburgh Review*, XXIV (November 1814), 1–31. Jeffrey's review is reprinted in Robert Woof (ed.), *William Wordsworth: The Critical Heritage. Vol. I: 1793–1820* (London and New York: Routledge, 2001), 381–404.

25. STC, *Table Talk* (as note 2), I, 307. Entry for 21 July 1832.

26. WW to James Webbe Tobin, 6 March [1798]; WW to James Losh, 11 March [1798]. *WL*, I, 210–12; 212–14. Wordsworth's most ambitious statement was made in the lines later printed as the Prospectus to *The Recluse* in *The Excursion* (1814), dated by scholars between 1800 and 1802. See Darlington, *Home at Grasmere*, 19–22.

27. Unpublished Preface, written 1818, to Cantos I and II of *Don Juan*. *Lord Byron, The Complete Poetical Works*, ed. Jerome J. McGann, 7 vols. (Oxford: Clarendon Press, 1980–93), VI, 81–2. Joanna Southcott established her own sect and in late middle age declared she was to give birth to a new Messiah, 'Shiloh'. The Reverend Tozer was one of her followers. Swedenborg was a Swedish philosopher and mystic. Richard Brothers was the self-proclaimed prophet of God's revelation that the French Revolution was fulfilling biblical prophecy. See Jon Mee, *Romanticism, Enthusiasm and Regulation* (Oxford: Oxford University Press, 2003), esp. 95–9.

28. *The Prelude, 1798–1799*, I, 457–8. Further line references in text. The poem is also often referred to as *The Two-Part Prelude*. It needs to be remembered that these titles are the invention of late twentieth-century scholars; Wordsworth never called his autobiographical work *The Prelude*, let alone *The Two-Part Prelude*.

29. For Jeffrey, see note 25. Thomas Babington Macaulay's journal entry for 28 July 1850 is reproduced in the *Norton Prelude*, 560.

30. Donald E. Hayden provides a splendidly illustrated and helpful account of all Wordsworth's explorations from 1801 to 1833 in *Wordsworth's Travels in Scotland*, Monograph Series, 21 (Tulsa, Okla.: University of Tulsa, 1985).

31. T. W. Thompson, *Wordsworth's Hawkshead*, ed. Robert Woof (London: Oxford University Press, 1970), 239. 'Scotland teemed with men carrying books from town to town, and they now crossed to England. One of these Scottish pedlars made a deep impression on the mind of the young Wordsworth.' William St Clair, *The Reading Nation in the Romantic Period* (Cambridge: Cambridge University Press, 2004), 114.

32. Butler, *The Ruined Cottage*, 476–80, presents all Wordsworth's comments about the Pedlar together with important ancillary material. In 1843 the poet insisted that while the Pedlar figure was of course 'in some degree a Composition; I will not & need not call it an invention—it was no such thing' (p. 477).

33. IF Note to *The Excursion*. Curtis, *Fenwick Notes*, 79. Sara Hutchinson knew James Patrick for four years before his death on 2 March 1787.

34. Robert Heron, *Observations Made in a Journey through the Western Counties of Scotland*, 2 vols. (Perth, 1793). The 1814 note was considerably enlarged from the 1827 edition onwards by additional quotation from the *Observations*. Heron's *A Memoir of the Life of the Late Robert Burns* first appeared in the *Monthly Magazine* in June 1797. See *Robert Burns: The Critical Heritage*, ed. Donald A. Low (London: Routledge & Kegan Paul, 1974), 117–27.

35. Butler, *The Ruined Cottage*, 331.

36. 'Pure livers' echoes 'grave Livers' in 'Resolution and Independence', written 1802. Fiona Stafford points out the link to the sonnets of this period in which Wordsworth summons his English countrymen to their moral duty in ' "Inhabited Solitudes": Wordsworth in Scotland, 1803', in David Duff and Catherine Jones (eds.), *Scotland, Ireland, and the Romantic Aesthetic* (Lewisburg: Bucknell University Press, 2009), 93–113.

37. Butler, *Ruined Cottage*, MS B Reading Text, p. 46. Following references to line numbers in text.

38. *Prose*, I, 122 and 124.

39. References are to *Othello*, I, iii, 135 (Arden Shakespeare, ed. M. R. Ridley, 1958); *Hart-Leap Well*, l. 97; Preface to *Lyrical Ballads* 1800 (*Prose*, I, 122–8); 'Michael', l. 19. The 'Michael' line also seems to echo the same scene in *Othello*: 'I will a round unvarnish'd tale deliver' (l. 90).

40. Pages references to *Prose*, I, are given in the body of the text.

41. Butler, *The Ruined Cottage*, 46. *The Prelude*, III, 121–7.

42. *DWJ*, 63; 66–7.

43. The passage was added to the manuscript prepared for Coleridge to take on his Mediterranean travels, MS M. Butler, *The Ruined Cottage*, 391.

44. *Prose*, III, 258–9.

45. 'When to the attractions of the busy world', l. 82. Published 1815. Curtis, *P2V*, 570. See also WW to Sir George Beaumont, 11 February 1805, on John: 'meek, affectionate, silently enthusiastic, loving all quiet things, and a Poet in every thing but words'. *WL*, I, 541.

46. John Stoddart, *Remarks on Local Scenery and Manners in Scotland during the Years 1799 and 1800*, 2 vols. (London: William Miller, 1801). Stoddart's dedicatory preface offers what is almost a precis of the 'Not Useless' lines: 'I do not call these forms inanimate; because I think such term

would ill apply to that which fills the mind with life and animation' (I, p. xii).

47. See Hayden, *Wordsworth's Travels in Scotland*, and, highly recommended as well annotated and illustrated, Dorothy Wordsworth, *Recollections of a Tour Made in Scotland*, ed. Carol Kyros Walker (New Haven and London: Yale University Press, 1997). Fiona Stafford's ' "Inhabited Solitudes": Wordsworth in Scotland, 1803', is the most insightful account yet of the significance of the tour.

48. Butler, *The Ruined Cottage*, 46. MS B, ll. 70–4. Following citation in text to Butler page references only.

49. The first complete version of *The Ruined Cottage*, MS B, carries as epigraph a quotation from Burns's *Epistle to J. L. L.*****k, An Old Scotch Bard*, ll. 734, 77–8. The epigraph disappears in the 1799 MS D, but Burns's presence continues vestigially in an allusion at l. 295 to his poem, *To W. S****n, Ochiltree*, stanza xv, l. 3, which survives through all later versions.

50. One small but telling textual change conforms to the change from the Lake District to Scotland. While the Pedlar is conceived of as a Cumbrian, he is said to have read greedily of 'Whate'er the rustic Vicar's shelf supplied, | The life and death of martyrs'. Given the wholly English 'Vicar', the reference could easily be to Foxe's *Book of Martyrs*. Once the Pedlar has become Scottish, however, 'Vicar' becomes 'Minister' and the reference is (specifically in MS M) to the martyrs of the Covenant.

51. This is but one of the many places in this chapter where it would be appropriate to acknowledge William Ulmer's *The Christian Wordsworth 1798–1805* (Albany: State University of New York Press, 2001) and the chapter 'Nature's Priest' in Robert Ryan's *The Romantic Reformation: Religious Politics in English Literature 1789–1824* (Cambridge: Cambridge University Press, 1997). Both of these revisionary studies greatly advance our understanding of Wordsworth's course as a religious poet.

52. St Paul's First Epistle to the Thessalonians, 4: 13. The importance of the previously unnoticed allusion in 'Elegiac Stanzas' was pointed out by Edward Wilson in *Review of English Studies* NS 43 (1992), 75–80.

53. MW to HCR, 7 April 1844. *WL*, VII, 542. A month earlier Quillinan had also commented to HCR that Wordsworth had been 'working very hard lately, to very little purpose, to mend the versification of the Excursion'. Quoted *WL*, VII, 542. I am grateful to Ruth Abbott for drawing my attention to these reports.

54. In *Georgic Modernity and British Romanticism* (Cambridge: Cambridge University Press, 2004), Kevis Goodman aptly describes 'The Wanderer . . . as the self-sufficing *fortunatus* or "happy man" of Virgilian and Horatian descent; his affections have grown with an apparent natural spontaneity tempered by the careful discipline of a frugal mind'

(p. 120). On the relation of WW's 'philosophy' to that of the Wanderer, see Sally Bushell's seminal *Re-Reading The Excursion: Narrative, Response and the Wordsworthian Dramatic Voice* (Aldershot: Ashgate, 2002), esp. 85–115, 'A Performative Philosophy'.

55. Keats famously declared to Benjamin Robert Haydon that *The Excursion* was one of the 'three things to rejoice at in this Age' (10 January 1818). See *John Keats: Selected Letters*, ed. Robert Gittings; rev. edn. Jon Mee (Oxford: Oxford University Press, 2002). For the Shelleys' judgement, 'He is a slave', see *Journals of Mary Shelley*, ed. Paula R. Feldman and Diana Scott-Kilvert, 2 vols. (Oxford: Clarendon Press, 1987), I, 25. For Tennyson, Darwin, and Arnold see Gill, *Wordsworth and the Victorians*.

56. Woof, *Critical Heritage*, 386. For a seminal discussion of Jeffrey's attitude to Wordsworth, see L. G. Mitchell, 'The *Edinburgh Review* and the Lake Poets 1802–1810', *Essays Presented to C. M. Bowra* (Oxford: Alden Press, 1970), 24–38.

57. Parrish, *1799*, 126.

58. John Locke, *The Reasonableness of Christianity* (1695), ed. I. T. Ramsey (London: Adam and Charles Black, 1958), 57.

59. I am not, of course, suggesting that Wordsworth was content to rest in Paley. To the contrary, in a letter to Catherine Clarkson of January 1815 he crossly disassociated himself from Paley's famous analogy of 'the Supreme Being as bearing the same relation to the universe as a watchmaker bears to a watch'. *WL*, III, 189.

60. James Montgomery, *Eclectic Magazine*, III (January 1815), 13–39; Woof, *Critical Heritage*, 424. Montgomery (1771–1854) was the author of, amongst much other poetry, *The World Before the Flood* (1812).

61. John Taylor Coleridge, *British Critic*, III (May 1815), 449–67; Woof, *Critical Heritage*, 445 and 457. John Taylor Coleridge, 1790–1876, was Coleridge's nephew and an Oxford friend of such as John Keble and Thomas Arnold.

62. John Taylor Coleridge, *British Critic*, XV (February 1821), 113–35; Woof, *Critical Heritage*, 807.

63. *Blackwood's Edinburgh Magazine*, XXIV (December 1828), 917–38. The article on 'Sacred Poetry' was substantially enlarged and revised for *The Recreations of Christopher North*, 3 vols. (Edinburgh: William Blackwood and Sons, 1842), 320–403, but the passages on Wordsworth remained intact. The quoted passage from *Recreations*, II, 348–9, is cited by Jonathan Wordsworth, *The Music of Humanity*, 26.

64. *Dearden's Miscellany*, III (1840), 93–108. The Reverend Henry Alford (1810–71) sent Wordsworth a copy of the article. WW replied [*c.*20 Feb. 1840], not surprisingly, that it was 'highly gratifying' to him. *WL*, VII, 22–4.

65. Such questioning troubled Wordsworth. In 1843 he clearly had in mind John Taylor Coleridge's comments of two decades earlier when

he dictated this part of the Fenwick Note to the 'Ode: Intimations of Immortality': 'I think it right to protest against a conclusion which has given pain to some good & pious persons that I meant to inculcate such a belief [in pre-existence]. It is far too shadowy a notion to be recommended to faith as more than an element in our instincts of immortality. But let us bear in mind that, tho' the idea is not advanced in revelation, there is nothing to contradict it, & the fall of Man presents an analogy in its favor. Accordingly, a preexistent state has entered into the popular creeds of many nations . . . I took hold of the notion of preexistence as having sufficient foundation in humanity for authorizing me to make for my purpose the best use of it as I could as a Poet.' Curtis, *Fenwick Notes*, 61–2.

66. John Wyatt, *Wordsworth and the Geologists* (Cambridge: Cambridge University Press, 1995). See also Tess Cosslett (ed.), *Science and Religion in the Nineteenth Century* (Cambridge: Cambridge University Press, 1984).

67. Robert Southey's *The Book of the Church* (1824) follows a similar trajectory, from Druidical practices among the Britons to the Settlement with William and Mary. Southey's history gives a disproportionate amount of space to a highly sympathetic account of the martyrdom of Archbishop Laud and concludes with words with which Wordsworth would have by this date entirely concurred: 'From the time of the Revolution the Church of England has partaken of the stability and security of the State. . . . It has rescued us, first from heathenism, then from papal idolatry and superstition; it has saved us from temporal as well as spiritual despotism. We owe to it our moral and intellectual character as a nation; much of our private happiness, much of our public strength. Whatever should weaken it, would in the same degree injure the common weal; whatever should overthrow it, would in sure and immediate consequence bring down the goodly fabric of the Constitution, whereof it is a constituent and necessary part. If the friends of the Constitution understand this as clearly as its enemies then will the Church and State be safe, and with them the liberty and the prosperity of our country.'

68. In 1820 Wordsworth had dedicated his *River Duddon* collection to his brother Christopher and included in it a poem addressed to him which both recognizes and broadcasts the brilliance of his brother's career to date. See my 'Wordsworth and the *River Duddon*', *Essays in Criticism*, 57, i (January 2007), 22–41. For a concise account of the importance of the two Christophers, see Alan G. Hill, 'Poetry and Ecumenism: The Legacy of the Wordsworths', *Lambeth Palace Library Annual Review* (1992), 49–64.

69. Gill, *Wordsworth and the Victorians*, 23. 'The ecclesiological movement of the 1830s and 1840s was . . . one which endeavoured to harness

medievalism and romanticism to be of practical benefit to the ecclesiastical community.' Nigel Yates, *Anglican Ritualism in Victorian Britain 1830–1910* (Oxford: Oxford University Press, 1999), 44. What would particularly have commended Wordsworth to the members of the Camden Society are the sonnets in *Ecclesiastical Sketches* concerning church architecture and a long note about the importance of the parsonage-house. See Jackson, *Sonnet Series*, esp. 199–202 and 231–2.

70. Should a Cross (let alone a Crucifix) be permitted within a church? Should it stand on the communion table—or is it to be called the altar? Should the latter, by whatever name, be moveable or fixed, wood or stone? Should a cross be permitted ornamentation on vestments? These questions were given renewed vigour with the rise of the Oxford Movement and continued to inflame during the major period of Anglo-Catholic ritualism. See Peter B. Nockles, *The Oxford Movement in Context: Anglican High Churchmanship 1760–1857* (Cambridge: Cambridge University Press, 1994); Yates, *Anglican Ritualism*; John Shelton Reed, *Glorious Battle: The Cultural Politics of Victorian Anglo-Catholicism* (Nashville: Vanderbilt University Press, 1996).

71. The Maynooth Endowment Grant was intended to put the finances of the Maynooth Seminary (founded 1795) on a sounder footing, at least in part by making a substantially enhanced grant annual and permanent. Wordsworth was not alone in thinking that 'in the present state of things I can not see that any good can be done by what Sir R. Peel and others call conciliation'. See WW's letter of 10 April 1845 to Christopher Wordsworth, junior, author of three pamphlets on the topic. *WL*, VII, 667; and very helpful notes, 666–8.

72. See Timothy Webb, 'Catholic Contagion: Southey, Coleridge and English Romantic Anxieties', in Gavin Hopps and Jane Stabler (eds.), *Romanticism and Religion from William Cowper to Wallace Stevens* (Aldershot: Ashgate, 2006), 75–92. Although not centrally on Wordsworth, this fine article touches on most of his concerns.

73. As already mentioned, the Postscript of 1835 ended with a long passage of blank verse originally referring to the worth of such lowly people as Lake District shepherds. It is a striking example of how determinedly Wordsworth brought earlier work into relation to later, that he should have excerpted the passage from *The Prelude* to add weight to this much later consideration of men little regarded by the world, but of great worth, curates, shepherds of their flock.

74. For an account of the occasion and for the Oxford Movement's embrace of the poet, see my *Wordsworth and the Victorians*, and Mark Knight and Emma Mason, *Nineteenth-Century Religion and Literature: An Introduction* (Oxford: Oxford University Press, 2006), ch. 3.

75. Christopher Wordsworth, senior, to his son, Christopher Wordsworth, 6 July 1844. Cited Nockles, *Oxford Movement*, 183.

76. 'To the Rev. Christopher Wordsworth, D.D., Master of Harrow School.' Published in the 1845 edition of the Collected Poetical Works. Curtis, *Last Poems*, 386.
77. In a letter to Elizabeth Monkhouse of 6 December [1812], for example, about the death of his son, Thomas, Wordsworth speaks of 'the blessing of God', the 'will of God' and says that 'nothing can sustain us under our affliction but reliance in God's Goodness, and a firm belief that it is for *our* Good, as we cannot doubt it was for his, that he should be removed from this sinful and troublesome world'. *WL*, VIII, 140–1.
78. 'To the Lady —, On Seeing the Foundation Preparing for the Erection of — Chapel, Westmoreland', 68. Curtis, *Last Poems*, 31; 'A Grave-Stone Upon the Floor in the Cloisters of Worcester Cathedral', 14. Ibid. 96.
79. '. . . it was my wish, & I might say intention, that we should resume our wanderings & pass the borders into his native country where as I hoped he might witness in the Society of the Wanderer some religious ceremony—a sacrament say, in the open fields, or a preaching among the Mountains, which by recalling his mind to the days of his early Childhood, when he had been present on such occasions in company with his Parents & nearest Kindred, might have dissolv'd his heart into tenderness & so done more towards restoring the Christian Faith in which he had been educated, & with that, contentedness & even chearfulness of mind, than all that the Wandererer & Pastor by their several effusions & addresses had been unable [*sic*] to effect . . .'. Curtis, *Fenwick Notes*, 91.
80. R. P. Graves to WW, 14 March 1844. Quoted Alan G. Hill, *Wordsworth's 'Grand Design'*, British Academy Warton Lecture on English Poetry, *Proceedings of the British Academy*, 72 (1986), 194. I am grateful to Professor Hill for drawing my attention to this very helpful lecture.
81. For further details of Faber's influence on Wordsworth, see my *Wordsworth and the Victorians*, 70–80.
82. James Anthony Froude, *Thomas Carlyle: A History of His Life in London 1834–1881*, 2 vols. (London: Longmans, Green & Co., 1884), I, 291.

CHAPTER THREE

1. *Prelude* (1805), II, 28–33. All references in this chapter to the 1805 *Prelude* are to *The Thirteen-Book Prelude*, ed. Mark L. Reed, 2 vols. (Ithaca and London: Cornell University Press, 1991). References to the earlier version of the poem are to *The Prelude, 1798–1799*, ed. Stephen Parrish (Ithaca and London: Cornell University Press, 1977). Abbreviated references on occasion to *1799* or *1805* are self-explanatory.
2. Christopher Wordsworth is often referred to as one of the poet's executors. He was not. The executors, named in Wordsworth's will, dated 31 August 1847, were his son, William Wordsworth, William Strickland Cookson, of Lincoln's Inn, and John Carter.

3. Dora Wordsworth to Maria Kinnaird, 7 February 1832. Quoted *Norton Prelude*, 536.

4. Christopher Wordsworth, *Memoirs of William Wordsworth*, 2 vols. (London: Edward Moxon, 1851), I, 313. Mary Jacobus discusses the passage and the act of naming the poem as 'at once a legitimation, an act of propriety, and an appropriation' in *Romanticism, Writing, and Sexual Difference: Essays on The Prelude* (Oxford: Clarendon Press, 1989), 188–9.

5. William Knight published *The Poetical Works of William Wordsworth*, 8 vols. (Edinburgh: William Paterson, 1882–6), and again in 8 vols. (London: Macmillan, 1896); *The Prelude* in vol. 3 in both editions. For an account of Knight as editorial pioneer see my *Wordsworth and the Victorians* (Oxford: Clarendon Press, 1998).

6. *The Prelude*, ed. Ernest De Selincourt (Oxford: Clarendon Press, 1926; 2nd rev. edn. Helen Darbishire, 1959). De Selincourt writes with confidence about 'later improvements' and 'lapses' and 'later deterioration' of the poem, his overall position being that the revised 1850 Prelude 'has falsified our estimate of the authentic Wordsworth, the poet of the years 1798–1805' (p. lxi). When Oxford University Press issued the 1805 text separately in 1933, De Selincourt's introduction was repeated.

7. Parrish's edition of *The Prelude, 1798–1799* (see note 1) was followed by the Norton edition of *The Prelude 1799, 1805, 1850*, ed. Jonathan Wordsworth, M. H. Abrams, and Stephen Gill (New York and London: W. W. Norton, 1979).

8. *The Five-Book Prelude*, ed. Duncan Wu (Oxford: Blackwells, 1997); *The Prelude: The Four Texts (1798, 1799, 1805, 1850)* (London: Penguin, 1995), pp. xxv–xxvi. The 'Was it for this' lines were first printed by Helen Darbishire as draft materials only recently discovered in an appendix to her revised edition of the parallel text *Prelude* in 1959.

9. For evidence of Wordsworth's changing role in national culture see my *Wordsworth and the Victorians*.

10. Keats to B. R. Haydon, 10 January 1818. *John Keats: Selected Letters*, ed. Robert Gittings; rev. edn. Jon Mee (Oxford: Oxford University Press, 2002), 47.

11. DW to Catherine Clarkson, 27 March [1821]. *WL*, IV, 50.

12. The most important discussions of the textual issues are Jonathan Wordsworth, 'The Five-Book *Prelude* of Early Spring 1804', *JEGP*, LXXVI (January 1977); and the Reed and Wu editions already noted.

13. STC to Lady Beaumont, 26 March 1804. *STCL*, II, 1104.

14. WW to Francis Wrangham, 24 January–7 February 1804. *WL*, I, 436.

15. STC to WW, 12 October 1799. *STCL*, I, 538.

16. WW to Richard Sharp, 29 April 1804. *WL*, I, 470.

17. The manuscript is DC MS 44 at the Wordsworth Library, Grasmere. For a brief description, see Curtis, *P2V*, p. xxi.

18. Book Four, 143–6, in *The Five-Book Prelude*, ed. Wu, p. 111.

19. WW to James Webbe Tobin, 6 March [1798]. *WL*, I, 212. Second quotation *1799*, II, 478–9.

20. *Home at Grasmere*, 892, where the striking formulation 'Strange question . . .' appears in a very similar context: Wordsworth has just ringingly announced that 'something must be done' (l. 776), only to ask, in effect, 'Yes, but what?'

21. See Alexandra Franklin and Mark Philp's absorbing exhibition catalogue, *Napoleon and the Invasion of Britain* (Oxford: Bodleian Library, 2003), and Frank McLynn, *Napoleon: A Biography* (London: Jonathan Cape, 1997), 324.

22. DW to Catherine Clarkson, 9 October [1803]. *WL*, I, 403.

23. Quotations from *Prelude*, IX, 124–5 and X, 215–16.

24. 'Composed by the Sea-Side, near Calais.' Curtis, *P2V*, 155.

25. 'Composed in the Valley, near Dover.' Curtis, *P2V*, 162–3.

26. 'Anticipation.' Curtis, *P2V*, 173. For discussion of this sonnet, see Colin Pedley, 'Anticipating Invasion: Some Wordsworthian Contexts', *Wordsworth Circle*, 21 (1990), 64–70; and for very valuable wider discussion, Simon Bainbridge's *Napoleon and English Romanticism* (Cambridge: Cambridge University Press, 1995), 54–94 and the same author's *British Poetry and the Revolutionary and Napoleonic Wars: Visions of Conflict* (Oxford: Oxford University Press, 2003), esp. 99–119.

27. For details see Nicholas Roe, *Wordsworth and Coleridge: The Radical Years* (Oxford: Clarendon Press, 1988) and Albert Goodwin, *The Friends of Liberty: The English Democratic Movement in the Age of the French Revolution* (London: Hutchinson, 1979).

28. STC to John Thelwall, 13 May 1796. *STCL*, I, 215.

29. STC to John Prior Estlin, 10 June 1797. *STCL*, I, 327.

30. Osborn, *The Borderers*, 210. The Early Version (1797–9), III, v, 30–3.

31. The literature on this topic is huge. David Bromwich's *Disowned by Memory: Wordsworth's Poetry of the 1790s* (Chicago and London: University of Chicago Press, 1998) is an excellent starting point in that, while Bromwich has a thesis of his own to promote, he is scrupulous in attending to past discussions of the subject.

32. DW to Mary Hutchinson [June 1797]. *WL*, I, 189.

33. Butler, *The Ruined Cottage* [MS B, 60–5], p. 46.

34. By presenting the Druids both as bloodthirsty tyrants and as proto members of the Royal Society WW was, according to Ronald Hutton, 'mirror[ing] in his poetry the spectrum of pre-existing attitudes to Druids that had emerged in British culture by his time'. *Blood and Mistletoe: The History of the Druids in Britain* (New Haven and London: Yale University Press, 2009), 209.

35. Quotation from the 'Prospectus' to *The Recluse*, first published in the Preface to *The Excursion* (1814) but originally part of the conclusion to Book One of the first part of *The Recluse*, 'Home at Grasmere'

(unpublished in WW's lifetime). Date of composition tantalizingly uncertain. See Darlington, *Home at Grasmere*.

36. Samuel Taylor Coleridge, *Biographia Literaria*, ed. James Engell and W. Jackson Bate, 2 vols. (London: Routledge & Kegan Paul, 1983), I, 78–80.

37. For a discussion of these matters, which arrives at different conclusions from mine, see Lucy Newlyn, *Coleridge, Wordsworth, and the Language of Allusion* (Oxford: Clarendon Press, 1986), 3–7; 183–5.

38. WW to Francis Wrangham, 20 November [1795]. *WL*, I, 159.

39. Reed, *1805*, I, 78–80.

40. 'C-Stage Text', 434–5. Reed, *1805*, II, 104. All following quotations are from Reed's text of the 1819 interpolation.

41. For a detailed account of the 1819 composition, see Reed, *1805*, II, 995–7. For a discussion of the interpolation's place in the structure of the poem overall, see Joseph Kishel, 'Wordsworth and the Grande Chartreuse', *Wordsworth Circle*, 12 (1981), 82–8.

42. DW to HCR, 21 December 1822. *WL*, IV, 176.

43. WW to DW, 6 and 16 September 1790. *WL*, I, 33. When he declared to his sister in this letter that 'Among the more awful scenes of the Alps, I had not a thought of man, or a single created being; my whole soul was turned to him who produced the terrible majesty before me' (p. 34), he was doing no more than repeat a celebrated remark in Gray's letter of 16 November 1739 about the Grande Chartreuse, 'Not a precipice, not a torrent, not a cliff, but is pregnant with religion and poetry. There are certain scenes that would awe an atheist into belief, without the help of other argument.' Thomas Gray, *Correspondence*, ed. Paget Toynbee and Leonard Whibley, 3 vols. (Oxford: Clarendon Press, 1935); with additions and corrections by H. W. Starr, 3 vols. (Oxford: Clarendon Press, 1971), I, 128. Wordsworth knew the letters from William Mason's edition of Gray's poems (2 vols., 1775), which included a Memoir of His Life and Writings.

44. *Descriptive Sketches*, ed. Eric Birdsall, with the assistance of Paul M. Zall (Ithaca and London: Cornell University Press, 1984), 44.

45. Thomas Gray to Mrs Gray, 13 October 1739. *Correspondence*, I, 122.

46. *The Tuft of Primroses, with Other Late Poems for The Recluse*, ed. Joseph F. Kishel (Ithaca and London: Cornell University Press, 1986), 47. James A. Butler's 'Wordsworth's *Tuft of Primroses*: "An Unrelenting Doom"', *Studies in Romanticism*, 14 (1975), 237–48, and Kenneth R. Johnston, *Wordsworth and The Recluse* (New Haven and London: Yale University Press, 1984), 243–60, remain the best critical discussions of the poem.

47. Gill, *SPP*, 38.

48. *Prose*, III, 137–228. Page references to brief quotations are given in the text.

49. Sara Hutchinson to Thomas Monkhouse, 13 April 1818. *The Letters of Sara Hutchinson*, ed. Kathleen Coburn (London: Routledge & Kegan Paul, 1954), 132.

50. The *Addresses* conclude with the words quoted in block capitals. *Prose*, III, 189.

51. Despite having issued 'Vaudracour and Julia' separately, Wordsworth could not quite excise the story altogether from *The Prelude*. A very stilted passage in the 1850 text (IX, 553–85) refers to the existence of this other poem which the reader must be assumed to know.

52. Robert Woof (ed.), *Wordsworth: The Critical Heritage. Vol. I: 1793–1820* (London: Routledge, 2001), 774; 765–6.

53. F. M. Todd, *Politics and the Poet: A Study of Wordsworth* (London: Methuen, 1957), 217–28; Helen Maria Williams, *Letters Written in France, In the Summer 1790*, ed. Neil Fraistat and Susan S. Lanser (Peterborough, Ont.: Broadview Press, 2001).

54. See my *Wordsworth and the Victorians*, 230–4 for an account of the scholarly uncovering of the story of Wordsworth's French daughter by George McLean Harper, which became public knowledge in 1916 with the publication of his *William Wordsworth: His Life, Works, and Influence*, 2 vols. (London, 1916), but which had been known to a few scholars for some years.

55. The note of caution in 'almost certainly' is introduced by an important unsettled question in Wordsworth's biography. In late life he indicated that he had witnessed the execution of the Girondin journalist Antoine Gorsas on 7 October 1793. Scholars are divided as to whether Wordsworth can possibly have made a further hasty and very hazardous visit to France late in 1793. See my *William Wordsworth: A Life* (Oxford: Clarendon Press, 1989), 77–8 and Kenneth R. Johnston, *The Hidden Wordsworth: Poet-Lover-Rebel-Spy* (New York and London: W. W. Norton, 1998), 358–400.

56. Strong essays on the episode are 'Genre, Gender, and Autobiography: Vaudracour and Julia', in Jacobus, *Romanticism, Writing, and Sexual Difference*, and Deborah Kennedy, 'Revolutionary Tales: Helen Maria Williams's *Letters from France* and William Wordsworth's "Vaudracour and Julia"', *Wordsworth Circle*, 21 (1990), 109–14. See also Richard Gravil's landmark discussion, 'Helen Maria Williams: Wordsworth's Revolutionary *Anima*', *Wordsworth Circle*, 40 (2009), 55–64.

57. See David Duff's account of 'Wordsworth in 1815' in his *Romanticism and the Uses of Genre* (Oxford: Oxford University Press, 2009), 89–94.

58. See *The White Doe of Rylstone; or The Fate of the Nortons*, ed. Kristine Dugas (Ithaca and London: Cornell University Press, 1988), for a full account of the tortuous publication history of this poem.

59. *Benjamin the Waggoner*, ed. Paul F. Betz (Ithaca: Cornell University Press, 1981). *Peter Bell*, ed. John F. Jordan (Ithaca and London:

Cornell University Press, 1985). Quotation from Wordsworth's Preface, p. 41.

60. *The Excursion*, ed. Sally Bushell, James A. Butler, and Michael C. Jaye (Ithaca and London: Cornell University Press, 2007), 124.

61. For example: *The Excursion*, II, 587–9, 'What traveller . . . does not own | The bond of brotherhood', echoes *The Ruined Cottage*, MS B, 136–7, 'the bond | Of brotherhood is broken'; *The Excursion*, III, 709–10, 'The intellectual Power, through words and things, | Went sounding on, a dim and perilous way!', repeats *The Borderers* [1797–9 version], IV, ii, 102–3, 'Three sleepless nights I passed in sounding on | Through words and things, a dim and perilous way'.

62. The use of 'abstruse' also strikingly recalls the Alfoxden period Coleridge of 'Frost at Midnight'—'abstruser musings'—and the Coleridge of 'Dejection: An Ode'—'abstruse research'.

63. Quotation from the Preface to *The Excursion* (1814) in which Wordsworth explains the origins of the poem.

64. The sonnet had been published in the *European Magazine*, XI (1787), 202, under the pseudonym 'Axiologus', a Greek/Latin play on his surname. For an account of the meeting, see Mary Moorman, *William Wordsworth: A Biography. The Later Years 1803–1850* (Oxford: Clarendon Press, 1965), 387.

65. *European Magazine*, LXXVII (June 1820), 523. Woof, *Critical Heritage*, 765.

66. And not just for Wordsworth. The long period of the Regency came to a close in January 1820 with the death of George III.

CHAPTER FOUR

1. *1805*, I, 352–61.

2. Owen, *1850*, 5.

3. Darlington, *Home at Grasmere*, 27.

4. Ibid.

5. Dora Wordsworth to Maria Jane Jewsbury, 3 December 1831. Quoted Darlington, *Home at Grasmere*, 8.

6. WW to James Webbe Tobin, 6 March [1798]. *WL*, I, 212; Preface to *The Excursion, being a portion of The Recluse, a Poem* (1814).

7. *WL*, IV, 358–65.

8. WW to Hugh James Rose [late January 1829]. *WL*, V, 20.

9. *WL*, V, 488–91. The letter is of a kind all too easily dismissed as the high Tory vapourings of an agitated old man. In fact it is a good example of Wordsworth's continuing command at a high level of both political detail and general discussion.

10. WW to Christopher Wordsworth, 1 April [1832]. *WL*, V, 517.

11. For a detailed account see Michael Brock, *The Great Reform Act* (London: Hutchinson, 1973).

12. Orville Dewey, *The Old World and the New* (New York: 1836), 90. Quoted F. M. Todd, *Politics and the Poet* (London: Methuen, 1957), 11.
13. W W to Benjamin Robert Haydon, 23 April [1831]. *WL*, V, 378.
14. *Prose*, III, 260.
15. Both quotations, I V, 263 and 254–5, are taken from one of the finest of the poem's many attempts to convey the difficulties inherent in seeking truth through recollection.
16. *1805*, II, 28–33.
17. Conor Cruise O'Brien, *The Great Melody: A Thematic Biography of Edmund Burke* (London: Sinclair-Stevenson, 1992), 415.
18. W W to George Huntly Gordon [March 1832]. *WL*, V, 504–5.
19. *Prose*, I, 31.
20. Quotation from *Letter* is *Prose*, I, 31. In letters to William Mathews of 23 May, 8 June, and 24 December 1794 Wordsworth also proclaimed the political views that moved his brother, Richard, to counsel him in May 1794: 'I hope you will be cautious in writing or expressing your political opinions. By the suspension of the Habeas Corpus Acts the Ministers have great powers.' See *WL*, I, 121. For evidence that Richard's fears were well founded, see Albert Goodwin, *The Friends of Liberty: The English Democratic Movement in the Age of the French Revolution* (London: Hutchinson, 1979) and John Barrell's two related studies, *Imagining the King's Death* (Oxford: Oxford University Press, 2000) and *The Spirit of Despotism* (Oxford: Oxford University Press, 2006).
21. *Wordsworth's Second Nature: A Study of the Poetry and Politics* (Chicago and London: University of Chicago Press, 1984), 22.
22. *Reflections on the Revolution in France. The Writings and Speeches of Edmund Burke*, V III, *The French Revolution 1790–1794*, ed. L. G. Mitchell (Oxford: Clarendon Press, 1989), 84. Page references for further quotation are from this edition and given in the text.
23. The title of the 1794 first edition of Godwin's novel was *Things As They Are: or, The Adventures of Caleb Williams*.
24. Quoted phrases are from the *Letter*, *Prose*, I, 39, 43, 48, 34.
25. Wordsworth to Benjamin Robert Haydon, *c.*8 July 1831; second quotation from letter of 6 October [1832] to Robert Eaglesfield Griffith. *WL*, V, 408, 557. 'Blood and vital juices' comes from Wordsworth's *Essay on Morals* (the title is editorial) of 1798 and is apposite, because in it he contrasts the inefficacy of 'publications in which we formally & systematically lay down rules for the actions of Men', with books 'written with sufficient power to melt into our affections, to incorporate [themselves] with the blood & vital juices of our minds'. *Prose*, I, 103.
26. In *Paradise Lost*, II, 391, Satan addresses the fallen angels as 'Synod of Gods'. Wordsworth invokes Pandaemonium and its primary actors

throughout the treatment of the French developments in Books IX–X of *The Prelude*.

27. Jean-Baptiste Louvet de Couvrai (1760–97) was a novelist and political writer, who when elected to the Assembly in 1791 associated himself with the Girondists. He fled from Paris in 1793, but returned after the fall of Robespierre.

28. For a thoughtful consideration of Wordsworth's state of mind at this time, see Nicholas Roe, *Wordsworth and Coleridge: The Radical Years* (Oxford: Clarendon Press, 1988), esp. 69–79.

29. '. . . I had so often seen Mr. Pitt upon his own ground at Cambridge & upon the floor of the House of Commons.' Note to 'Monument of Mrs Howard'. Curtis, *Fenwick Notes*, 54.

30. See L. G. Mitchell, *Charles James Fox* (Oxford: Oxford University Press, 2002), esp. 114–15; and Conor Cruise O'Brien, *The Great Melody*, esp. 414–31.

31. In *The Later Wordsworth* (Cambridge: Cambridge University Press, 1933), 156–7, Edith C. Batho draws attention to the lines on Fox, but somewhat misrepresents them by failing to note their unfinished state. Batho implies that the passage became part of the poem, only to be cut out at a later stage, but such is not the case.

32. WW to Charles James Fox, 14 January 1801. *WL*, I, 312–15.

33. After 1832 the line, 'But when the Mighty pass away' was changed to 'But when the great and good depart'.

34. *Prose*, III, 157–8.

35. Conor Cruise O'Brien, *The Great Melody*, 425.

36. Mitchell, *Charles James Fox*, 116–36.

37. WW to Lord Lonsdale [*c.*23 December, 1831]. *WL*, V, 469.

38. Edmund Burke, *Reflections on the Revolution in France*, ed. L. G. Mitchell (Oxford, 1989), 127.

39. Isabella Fenwick to Henry Taylor, 28 March 1839. *Correspondence of Henry Taylor*, ed. Edward Dowden (London: Longmans, Green, 1888), 117.

40. WW to Dora Wordsworth and Dorothy Wordsworth [*c.*May 1839]. *WL*, VI, 693. Quoted Owen, *1850*, 9.

41. Samuel Taylor Coleridge, *The Notebooks*, ed. Kathleen Coburn, 6 vols. (London: Routledge & Kegan Paul, 1957–2002), I, entry 1801.

42. Isabella Fenwick to Henry Taylor, 18 August 1838. *Correspondence of Henry Taylor*, 95.

43. STC to WW, 12 October 1799. *STCL*, I, 538. WW to STC, 6 March 1804. *WL*, I, 452.

44. *Biographia Literaria* (1817), ed. James Engell and Walter Jackson Bate, 2 vols. (London: Routledge & Kegan Paul, 1983), II, 156.

45. *The Friend*, ed. Barbara E. Rooke, 2 vols. (London: Routledge & Kegan Paul, 1969), II, 146–8; 258–9. Wordsworth published the skating episode in his 1815 collection as 'Influence of Natural Objects In calling

forth and strengthening the Imagination in Boyhood and early Youth; From an unpublished Poem'.
46. *Prose*, III, 238–59.
47. *The Works of Thomas De Quincey*, ed. Grevel Lindop, 21 vols. (London: Pickering and Chatto, 2000–3), Vol. 11, ed. Julian North, 40–109, esp. 87–90. Alan Lang Strout, 'William Wordsworth and John Wilson: A Review of their Relations between 1807–1817', *PMLA*, 49 (1934), 143–83; quotation p. 152.
48. *Prose*, III, 353–4. The passage made a great impression on Tennyson. See Stephen Gill, *Wordsworth and the Victorians* (Oxford: Clarendon Press, 1998), 192.
49. WW to Richard Sharp, 29 April 1804. *WL*, I, 470.
50. WW to Thomas Noon Talfourd [*c*.10 April 1839]. *WL*, VI, 679–80.
51. Michael Millgate, *Testamentary Acts* (Oxford: Clarendon Press, 1992), 186–7.
52. WW to Edward Moxon [1 April 1842]. *WL*, VII, 314.
53. 'Condition of England' is, of course, the memorable phrase from the opening sentence of *Past and Present* (1843), but Carlyle had anticipated it in the opening to *Chartism* four years earlier.
54. *The Works of Thomas De Quincey*, Vol. 15, ed. Frederick Burwick, 234–5.
55. For Price's utterance of *Nunc Dimittis*, see Marilyn Butler (ed.), *Burke, Paine, Godwin, and the Revolution Controversy* (Cambridge: Cambridge University Press, 1984), 31.
56. Stopford A. Brooke, *Life and Letters of Frederick W. Robertson, M.A.*, 2 vols. (London: Smith, Elder, and Co., 1865), I, 140. For more on Robertson, see Gill, *Wordsworth and the Victorians*, 58–62.
57. The quotation is from the memorial in Grasmere Church raised after Wordsworth's death, quoted more fully above, p. 8, and in Gill, *Wordsworth and the Victorians*, 30–1, 37.
58. The reference is to the extract from *The Prelude* published first by Coleridge in *The Friend* in 1809 and subsequently by Wordsworth in 1815 as 'French Revolution As It Appeared To Enthusiasts At Its Commencement'. The passage, beginning 'Oh! pleasant exercise of hope and joy!' includes the much-quoted lines, 'Bliss was it in that dawn to be alive, | But to be young was very heaven!'
59. *Prose*, III, 260.
60. 'It is not to be thought of that the Flood', 11–14. Curtis, *P2V*, 167.
61. Cited by Thomas Carlyle in Book III, Chapter III, 'Gospel of Mammonism' in *Past and Present* (1843). For many other examples, see Sheila M. Smith, *The Other Nation: The Poor in English Novels of the 1840s and 1850s* (Oxford: Clarendon Press, 1980).
62. See Brian W. Martin, *John Keble: Priest, Professor and Poet* (London: Croom Helm, 1976), 81. For Macaulay's Journal entry of 28 July 1850,

see George Otto Trevelyan, *The Life and Letters of Lord Macaulay*, 2 vols. (London: Longmans, Green, and Co., 1876), II, 279.

CHAPTER FIVE

1. WW to R. P. Gillies, 23 November 1814. *WL*, III, 170. Some of the material in this chapter derives from earlier work of mine, 'Wordsworth, Scott, and "Musings Near Aquapendente"', *Centennial Review*, 36 (1992), 221–30.

2. In the Fenwick note WW revealed that he had drawn on a sentence in the MS journal of his friend Thomas Wilkinson—later published as *Tours to the British Mountains, with the Descriptive Poems of Lowther and Emont Vale* (London: Taylor and Hessey, 1824): 'Passed a female who was reaping alone: she sung in Erse as she bended over her sickle; the sweetest human voice I ever heard: her strains were tenderly melancholy, and felt delicious, long after they were heard no more.' See Curtis, *P2V*, 415.

3. Blake's annotation to the final paragraph of WW's 'Essay, Supplementary to the Preface' to *Poems* (1815). See *The Poetry and Prose of William Blake*, ed. David V. Erdman and Harold Bloom (New York: Doubleday, 1965), 655.

4. See Butler and Green, *Lyrical Ballads*, 332 and 336–7.

5. For a splendidly illustrated account of the 1837 tour, see Donald E. Hayden, *Wordsworth's Travels in Europe II*, Monograph Series, 23 (Tulsa, Okla.: University of Tulsa, 1985), 49–110. For a discussion of the poems memorializing the tour, see John Wyatt, *Wordsworth's Poems of Travel, 1819–1842* (Basingstoke: Macmillan Press, 1999), 118–36.

6. WW to Samuel Rogers [30 July 1830]. *WL*, V, 310.

7. As Peter Manning says, 'the poem is a proleptic elegy for Scott'. For a discussion of these poems, which ranges beyond the concerns of this chapter, see Manning's enormously informative and thought-provoking essay, 'The Other Scene of Travel: Wordsworth's "Musings Near Aquapendente"', in Helen Rugueiro Elam and Frances Ferguson (eds.), *The Wordsworthian Enlightenment: Romantic Poetry and the Ecology of Reading* (Baltimore: Johns Hopkins University Press, 2005), 191–211.

8. Why was the night uncomfortable? See Mark L. Reed, *Wordsworth: The Chronology of the Middle Years 1800–1815* (Cambridge, Mass.: Harvard University Press, 1975), 296: 'W and Scott are kept from their beds, which are to be spread on the floor, by a group of ladies who retain possession of their room until 12:30 am, although W and Scott call out the half-hours like watchmen under their windows.'

9. Information and quotation about this day are taken from the IF notes to 'Yarrow Revisited' and 'Musings Near Aquapendente'.

10. WW to Walter Scott, 7 November 1805. *WL*, I, 641. For the Scottish tour see Hayden, *Wordsworth's Travels in Scotland*, 9–30.

11. WW to Walter Scott, 16 January 1805. *WL*, I, 530.

12. DW to Lady Beaumont, 4 May 1805. *WL*, I, 590.

13. *The Tea-Table Miscellany: or, Allan Ramsay's Collection of Scots Sangs* (1730); Thomas Percy, *Reliques of Ancient English Poetry* (1765); David Herd, *Ancient and Modern Scottish Songs* (1776); Walter Scott, *Minstrelsy of the Scottish Border* (1802). R. Borland's *Yarrow: Its Poets and Poetry* (Galashiels: A. Walker & Son, 1890; 2nd edn., 1908) is informative and remains of historic interest. The best discussions known to me of W's Yarrow poems and their relation to Scott are those in Michael Baron's *Language and Relationship in Wordsworth's Writing* (London: Longman, 1995), 235–52 and Peter T. Murphy, *Poetry as an Occupation and an Art in Britain 1760–1830* (Cambridge: Cambridge University Press, 1993), 208–23.

14. *Minstrelsy of the Scottish Border* (1802), ed. T. F. Henderson, 4 vols. (Edinburgh and London: William Blackwood & Sons; New York: Charles Scribner's Sons, 1902), III, 175.

15. Walter Scott to WW, 16 March 1805. *The Letters of Sir Walter Scott*, ed. H. J. C. Grierson, 12 vols. (London: Constable, 1932–7), I, 241.

16. See Scott to Joseph Ritson, 11 September 1803, *Letters*, 201; and [J. G. Lockhart], *Memoirs of the Life of Sir Walter Scott, Bart.*, 7 vols. (Edinburgh: Robert Cadell; London: John Murray and Whittaker & Co., 1837–8), IV, 265–6.

17. As note 15.

18. See letters of DW to Catherine Clarkson, 9 June 1806 and WW to Scott [before 15 June 1806]. *WL*, II, 38 and 40.

19. Curtis, *Fenwick Notes*, 27–8.

20. Ibid. 28. Robert Anderson, *The Works of the British Poets. With Prefaces, Biographical and Critical*, 13 vols. (London and Edinburgh, 1792–5). John Wordsworth's set is in the Wordsworth Library. For the lament, 'Distressful gift!', which WW did not publish, see Curtis, *P2V*, 617. For 'silent poet' see 'When, to the attractions of the busy World' (pub. 1815), l. 82. Curtis, *P2V*, 570.

21. Ketcham, *Shorter Poems*, 528.

22. *DWJ*, 104. Entry for 3 June 1802.

23. See my '"The Braes of Yarrow": Poetic Context and Personal Memory in Wordsworth's "Extempore Effusion Upon the Death of James Hogg"', *Wordsworth Circle*, XVI (1985), 120–5. Logan appears in Anderson's *British Poets*, XI, 1027–49. 'The Braes of Yarrow' had also been published in the 2nd edition of Herd's *Ancient and Modern Scottish Songs* (1791).

24. In a letter to Scott [before 15 June 1806] W reports, 'I heard of you and your Last Minstrel every where in London; your Poem is more popular and more highly spoken of than you can possibly be aware.' Just one sentence later W remarks that he is thinking to publish some

miscellaneous poems in the coming spring. When he does, the collection, *Poems, in Two Volumes*, is greeted with derision and, compared with *The Lay of the Last Minstrel*, sells miserably.

25. WW to EQ, 23 August [183]. *WL*, V, 421.
26. The event and Scott's words are recorded in the IF note to 'Yarrow Revisited'; Jackson, *Sonnet Series*, 526. For an account of the entry and a photograph of it, see F. V. Morley, *Dora Wordsworth: Her Book* (London: Selwyn & Blount, 1924), 73–80. For an appreciative account of the poetry of this time, see Jill Rubenstein, 'Wordsworth and "Localised Romance": The Scottish Poems of 1831', *Studies in English Literature*, 16 (1976), 579–90.
27. WW to Samuel Rogers [30 July 1830]. *WL*, V, 310. In the essay cited in note 7 Peter Manning examines the degree of competitiveness in these late poems about Scott, judiciously bringing out W's reservations about Scott *as a poet*.
28. In an edition of *Minstrelsy of the Scottish Border* brought out in 1833, Lockhart appended a note to the introduction to 'The Dowie Dens of Yarrow', emphasizing the connection between his father-in-law and Wordsworth: 'It may now be added, that Hamilton's ballad, and the scenery of the tragic tale, have inspired Mr Wordsworth to two of his most exquisite poems—"Yarrow Unvisited," and "Yarrow Visited;" and that he has more lately immortalized an excursion to the Yarrow, in which he was accompanied by Sir Walter Scott, only two days before Sir Walter left Scotland in September, 1831, in a most affecting piece, not yet published, entitled, "Yarrow Revisited."' This note intrigued a certain Thomas Forbes Kelsall, a long-time admirer, who wrote to Wordsworth requesting a copy. Astonishingly Wordsworth complied (*c*.30 October 1833, *WL*, V, 655–6). The poem was eventually published in the collection to which it gives its name, *Yarrow Revisited*, in 1835.
29. The phrase—it is to be hoped that it is WW's—is recorded in Aubrey de Vere's 'Recollections of Wordsworth' published in *The Prose Works of William Wordsworth*, ed. Alexander B. Grosart, 3 vols. (London: Edward Moxon, Son & Co., 1876), III, 487.
30. The first mentioned quotation is l. 295 of MS D of *The Ruined Cottage*. Butler, *The Ruined Cottage*, 63. The *Duddon* Postscript reads in part, 'The power of waters over the minds of Poets has been acknowledged from the earliest ages;—through the "Flumina amem sylvas que inglorius" of Virgil, down to the sublime apostrophe to the great rivers of the earth, by Armstrong, and the simple ejaculation of Burns, (chosen, if I recollect right, by Mr. Coleridge, as a motto for his embryo "Brook")

> "The Muse nae Poet ever fand her,
> Till by himsel' he learned to wander,

> Adown some trotting burn's meander,
> AND NA' THINK LANG." '

Jackson, *Sonnet Series*, 77. The lines quoted in the *Kendal and Windermere Railway* are "O Nature, a' thy shows an' forms, | To feeling pensive hearts hae charms!" *Prose*, III, 346.

31. For the best account to date, see Fiona Stafford, ' "Inhabited Solitudes": Wordsworth in Scotland, 1803', in David Duff and Catherine Jones (eds.), *Scotland, Ireland, and the Romantic Aesthetic* (Lewisburg: Bucknell University Press, 2007), 93–113.

32. W W to Allan Cunningham, 14 June [1834]. *WL*, V, 722.

33. DW to Jane Pollard, [*c*.6 and 16 December 1787]. *WL*, I, 13.

34. Henry Crabb Robinson to Thomas Robinson, 6 October 1833. *The Correspondence of Henry Crabb Robinson with the Wordsworth Circle*, ed. Edith J. Morley, 2 vols. (Oxford: Clarendon Press, 1927), I, 247.

35. *Home at Grasmere* [MS B], ll. 109–13:

> Where'er my footsteps turned
> Her Voice was like a hidden Bird that sang;
> The thought of her was like a flash of light
> Or an unseen companionship, a breath
> Of fragrance independent of the wind.

36. Isabella Fenwick to Henry Taylor, 20 May 1841. Quoted *WL*, VII, 198.

37. W W to Edward Moxon, 10 December 1835. *WL*, VI, 135.

38. There is no reason to doubt Wordsworth's recollection that the first version of the poem itself was 'written extempore, immediately after reading a notice of the Ettrick Shepherd's death in the Newcastle paper, to the Editor of which I sent a copy for publication'. See Curtis, *Fenwick Notes*, 58.

39. Dorothy Wordsworth, *Recollections of a Tour Made in Scotland*, ed. Carol Kyros Walker (New Haven and London: Yale University Press, 1997), 41–2.

40. For texts and an account of their complex history, see Curtis, *P2V*, 534–5 and Curtis, *Last Poems*, 307–12; 471–6.

41. Curtis, *P2V*, 534–5.

42. Dorothy Wordsworth, *Recollections of a Tour Made in Scotland*, 44.

43. Ibid. 42. DW slightly misremembers ll. 5–6, which read in Burns's Kilmarnock edition, 'Here pause—and thro' the starting tear, | Survey this grave.'

44. Reflecting on the death of Richard Sharp in 1835, W wrote to Rogers (5 April), 'How a thought of the presence of living friends brightens particular spots, and what a shade falls over them when those friends have passed away!' *WL*, VI, 41.

45. Curtis, *Last Poems*, 307–10.

46. WW to David Laing, 11 December 1835. *WL*, VI, 136.
47. Curtis, *Fenwick Notes*, 63; 169–70.

CHAPTER SIX

1. WW alluded to Akenside in 1785 in his earliest surviving poem, 'Lines on the Bicentenary of Hawkshead School', and became increasingly familiar with his work in the following decade. See Duncan Wu, *Wordsworth's Reading 1770–1799* (Cambridge: Cambridge University Press, 1993), 1–2; Landon and Curtis, *Early Poems*, 354–61. The epigraph is *The Pleasures of the Imagination*, V, 101–3. See *The Poetical Works of Mark Akenside*, ed. Robin Dix (Madison: Fairleigh Dickinson University Press, 1996), 232.
2. Wu, *Wordsworth's Reading*, 117.
3. In *Wordsworth and Word-Preserving Arts: Typographic Inscription, Ekphrasis and Posterity in the Later Work* (Basingstoke: Palgrave Macmillan, 2007), 126–8, Peter Simonsen comments in some detail on the significance of the dedication to Rogers, noting that WW received 'no less than three complimentary copies of the illustrated edition of *Italy* in 1830, and . . . three copies of the profusely and brilliantly illustrated *Poetical Works* in 1834'.
4. WW to Samuel Rogers, 14 January [1834]. *WL*, V, 688. The young Rogers was radically inclined and visited Paris in 1791. He and Wordsworth first met in 1801. See also *WL*, VII, 210, where, in a letter to Isabella Fenwick of 29 June 1841, an account of visiting Hampton Court with Rogers brings back to WW's mind an earlier visit with Scott and members of his family. In 1841 also WW had the shock of discovering that in some quarters he was thought to be already dead. A now unknown correspondent included a series of 'Epitaphs upon Authors not long since dead', written by an acquaintance, among which was one upon W. See WW to Unknown, 16 February 1841. *WL*, VII, 180.
5. WW to Edward Moxon, 28 January 1837. *WL*, VI, 353.
6. For an account of the ceremony and its significance, see my *Wordsworth and the Victorians* (Oxford: Clarendon Press, 1998), 19–20.
7. Published 1841. WW contributed 'Extract from Troilus and Cressida' and the pseudo-Chaucerian 'The Cuckoo and the Nightingale'. See Bruce E. Graver (ed.), *Translations of Chaucer and Virgil* (Ithaca and London: Cornell University Press, 1998).
8. WW to Thomas Powell, 18 January [1840]. *WL*, VII, 8. Powell was a literary con-man and embezzler, who had to flee to America. For Horne see Ann Blainey, *The Farthing Poet: A Biography of Richard Hengist Horne, 1802–84* (London: Longmans, 1968).
9. Gill, *SPP*, 215–16.

10. Quotations in this paragraph are from WW to John Peace, 4 September 1841, *WL*, VII, 242; Mary Wordsworth to Susan Wordsworth, 15 May 1841 and to Isabella Fenwick, 2 June [1841]. *Letters of Mary Wordsworth*, ed. Mary E. Burton (Oxford: Clarendon Press, 1958), 245; 246. Isabella Fenwick to Henry Taylor, 20 May 1841. Quoted *WL*, VII, 198. See also *WL*, VII, 214 for a quotation from a letter from Sir John Stoddart to WW, 17 July 1841, in which his old friend laments that they did not meet on W's recent visit south: 'I have resolved to make an attempt to see you once more—since as you feelingly say, after the death of our old and valued friends Lamb and Coleridge and Scott, we know not "who next may drop and disappear." . . . I shall be anxious to talk over with you the old Grasmere recollections . . .'.

11. Joseph Cottle, *Early Recollections, Chiefly Relating to the Late Samuel Taylor Coleridge, During his Long Residence in Bristol*, 2 vols. (London: Longman, Rees and Co. and Hamilton Adams and Co., 1837), I, 314.

12. See MW to HCR, 1 November 1836. *WL*, VI, 314.

13. John Kenyon (1784–1856) was an independently wealthy man whose London home became a mecca for the intelligentsia and foreign travellers. In 1841, as requested, Kenyon, at her request, obtained a Wordsworth relic for Elizabeth Barrett, a piece of greenery from Rydal Mount.

14. See Mrs Henry Sandford, *Thomas Poole and His Friends*, 2 vols. (London: Macmillan, 1888) and Berta Lawrence, *Coleridge and Wordsworth in Somerset* (Newton Abbot: David and Charles, 1970).

15. WW to Thomas Poole, 19 April [1836]. *WL*, VI, 205.

16. John Kenyon, *Poems: For the Most Part Occasional* (London: Edward Moxon, 1838), 12–14. 'Moonlight' has no line numbering.

17. WW to John Kenyon [summer 1838]. *WL*, VI, 616.

18. WW to Samuel Carter Hall, 15 January 1837. *WL*, VI, 348.

19. DW to Jane Pollard, 30 August [1793]. *WL*, I, 109.

20. *Poems, Chiefly of Early and Late Years* (1842), 3–4. Gill, *SPP*, 215–17.

21. 'How sweet the walk along the woody steep', 15–19. Landon and Curtis, *Early Poems*, 744.

22. Curtis, *Fenwick Notes*, 62–3.

23. *Poems, Chiefly of Early and Late Years* (1842) was issued with an alternative title-page to allow readers who already had the current six-volume edition of the Collected Works (1840) to bind their new purchase uniformly as a seventh volume. This meant, of course, that they had paid for 'The Female Vagrant' twice—once in its appearance amongst the 'Juvenile Pieces' in Volume One of the collective edition and once as part of *Guilt and Sorrow*. WW was sensitive about the bibliographical-moral problem he was creating here, as his anxious letters to Moxon about it reveal, and separate printing of 'The Female Vagrant' was discontinued in future collective editions.

24. WW to William Mathews, 7 November 1794. *WL*, I, 136.

25. All quotation will be from 'Salisbury Plain' in Gill, *SPP*.

26. In her pioneering *Salisbury Plain: A Study in the Development of Wordsworth's Mind and Art* (Oxford: Basil Blackwell, 1966), Enid Welsford was led into numerous errors by her unavoidable reliance on the piecemeal presentation of 'Salisbury Plain' in the notes to *Guilt and Sorrow*, pp. 334–41, in the first volume of the De Selincourt–Darbishire edition of the *Poetical Works*.

27. WW to Samuel Carter Hall, 15 January 1837. *WL*, VI, 348. WW refers to Oliver Goldsmith's *The Deserted Village* (1770), John Langhorne's *The Country Justice* (1774), and Shenstone's *The Schoolmistress* (1742), all poems he had known since school-days.

28. DW to Jane Pollard [10 and 12 July 1793]. *WL*, I, 100–1. See also Everard H. King, *James Beattie's 'The Minstrel' and the Origins of Romantic Autobiography* (Lewiston, Lampeter, and Queenston: The Edwin Mellen Press, 1992), 61–111.

29. Literary and political analogues to early Wordsworth have been widely discussed—foundational studies relevant to the observations made in this chapter are Mary Jacobus, *Tradition and Experiment in Wordsworth's Lyrical Ballads* (Oxford: Clarendon Press, 1976) and Nicholas Roe, *Wordsworth and Coleridge: The Radical Years* (Oxford: Clarendon Press, 1988). See also for details mentioned in this paragraph, Paul Kelley, 'Rousseau's "Discourse on the Origins of Inequality" and Wordsworth's "Salisbury Plain"', *Notes and Queries* (July–August, 1977), 323; Francis Celoria, 'Chatterton, Wordsworth and Stonehenge', *Notes and Queries* (March 1976), 103–4; John Barrell, *The Spirit of Despotism: Invasions of Privacy in the 1790s* (Oxford: Oxford University Press, 2006), esp. 214–24; Philip Shaw (ed.), *Romantic Wars: Studies in Culture and Conflict, 1793–1822* (Aldershot: Ashgate, 2000), 2; Stephen C. Behrendt, '"A few harmless Numbers": British Women Poets and the Climate of War, 1793–1815', ibid. 19; Tom Duggett, 'Celtic Night and Gothic Grandeur: Politics and Antiquarianism in Wordsworth's *Salisbury Plain*', in his *Gothic Romanticism: Architecture, Politics, and Literary Form* (New York: Palgrave Macmillan, 2010), 67–95.

30. Richard Gravil, *Wordsworth's Bardic Vocation, 1787–1842* (Basingstoke: Palgrave Macmillan, 2003), 80.

31. Quotation from Price's *Discourse* taken from Marilyn Butler (ed.), *Burke, Paine, Godwin, and the Revolution Controversy* (Cambridge: Cambridge University Press, 1984), 32.

32. In his *British Poetry and the Revolutionary and Napoleonic Wars* (Oxford: Oxford University Press, 2003), Simon Bainbridge, drawing on Betty T. Bennett's *War Poetry in the Age of Romanticism: 1793–1815* (New York and London: Garland, 1976), discusses the ways in which the poetry that was published—a great quantity—served as 'a crucial form for the mediation of the wars to the British public' (p. vii).

33. The history of the government's wide-ranging and very effective controls on all activity deemed subversive is too familiar to need rehearsing here. See Albert Goodwin, *The Friends of Liberty: The English Democratic Movement in the Age of the French Revolution* (London: Hutchinson, 1979). For a study which focuses on the effect of these measures on Wordsworth and Coleridge and radical activists known to them, see Roe, *Wordsworth and Coleridge: The Radical Years*. By the end of the decade Wordsworth's first publisher, Joseph Johnson, would be imprisoned for selling a 'seditious' pamphlet. See Helen Braithwaite, *Romanticism, Publishing and Dissent: Joseph Johnson and the Cause of Liberty* (Basingstoke: Palgrave Macmillan, 2003).

34. WW to William Mathews, 23 May [1794]. *WL*, I, 119. See also WW's further long avowal to Mathews, [8] June [1794].

35. Butler (ed.), *Burke, Paine, Godwin*, 32.

36. William Godwin, *Cursory Strictures on the charge delivered by Lord Chief Justice Eyre to the Grand Jury, Oct. 2, 1794*, 24. In *The Friends of Liberty* Goodwin describes *Cursory Strictures* as 'perhaps the most signal service Godwin ever rendered to the cause of radicalism' (p. 341).

37. In his 1995 Nobel Prize acceptance address, 'Crediting Poetry', Seamus Heaney discussed the place of poetry at times of crisis, invoking Wordsworth in his exposition of the 'adequate' (reprinted in *Opened Ground: Poems 1966–1996* (London: Faber and Faber, 2002), 447–67). Heaney's optimistic vision in this lecture is the starting-point for Fiona Stafford's important study, *Local Attachments: The Province of Poetry* (Oxford: Oxford University Press, 2010). See *passim*, but esp. 96–134.

38. Greg Kucich, *Keats, Shelley, and Romantic Spenserianism* (University Park, Pa.: Pennsylvania State University Press, 1991), 71. For further consideration of the significance of the poem's verse form, see Kurt Fosso, 'The Politics of Genre in Wordsworth's *Salisbury Plain*', *New Literary History*, 30 (1999), 159–77; revised as 'Genre, Politics, and Community in the Salisbury Plain Poems', in Kurt Fosso, *Buried Communities: Wordsworth and the Bonds of Mourning* (Albany: State University of New York Press, 2004), 67–96.

39. WW to Catherine Grace Godwin [spring 1829]. *WL*, V, 58. Godwin was a prolific poet, who dedicated her 1829 collection, *The Wanderer's Legacy*, to Wordsworth.

40. See James Averill (ed.), *An Evening Walk* (Ithaca and London: Cornell University Press, 1984). It might be noted that the process of dismembering, figuratively speaking, the 1793 poem for revision did involve literal dismemberment of a copy of the first edition quarto.

41. WW to Francis Wrangham, 20 November 1795. *WL*, I, 159.

42. WW to William Mathews, [*c*.24 December and 7 January 1795]. *WL*, I, 137.

43. *Prose*, I, 39.

44. See V. A. C. Gattrell, *The Hanging Tree: Execution and the English People 1770–1868* (Oxford: Oxford University Press, 1994).

45. In 1795 two 'Quota Acts' were passed requiring counties to provide men for service in the navy.

46. Faced with the distress caused to the agricultural poor by the soaring price of bread, in May 1795 the justices of Speenhamland in Berkshire decided to give direct help (so-called 'outdoor relief) to poor families on a sliding scale in proportion to the cost of a loaf.

47. WW to William Mathews, [20] and 24 October [1795]. *WL*, I, 154. DW to Jane Marshall, 30 November [1795]. *WL*, I, 162.

48. Debate 5 January 1795. *The Parliamentary History of England, From the Earliest Period to the Year 1803* (London, 1818), XXXI (14 March 1794–22 May 1795), 1070–1.

49. DW to Jane Marshall [7 March 1796]. *WL*, I, 166.

50. WW to Francis Wrangham, 20 November [1795]. *WL*, I, 159.

51. The epigraph to *Adam Bede* (1859) is taken from the Pastor's words in *The Excursion*, VI, 651–8: 'So that ye may have | Clear images before your gladden'd eyes | Of nature's unambitious underwood . . .'.

52. Toby R. Benis, *Romanticism on the Road: The Marginal Gains of Wordsworth's Homeless* (Basingstoke: Macmillan Press, 2000), very interestingly probes the Salisbury Plain poems in the context of the developing concern about vagrancy (see esp. 4–10 and 57–93). Mary Jacobus, *Tradition and Experiment in Wordsworth's Lyrical Ballads 1798* (Oxford: Clarendon Press, 1976) remains a fine introduction to the literary representation of the vagrant poor in Wordsworth and others such as Langhorne and Cowper and their contribution to what Gary Harrison, *Wordsworth's Vagrant Muse* (Detroit: Wayne State University Press, 1994), calls the 'Discourse on Poverty'.

53. WW to Charles James Fox, 14 January 1801. *WL*, I, 315.

54. See Gill, *SPP*, 7–8 for further details and references. According to Azariah Pinney, Coleridge was so intent on serious inspection of the poem that he 'interleaved it with white paper to mark down whatever may strike him as worthy your notice'. See Stephen Gill, *William Wordsworth: A Life* (Oxford: Clarendon Press, 1989), 100. The interleaved manuscript would be a treasure, but since there has never been any sight of it recorded, one may doubt whether in fact it ever existed.

55. For the new material see Gill, *SPP*, 287–303 and Landon and Curtis, *Early Poems*, 28–9. Letter reference: DW to Unknown, 24 October 1796. *WL*, I, 172.

56. WW to Joseph Cottle, 9 May 1798. *WL*, I, 218.

57. For a scrupulously full account see Butler and Green, *Lyrical Ballads*, 459–63.

58. The few lines that do survive are found in Butler and Green, *Lyrical Ballads*, 317. Believing the poem to be without merit and likely

to damage the poet's reputation, William Knight and Gordon Graham
Wordsworth at different times destroyed manuscript copies of it.

59. WW to STC, 27 February [1799]. *WL*, I, 256–7.

60. In the fair-copy manuscript DW made in late 1799 the Woman's story
('The Female Vagrant') is omitted, but three stanzas are entered about
the Woman, now called Rachel. See Gill, *SPP*, 207–9.

61. WW alludes, of course, to *Othello*, I, iii, 135. For a discussion of the
conflicted aspects of W's attitude to 'gross and violent stimulants' at this
time, see Michael Gamer, *Romanticism and the Gothic* (Cambridge:
Cambridge University Press, 2000), 90–126.

62. WW to STC [late November–early December 1798]. *WL*, I, 234. See
also WW's letter to John Wilson [7 June 1802], in which he insists that
the poet's role is 'to a certain degree to rectify men's feelings, to give
them new compositions of feeling, to render their feelings more sane
pure and permanent'. *WL*, I, 355.

63. *Prose*, I, 128.

64. Preface to *Lyrical Ballads* (1800). *Prose*, I, 130.

65. WW to John Taylor and to Anne Taylor, both 9 April 1801. *WL*, I,
325–6 and 328–9. The phrase 'jacobinical pathos' was John Taylor's.

66. *Prose*, I, 130–2.

67. Basil Willey, *The Eighteenth Century Background* (London: Chatto and
Windus, 1940), 264.

68. In the first draft of the 'Advertisement' WW also remarked that the
poem was precious to him 'from a remembrance of its having acted
upon the youthful imagination of my friend Coleridge in a way that he
used to speak of with delight', thus complementing STC's tribute in
Biographia Literaria, discussed above. See Gill, *SPP*, 216.

69. WW to William Mathews, 23 May [1794] and 8 June [1794]. *WL*, I,
118–20, 123–9. 'I am of that odious class of men called democrats, and
of that class I shall for ever continue.' 'Hereditary distinctions and priv-
ileged orders of every species I think must necessarily counteract the
progress of human improvement: hence it follows that I am not amongst
the admirers of the British constitution.'

70. STC to Joseph Cottle [28 May 1798]. *STCL*, I, 412.

71. In his account of why the Wordsworths were ejected from Alfoxden in
1798 Cottle repeats, '(as Mr. Coleridge informed me)', a series of whim-
sical anecdotes, thus following suit with STC's rendering of the spy
episode in *Biographia Literaria* as comic and without serious political
implications. Cottle, *Early Recollections*, I, 319–20.

72. Changes to 'The Female Vagrant' had been introduced since 1802 and
will have been spotted by attentive readers over the years in which
WW's collective editions appeared, but only now in 1842 could they
see how the woman's story meshed with a larger narrative about kinds
of victimhood.

73. See Gill, *SPP*, 257, and Stephen Gill, ' "Adventures on Salisbury Plain" and Wordsworth's Poetry of Protest 1795–97', *Studies in Romanticism*, 11 (1972), 48–65, esp. 59.
74. Richard Gravil, *Wordsworth's Bardic Vocation, 1787–1842* (Basingstoke: Palgrave Macmillan, 2003), 249. A revised version of Wordsworth's 1796–7 tragedy, *The Borderers*, also appeared in *Poems, Chiefly of Early and Late Years*, but in this case it does not seem that the revision was driven—at least, not in any obvious way—by engagement with contemporary issues. In *Disowned by Memory: Wordsworth's Poetry of the 1790s* (Chicago and London: University of Chicago Press, 1998), David Bromwich has argued, rather against received opinion, that the revision of the play 'is a triumph' (p. 45).
75. See Gill, *Wordsworth and the Victorians*, 26.
76. All quotation taken from *Prose*, III, 229–59.
77. WW to Robert Ferguson, 4 July [18]42. *WL*, VII, 350. Parts of this letter clearly echo the formulations of the 1835 'Postscript'. By the date of this letter Ferguson had become the Queen's gynaecologist.
78. Thomas Carlyle, *Past and Present* (1843), ed. Chris R. Bossche, Joel J. Brattin, and D. J. Trela (Berkeley, Los Angeles, and London: University of California Press, 2005), 3.
79. Fuller consideration of the discursive context of the contemporary debate about capital punishment would include *Oliver Twist* (1837–9), especially the chapter, 'The Jew's Last Night Alive'; and the exchange between Dickens and Thackeray sparked by the latter's article, 'Going to See a Man Hanged' in *Fraser's Magazine* for August 1840, about a public execution which both novelists had witnessed. See Stephen Gill (ed.), *Oliver Twist* (Oxford: Oxford University Press, 1999), Appendix 2, and Michael Slater, *Charles Dickens* (New Haven and London: Yale University Press, 2009), 153; 247–8.
80. *The Quarterly Review*, LXIX (December 1841 and March 1842), 1–51.
81. For further discussion of WW's growing attention to the figure of the Redeemer as evidence of personal change and of responsiveness to the *Zeitgeist*, see ch. 2 of Gill, *Wordsworth and the Victorians*, esp. 70–80.
82. Curtis, *Last Poems*, 364.
83. WW to William Mathews, 23 May [1794]. *WL*, I, 119.

Select Bibliography

PRIMARY SOURCES

Coleridge, Samuel Taylor, *Biographia Literaria*, ed. James Engell and W. Jackson Bate, 2 vols. (London and Princeton, 1983).
—— *Collected Letters of Samuel Taylor Coleridge*, ed. Earl Leslie Griggs, 6 vols. (Oxford, 1956–71).
—— *The Friend*, ed. Barbara E. Rooke, 2 vols. (London, 1969).
—— *The Notebooks*, ed. Kathleen Coburn, 5 vols. (London, 1957–2002).
—— *Table Talk*, ed. Carl Woodring, 2 vols. (London and Princeton, 1990).
Hutchinson, Sara, *The Letters of Sara Hutchinson*, ed. Kathleen Coburn (London, 1954).
Robinson, Henry Crabb, *The Correspondence of Henry Crabb Robinson with the Wordsworth Circle*, ed. Edith J. Morley, 2 vols. (Oxford, 1927).
Wordsworth, Christopher, *Memoirs of William Wordsworth*, 2 vols. (London, 1851).
Wordsworth, Dorothy, *The Grasmere Journals*, ed. Pamela Woof (Oxford, 1991).
—— *The Grasmere and Alfoxden Journals*, ed. Pamela Woof (Oxford, 2002).
—— *Recollections of a Tour Made in Scotland*, ed. Carol Kyros Walker (New Haven and London, 1997).
Letters of Mary Wordsworth, ed. Mary E. Burton (Oxford, 1958).
Wordsworth, William, *The Fenwick Notes of William Wordsworth*, ed. Jared Curtis (London, 1993).
—— *The Poetical Works of William Wordsworth*, ed. William Knight, 8 vols. (Edinburgh, 1882–6).
—— *The Poetical Works of William Wordsworth*, ed. William Knight, 8 vols. (London, 1896).
—— *The Prelude*, ed. Ernest De Selincourt (Oxford, 1926); 2nd revised edition, Helen Darbishire (Oxford, 1959).
—— *The Five-Book Prelude*, ed. Duncan Wu (Oxford, 1997).
—— *The Prelude: The Four Texts (1798, 1799, 1805, 1850)*, ed. Jonathan Wordsworth (London, 1995).
—— *The Prose Works*, ed. Alexander Grosart, 3 vols. (London, 1876).
—— *The Prose Works of William Wordsworth*, ed. W. J. B. Owen and Jane Worthington Smyser, 3 vols. (Oxford, 1974).

Wordsworth, William and Wordsworth, Dorothy, *The Letters of William and Dorothy Wordsworth*, 8 vols. (Oxford: Clarendon Press, 1967–93). Individual volumes: *The Early Years 1787–1805*, ed. Chester L. Shaver (1967); *The Middle Years, pt. 1: 1806–1811*, ed. Mary Moorman (1969); *The Middle Years, pt. 2: 1812–1820*, ed. Mary Moorman and Alan G. Hill (1970); *The Later Years, pt. 1: 1821–1828*, ed. Alan G. Hill (1978); *The Later Years, pt. 2: 1829–1834*, ed. Alan G. Hill (1979); *The Later Years, pt. 3: 1835–1839*, ed. Alan G. Hill (1982); *The Later Years, pt. 4: 1840–1853*, ed. Alan G. Hill (1988); *A Supplement of New Letters*, ed. Alan G. Hill (1993).

OTHER EIGHTEENTH- AND NINETEENTH-CENTURY SOURCES

Akenside, Mark, *The Poetical Works of Mark Akenside*, ed. Robin Dix (Madison, 1996).
Anderson, Robert, *The Works of the British Poets. With Prefaces, Biographical and Critical*, 13 vols. (London and Edinburgh, 1792–5).
Blake, William, *The Poetry and Prose of William Blake*, ed. David V. Erdman and Harold Bloom (New York, 1965).
Borland, R., *Yarrow: Its Poets and Poetry* (Galashiels, 1890; 2nd edn. 1908).
Brooke, Stopford, *Life and Letters of Frederick W. Robertson, M.A.*, 2 vols. (London, 1865).
Burke, Edmund, *Reflections on the Revolution in France. The Writings and Speeches of Edmund Burke*, VIII, *The French Revolution 1790–1794*, ed. L. G. Mitchell (Oxford, 1989).
Byron, Lord, *Lord Byron, The Complete Poetical Works*, ed. Jerome J. McGann, 7 vols. (Oxford, 1980–93).
Carlyle, Thomas, *Past and Present* (London, 1843), ed. Chris R. Bossche, Joel J. Brattin, and D. J. Trela (Berkeley, Los Angeles, and London, 2005).
Cottle, Joseph, *Early Recollections, Chiefly Relating to the Late Samuel Taylor Coleridge, During his Long Residence in Bristol*, 2 vols. (London, 1837).
De Quincey, Thomas, *The Works of Thomas De Quincey*, ed. Grevel Lindop, 21 vols. (London, 2000–3).
Dewey, Orville, *The Old World and the New; or, Journal of Reflections and Observations Made on a Tour in Europe*, 2 vols. (New York, 1836).
Field, Barron, *Memoirs of Wordsworth*, ed. Geoffrey Little (Sydney, 1975).
Froude, James Anthony, *Thomas Carlyle: A History of His Life in London 1834–1881*, 2 vols. (London, 1884).
Godwin, William, *Cursory Strictures on the charge delivered by Lord Chief Justice Eyre to the Grand Jury, Oct. 2, 1794* (London, 1794).
Gray, Thomas, *Correspondence*, ed. Paget Toynbee and Leonard Whibley, 3 vols. (Oxford, 1935); with additions and corrections by H. W. Starr, 3 vols. (Oxford, 1971).
Herd, David, *Ancient and Modern Scottish Songs* (1776), 2 vols. (Edinburgh and London, 1973).

Heron, Robert, *Observations Made in a Journey through the Western Counties of Scotland*, 2 vols. (Perth, 1793).

Keats, John, *John Keats: Selected Letters*, ed. Robert Gittings; rev. edn. Jon Mee (Oxford, 2002).

Kenyon, John, *Poems: For the Most Part Occasional* (London, 1838).

Lockhart, J. G., *Memoirs of the Life of Sir Walter Scott, Bart.*, 7 vols. (Edinburgh and London, 1837–8).

Percy, Thomas, *Reliques of Ancient English Poetry* (London, 1765).

Ramsay, Allan, *The Tea-Table Miscellany: or, Allan Ramsay's Collection of Scots Sangs* (Edinburgh, 1730).

Ruskin, John, *The Works of John Ruskin*, ed. E. T. Cook and Alexander Wedderburn, 39 vols. (London, 1903–12).

Sandford, Mrs Henry, *Thomas Poole and His Friends*, 2 vols. (London, 1888).

Scott, [Sir] Walter, *Minstrelsy of the Scottish Border* (Edinburgh, 1802), ed. T. F. Henderson, 4 vols. (Edinburgh, London, and New York, 1902).

—— *The Letters of Sir Walter Scott*, ed. H. J. C. Grierson, 12 vols. (London, 1932–7).

Shelley, Mary, *Journals of Mary Shelley*, ed. Paula R. Feldman and Diana Scott-Kilvert, 2 vols. (Oxford, 1987).

Stoddart, John, *Remarks on Local Scenery and Manners in Scotland during the Years 1799 and 1800*, 2 vols. (1801).

Taylor, Henry, *Correspondence of Henry Taylor*, ed. Edward Dowden (London, 1888).

Trevelyan, George Otto, *The Life and Letters of Lord Macaulay*, 2 vols. (London, 1876).

Wilkinson, Thomas, *Tours to the British Mountains* (London, 1824).

Williams, Helen Maria, *Letters Written in France, In the Summer 1790*, ed. Neil Fraistat and Susan S. Lanser (Peterborough, Ont., 2001).

Wilson, John, *The Recreations of Christopher North*, 3 vols. (Edinburgh, 1842).

Woof, Robert (ed.), *Wordsworth: The Critical Heritage. Volume I: 1793–1820* (London, 2001).

LATER SECONDARY SOURCES

Bainbridge, Simon, *Napoleon and English Romanticism* (Cambridge, 1995).

—— *British Poetry and the Revolutionary and Napoleonic Wars* (Oxford, 2003).

Baron, Michael, *Language and Relationship in Wordsworth's Writing* (London, 1995).

Barrell, John, *Imagining the King's Death: Figurative Treason, Fantasies of Regicide 1793–1796* (Oxford, 2000).

—— *The Spirit of Despotism: Invasions of Privacy in the 1790s* (Oxford, 2006).

Barron, Jonathan, and Johnston, Kenneth R., '"A Power to Virtue Friendly": The Pedlar's Guilt in Wordsworth's "Ruined Cottage"', in

Robert Brinkley and Keith Hanley (eds.), *Romantic Revisions* (Cambridge, 1992), 64–86.

Batho, Edith C., *The Later Wordsworth* (Cambridge, 1933).

Behrendt, Stephen C., ' "A few harmless Numbers": British Women Poets and the Climate of War, 1793–1815', in Shaw, *Romantic Wars*.

Benis, Toby R., *Romanticism on the Road: The Marginal Gains of Wordsworth's Homeless* (Basingstoke, 2000).

Bennett, Betty T., *War Poetry in the Age of Romanticism: 1793–1815* (London and New York, 1976).

Blainey, Ann, *The Farthing Poet: A Biography of Richard Hengist Horne, 1802–84* (London, 1968).

Braithwaite, Helen, *Romanticism, Publishing and Dissent: Joseph Johnson and the Cause of Liberty* (Basingstoke, 2003).

Brock, Michael, *The Great Reform Act* (London, 1973).

Bromwich, David, *Disowned by Memory: Wordsworth's Poetry of the 1790s* (Chicago, 1998).

Bushell, Sally, *Re-Reading The Excursion: Narrative, Response and the Wordsworthian Dramatic Voice* (Aldershot, 2002).

—— *Text as Process: Creative Composition in Wordsworth, Tennyson, and Dickinson* (Virginia, 2009).

Butler, James A., 'Wordsworth's *Tuft of Primroses*: "An Unrelenting Doom" ', *Studies in Romanticism*, 14 (1975), 237–48.

Butler, Marilyn (ed.) *Burke, Paine, Godwin, and the Revolution Controversy* (Cambridge, 1984).

Celoria, Francis, 'Chatterton, Wordsworth and Stonehenge', *Notes and Queries*, NS 23 (March 1976), 103–4.

Chandler, James, *Wordsworth's Second Nature: A Study of the Poetry and Politics* (Chicago and London, 1984).

Cookson, J. E., *The Friends of Peace: Anti-War Liberalism in England, 1793–1815* (Cambridge, 1982).

Cosslett, Tess (ed.), *Science and Religion in the Nineteenth Century* (Cambridge, 1984).

Cronin, Richard, *The Politics of Romantic Poetry* (Basingstoke, 2000).

Curtis, Jared, 'The Wellesley Copy of Wordsworth's *Poetical Works* 1832', *Harvard Library Bulletin*, 28 (1980), 5–15.

Duff, David, *Romanticism and the Uses of Genre* (Oxford, 2009).

Duggett, Tom, *Gothic Romanticism: Architecture, Politics, and Literary Form* (New York, 2010).

Elam, Helen Rogueiro, and Ferguson, Frances, *The Wordsworthian Enlightenment: Romantic Poetry and the Ecology of Reading* (Baltimore, 2005).

Erskine-Hill, Howard, *Poetry of Opposition and Revolution: Dryden to Wordsworth* (Oxford, 1996).

Fairer, David, *Organising Poetry: The Coleridge Circle, 1790–1798* (Oxford, 2009).

Fosso, Kurt, *Buried Communities: Wordsworth and the Bonds of Mourning* (Albany, 2004).

Franklin, Alexandra, and Philp, Mark, *Napoleon and the Invasion of Britain* (Oxford, 2003).

Gamer, Michael, *Romanticism and the Gothic* (Cambridge, 2000).

Gatrell, V. A. C., *The Hanging Tree: Execution and the English People 1770–1868* (Oxford, 1994).

Gill, Stephen, '"Adventures on Salisbury Plain" and Wordsworth's Poetry of Protest 1795–97', *Studies in Romanticism*, 11 (1972), 48–65.

—— '"Affinities Preserved": Poetic Self-Reference in Wordsworth', *Studies in Romanticism*, 24 (1985), 531–49.

—— '"The Braes of Yarrow": Poetic Context and Personal Memory in Wordsworth's "Extempore Effusion Upon the Death of James Hogg"', *Wordsworth Circle*, 16 (1985), 120–5.

—— *William Wordsworth: A Life* (Oxford, 1989).

—— 'Wordsworth, Scott, and "Musings Near Aquapendente"', *Centennial Review*, 36 (1992), 221–30.

—— 'Wordsworth's Poems: The Question of Text', in Robert Brinkley and Keith Hanley (eds.), *Romantic Revisions* (Cambridge, 1992), 43–63.

—— *Wordsworth and the Victorians* (Oxford, 1998).

—— 'Wordsworth and the *River Duddon*', *Essays in Criticism*, 57 (2007), 22–41.

Goodman, Kevis, *Georgic Modernity and British Romanticism* (Cambridge, 2004).

Goodwin, Albert, *The Friends of Liberty: The English Democratic Movement in the Age of the French Revolution* (London, 1979).

Gradon, W. McGowan, *Furness Railway: Its Rise and Development 1846–1923* (privately printed, 1946).

Graham, Jenny, *The Nation, the Law and the King: Reform Politics in England 1789–1799*, 2 vols. (Lanham, Md., 2000).

Gravil, Richard, *Wordsworth's Bardic Vocation, 1787–1842* (Basingstoke, 2003).

—— 'Helen Maria Williams: Wordsworth's Revolutionary *Anima*', *Wordsworth Circle*, 40 (2009), 55–64.

Gray, Douglas (ed.), *The Oxford Companion to Chaucer* (Oxford, 2003).

Harper, George McLean, *William Wordsworth: His Life, Works, and Influence*, 2 vols. (London, 1916).

Harrison, Gary, *Wordsworth's Vagrant Muse: Poetry, Poverty and Power* (Detroit, 1994).

Hayden, Donald E., *Wordsworth's Travels in Scotland* (Tulsa, 1985).

—— *Wordsworth's Travels in Europe, II* (Tulsa, 1988).

Hill, Alan G., *Wordsworth's 'Grand Design'*, British Academy Warton Lecture on English Poetry, *Proceedings of the British Academy*, 72 (1986).

—— 'Poetry and Ecumenism: The Legacy of the Wordsworths', *Lambeth Palace Library Annual Review* (1992), 49–64.

Housman, A. E., *The Letters of A. E. Housman*, ed. Archie Burnett, 2 vols. (Oxford: Clarendon Press, 2007).

Hutton, Ronald, *Blood and Mistletoe: The History of the Druids in Britain* (New Haven and London, 2009).

Jacobus, Mary, *Tradition and Experiment in Wordsworth's Lyrical Ballads 1798* (Oxford, 1976).

—— *Romanticism, Writing, and Sexual Difference: Essays on The Prelude* (Oxford, 1989).

Johnston, Kenneth R., *Wordsworth and The Recluse* (New Haven and London, 1984).

—— *The Hidden Wordsworth: Poet-Lover-Rebel-Spy* (New York and London, 1998).

Kelley, Paul, 'Rousseau's "Discourse on the Origins of Inequality" and Wordsworth's "Salisbury Plain"', *Notes and Queries*, NS 24 (July–August, 1977), 323.

Kennedy, Deborah, 'Revolutionary Tales: Helen Maria Williams's *Letters from France* and William Wordsworth's "Vaudracour and Julia"', *Wordsworth Circle*, 21 (1990), 109–14.

King, Everard H., *James Beattie's 'The Minstrel' and the Origins of Romantic Autobiography* (Lewiston, Lampeter, and Queenston, 1992).

Kishell, Joseph, 'Wordsworth and the Grande Chartreuse', *Wordsworth Circle*, 12 (1981), 82–8.

Knight, Mark, and Mason, Emma, *Nineteenth-Century Religion and Literature: An Introduction* (Oxford, 2006).

Kucich, Greg, *Keats, Shelley, and Romantic Spenserianism* (University Park, Pa., 1991).

Lawrence, Berta, *Coleridge and Wordsworth in Somerset* (Newton Abbot, 1970).

Leader, Zachary, *Revision and Romantic Authorship* (Oxford, 1996).

Low, Donald A. (ed.), *Robert Burns: The Critical Heritage* (London, 1974).

McLynn, Frank, *Napoleon: A Biography* (London, 1997).

Manning, Peter, 'The Other Scene of Travel: Wordsworth's "Musings Near Aquapendente"', in Helen Rugueiro Elam and Frances Ferguson (eds.), *The Wordsworthian Enlightenment: Romantic Poetry and the Ecology of Reading*, (Baltimore, 2005), 191–211.

Martin, Brian W., *John Keble: Priest, Professor and Poet* (London, 1976).

Matlack, Richard E., *The Poetry of Relationship: The Wordsworths and Coleridge, 1797–1800* (Basingstoke, 1997).

Mee, Jon, *Romanticism, Enthusiasm and Regulation* (Oxford, 2003).

Millgate, Michael, *Testamentary Acts* (Oxford, 1992).

Millward, Ray, and Robinson, Adrian, *The Lake District* (London, 1970; rev. edn. 1974).

Mitchell, L. G., 'The *Edinburgh Review* and the Lake Poets 1802–1810', *Essays Presented to C. M. Bowra* (Oxford, 1970), 24–38.

—— *Charles James Fox* (Oxford, 2002).

Moorman, Mary, *William Wordsworth: A Biography. The Early Years 1770–1803* (Oxford, 1957); *The Later Years 1803–1850* (Oxford, 1965).

Morley, F. V., *Dora Wordsworth: Her Book* (London, 1924).

Murphy, Peter T., *Poetry as an Occupation and an Art in Britain 1760–1830* (Cambridge, 1993).

Newlyn, Lucy, *Coleridge, Wordsworth, and the Language of Allusion* (Oxford, 1986; 2nd rev. edn. 2001).

Nockles, Peter B., *The Oxford Movement in Context: Anglican High Churchmanship 1760–1857* (Cambridge, 1994).

O'Brien, Conor Cruise, *The Great Melody: A Thematic Biography of Edmund Burke* (London, 1992).

Pedley, Colin, 'Anticipating Invasion: Some Wordsworthian Contexts', *Wordsworth Circle*, 21 (1990), 64–70.

Philp, Mark (ed.), *Resisting Napoleon: The British Response to the Threat of Invasion, 1797–1815* (Aldershot, 2006).

Reed, John Shelton, *Glorious Battle: The Cultural Politics of Victorian Anglo-Catholicism* (Nashville, 1996).

Reed, Mark L., *Wordsworth: The Chronology of the Early Years 1770–1779* (Cambridge, Mass., 1967)

—— *Wordsworth: The Chronology of the Middle Years 1800–1815* (Cambridge, Mass., 1975).

Rieder, John, *Wordsworth's Counterrevolutionary Turn: Community, Virtues, and Vision in the 1790s* (Newark, 1997).

Roe, Nicholas, *Wordsworth and Coleridge: The Radical Years* (Oxford, 1988).

Rubenstein, Jill, 'Wordsworth and "Localised Romance": The Scottish Poems of 1831', *Studies in English Literature*, 16 (1976), 579–90.

Ryan, Robert M., *The Romantic Reformation: Religious Politics in English Literature 1789–1824* (Cambridge, 1997).

Scrivener, Michael, *Poetry and Reform: Periodical Verse from the English Democratic Press 1792–1824* (Detroit, 1992).

Shaw, Philip, *Waterloo and the Romantic Imagination* (Basingstoke, 2002).

—— (ed.), *Romantic Wars: Studies in Culture and Conflict, 1793–1822* (Aldershot, 2000).

Simmons, Jack, *The Victorian Railway* (London, 1991).

Simonsen, Peter, *Wordsworth and Word-Preserving Arts: Typographic Inscription, Ekphrasis and Posterity in the Later Work* (Basingstoke, 2007).

Slater, Michael, *Charles Dickens* (New Haven and London, 2009).

Smith, Sheila, *The Other Nation: The Poor in English Novels of the 1840s and 1850s* (Oxford, 1980).

St Clair, William, *The Reading Nation in the Romantic Period* (Cambridge, 2004).

Stafford, Fiona, ' "Inhabited Solitudes": Wordsworth in Scotland, 1803', in David Duff and Catherine Jones (eds.), *Scotland, Ireland, and the Romantic Aesthetic* (Lewisburg, 2007), 93–113.

Stafford, Fiona, *Local Attachments: The Province of Poetry* (Oxford, 2010).

Strout, Alan Lang, 'William Wordsworth and John Wilson: A Review of their Relations between 1807–1817', *PMLA*, 49 (1934), 143–83.

Thompson, T. W., *Wordsworth's Hawkshead*, ed. Robert Woof (London, 1970).

Thomson, Douglass H., ' "Sport of Transmutations": The Evolution of Wordsworth's "To Lycoris" ', *Studies in English Literature*, 27 (1987), 581–93.

Todd, F. M., *Politics and the Poet: A Study of Wordsworth* (London, 1957).

Ulmer, William A., *The Christian Wordsworth 1798–1805* (Albany, 2001).

Walker, Eric C., *Marriage, Writing and Romanticism* (Stanford, 2009).

Webb, Timothy, 'Catholic Contagion: Southey, Coleridge and English Romantic Anxieties', in Gavin Hopps and Jane Stabler (eds.), *Romanticism and Religion from William Cowper to Wallace Stevens* (Aldershot, 2006), 75–92.

Welsford, Enid, *Salisbury Plain: A Study in the Development of Wordsworth's Mind and Art* (Oxford, 1966).

Wiley, Michael, *Romantic Geography: Wordsworth and Anglo-European Spaces* (Basingstoke, 1998).

Willey, Basil, *The Eighteenth Century Background* (London, 1940).

Wilson, Edward, 'An Echo of St Paul and Words of Consolation in Wordsworth's "Elegiac Stanzas" ', *Review of English Studies*, NS 43 (1992), 75–80.

Wordsworth, Jonathan, *The Music of Humanity* (London, 1969).

—— 'Startling the Earthworms', *Times Literary Supplement*, 3 Dec. 1976, p. 1524.

—— 'The Five-Book *Prelude* of Early Spring 1804', *JEGP*, 76 (1977), 1–25.

—— (ed.), *The Prelude: The Four Texts (1798, 1799, 1805, 1850)* (London, 1995).

Wu, Duncan, *Wordsworth's Reading 1770–1799* (Cambridge, 1993).

—— (ed.), *The Five-Book Prelude* (Oxford, 1997).

Wyatt, John, *Wordsworth and the Geologists* (Cambridge, 1995).

—— *Wordsworth's Poems of Travel, 1819–1842* (Basingstoke, 1999).

Yates, Nigel, *Anglican Ritualism in Victorian Britain 1830–1910* (Oxford, 1999).

General Index

Patrick, Mary 64
Peel, Sir Robert 228 n. 71
Peele Castle 22, 112
Percy, Thomas 162
philosophy 61, 62, 77, 143, 144,
        154
Pinney, Azariah 246 n. 54
Pitt, William 97, 128, 129, 136, 137,
        138, 192
poet, figure of the 1, 66, 68, 69–70
politics 112–14, 125–40, 154, 234 n.
        9; see also radicalism
Pollard, Jane 218 n. 13
Poole, Thomas 183, 199
poor, the 56, 150, 153, 191, 206–8,
        246 n. 46
Poor Law Amendment Act (1834) 8,
        125, 207
Powell, Thomas 19, 180–1
Prelude, The 4, 7, 10, 11, 12, 25, 29,
        31, 41–2, 46, 48, 50, 58, 68, 70,
        83–122, 123–54, 157, 163, 183,
        184–6, 187, 204, 228 n. 73
    The Two-Part Prelude (*1799*) 4–6,
        27, 45, 62–4, 75, 88
    1805; 83–122, 123, 138, 144, 145,
        207
Presbyterianism, Scottish 72
Price, Reverend Richard 150, 191–3
Priestley, Joseph 191, 192
publishing 32, 88–9, 147

Q
Quakerism 76
Quantock Hills 10, 86, 100, 141, 181,
        182
Quillinan, Edward 13, 218 n. 11, 225
        n. 53

R
Racedown 100, 104, 119, 182, 196,
        198
radicalism 98, 149, 153–4, 183, 191,
        245 n. 33
railways 2–4, 6, 90
Ramsay, Allan 162

readers 30, 32, 34–6, 38, 41, 47, 85,
        86, 105, 135, 141, 162, 201, 204,
        205, 209, 211
Reed, Mark 49, 107, 117, 238 n. 8
Reform Act (1832) 125, 126, 127,
        129, 130, 132, 135, 139, 149, 211
Relief Bill, Roman Catholic 124
religion 66, 72, 75–80, 81; *see
        also* Anglicanism; Catholic
        Emancipation; Christianity;
        Church of England; God; faith
retrospection 10, 42, 127, 156, 179
revision 12, 13–21, 25, 28, 36, 43, 44,
        48, 49, 69, 73, 148, 180, 194,
        196, 197, 202
revisitings 8–9, 10, 11, 12, 23, 28, 29,
        36–7, 38, 41, 43, 45, 56, 89, 90,
        92, 98, 99, 107, 109, 111, 123,
        127, 175, 178, 182, 188
Richards, Grant 217 n. 2
Rieder, John 222 n. 14
Robertson, Reverend F.W. 150
Robespierre, Maximilien 5, 6, 87,
        93, 134–5
Rogers, Samuel 158, 172, 179–80
Romanticism 20, 28
Rose, Hugh James 125
Rousseau, Jean Jacques 190
Routledge, George 47–8
Roy, Rob 71
Royal Institute of British
        Architects 216 n. 8
Ruskin, John 216 n. 8
Rydal Mount 2, 13, 18, 83, 113, 123,
        126, 153, 155, 172, 181, 183

S
Salisbury Cathedral 190
Salisbury Plain 31, 102–6, 148, 182,
        184, 185, 186, 187–8, 189, 197,
        203, 205, 208
science 78–9
Scotland 9, 43, 51, 64–5, 70–2, 98,
        160–9, 171–2, 174–5
Scott, Sir Walter 12, 71, 158–63,
        166–9, 170, 171, 180, 243 n. 10